The A B C of the Welsh Revolution

First impression: April 1982
© Derrick Hearne 1982

ISBN: 0 86243 015 1

Printed and published in Wales
by Y Lolfa Cyf., Talybont, Ceredigion SY24 5HE;
tel. Talybont (097086) 304.

The $\boxed{A}$ $\boxed{B}$ $\boxed{C}$ of the Welsh Revolution

Derrick Hearne

DERRICK HEARNE

Derrick Hearne lives in the Swansea Valley. He was born, educated and married in the Valley, but like many other of its sons, he has been forced to live and work in many other lands and has served many regimes: truly a victim of the "Welsh Disease" (as our betters in Whitehall laughingly put it).

Educated in the Grammar School, Ystalyfera, and King's College in London, he became involved with computers in their early days, and rapidly went through the normal career progression. In his mid-thirties, he threw up a "safe" job in the East End to begin a mendicant life of an "international" consultant. Working either for the United Nations Organizations, commercial firms or on direct hire to foreign governments, he has worked and travelled in Bulgaria, Iran, Libya, India, the West Indies, the GDR, the Gulf, Scandinavia and through most of the countries of Western Europe. He has spent long periods serving both Communist and Fascist governments. While no foreigner could ever, for one minute, be trusted by such regimes, there has been the occasional flash of lightning which has illuminated a broad stage. He is now back in his native valley engaged, in a very small way, in serving the needs of financial institutions of various sorts for systems of computer control, model making and forecasting.

He has written two other books, also published by Y Lolfa: *The Rise of the Welsh Republic* and *The Joy of Freedom* (see page 286).

ACKNOWLEDGEMENTS

The author wishes to record with respect and gratitude the influence of two French writers upon the ideas expressed in this book: Jacques Ellul and Roger Garaudy. One must admit to the continuing supremacy of the French intellectual tradition in ruthless analysis and bold construction of ideas.

I must acknowledge the kind permission to reproduce maps and statistics given by the Controller of Her Majesty's Stationery Office to produce material originally published in *Welsh Economic Trends* (Welsh Office) 1979 (Tables 102A, B, C and D).

Penguin Books for permission to quote from *The Alternative Future*, by Roger Garaudy.

J M Dent & Sons Limited, to be allowed to quote from Giraldus Cambrensis *Itinerary through Wales and Description of Wales*.

The Secretary of Plaid Cymru, to quote from the many Plaid Pamphlets and Dr D J Davies' works which first appeared as essays in Plaid Publications.

The Economist Newspaper, for permission to quote from their leading article of 5th November, 1977, *Blowing up a Tyranny* and the many statistics derived from numerous articles. (Although Welsh readers may not agree with all the views of this newspaper, it is still, without question, the best economic newspaper in the Western world, deserving of regular and diligent study.)

North West Community Newspapers and Rupert Cavendish for permission to quote extensively from *Differences and Similarities between Radical Liberalism and Plaid Cymru*, (1977). (This is recommended as a standard text for Plaid Party workers in order that they may be thoroughly familiar with arguments put forward by Liberals and Social Democrats.)

The author and publishers of *Adfer Enaid y Cymro*, Emyr Llewelyn, Llanbedr, 1974.

R S Thomas and Christopher Davies Press Swansea for permission to quote from the poem *His Condescensions are Short-lived*.

Edmund Wilson and Fontana Books for permission to quote from *To the Finland Station*.

Reverend John Mills and the publishers of *Gerald the Welshman* for permission to quote from this attractive little essay.

Finally, I must thank Mrs Meg Dafydd for her many struggles with the manuscript of this book during the typing of a difficult text.

AUTHOR'S NOTE ON WELSH UNEMPLOYMENT FIGURES APPEARING IN THE TEXT

It is with sadness that one must record the gross inaccuracies in the number of Welsh unemployed quoted in this text.

The book was written between 1977-1981 and it has been impossible to keep abreast of the figures.

God alone is able to judge the human misery that they hide: the broken marriages, the indignity and the lost years for young and old, and the sheer senseless waste.

May God give to this people a determination to destroy this régime once and for all, and to put in its place that free and prosperous Republic that all Welshmen secretly carry in their hearts. May God give to our whole people a happy issue out of all their afflictions.

TABLE OF
CONTENTS

INTRODUCTION

England, you can be sure, will have little regard for those interests which Welshmen themselves do not consider of sufficient importance to inspire them to unite in their defence, and for their cultivation and advancement. He who has no respect for himself, and his own life and interests, cannot complain if others do not give it.

Ithel Davies. *A TU Congress for Wales.*
Plaid pamphlet, 1944

If by the people, you understand the multitude, and it is no matter what they think: they are sometimes in the right, sometimes in the wrong: their judgement is a mere lottery.

Dryden

The Welsh people think of themselves as free, but are slaves to their own poor self-esteem. Seven hundred years after the brutal conquest of their country, they had so little pride left in them, that they cheerfully rejected a national assembly, which, whatever its shortcomings, would have given them some little voice, which could not be completely ignored when their fate was to be determined.

Was this a lack of judgement (as some would have us believe), or was it dislike of yet another bureaucracy, or was it the influence of the media? It may have been all or none of these, but it was compounded by a lack of pride. Those who have lost it can sink no lower. They are open to the violation of all comers, because they show that they will make only token protest.

Their signal was received with glee and acted upon with haste by an English power establishment which has always feared the Welsh (even in their bondage) and now are joyful to put them down with their own consent. Whitehall needed no second bidding. The surest way was to destroy what little support still remained to the Welsh working class. Despite all other factors, Welsh unemployment is in part a direct consequence of a No vote for the Welsh Assembly.

If it is true that a people get the government they deserve, then the Welsh people richly deserve their unemployment, and all which it brings with it. Were our people afraid to let go the Union connection? Let them eat it! A free Wales, however poor, would have been at liberty to bestir itself to put things right. That precious freedom the Welsh announced to the world, they did not want. Are they now begging, cap in hand, in the waiting rooms of influence in Whitehall, Brussels or Tokyo? They can be safely ignored. Theirs is only a maudlin rugby club nationalism of a light people of no consequence. They had their chance and threw it away. The bushmen of Africa knew better.

Do they protest that their land is now to become a dumping ground for nuclear waste? Do they demonstrate against Cruise missiles and army recruiting campaigns in their country? Did they think ahead to the consequences when they voted out a Welsh Assembly? Did they vote their sons into a war to shore up a collapsing capitalist order? Do they wring their hands for their lost jobs? Let them beware lest worse befall them! They may soon wring their hands for their dead sons!

There is in this land, however, a remnant who will not stand dutifully aside and accept a majority verdict. Nationalists may now be in an agony of reappraisal, but they are not part of it. Long ago, they went through their own struggle, and now, when others are in bewildered debate, they have the cool certainty that comes with conviction. This springs from the realisation that the age of votes, plebiscites and referenda is over. These are not the new reality. The Age of Scarcity is the age of revolution, because no other way exists of dealing with it. Monopoly capital has fossilised society so that it is too inflexible to respond to the needs of the Age of Scarcity without a revolution, but whose revolution? Ours or theirs? Will capitalism collapse in these islands, or will it be rescued, either by a war, or a fascist régime, which will head off the fall?

It is the contention of this book that it will be a close run thing. In Wales, we need to act very quickly indeed, unless we are to insulate ourselves from either catastrophe. The condition of the international economy gives grounds for fears even in the best governed states (and the English State is definitely not among that number). Capitalism will be brought near to collapse within the next 10 years. There is monetary chaos superimposed upon a structural crisis.

The monetary crisis is simple to understand. Since the 1944 Bretton Woods agreements, which govern settlements in the post-war period, broke down in 1971 due to pressure on the dollar, severe pressures have been brought to bear on the banking system. Large oil capital surpluses are looking for a safe investment haven, and there are no more to be found. The poor countries, who make up 20% of the world population and share out 1% of the world income are piling up enormous deficits, and the debt service on these overdrafts is so large that a default is possible. Much of the lending has been done by private banks. Several have suspended further lending, because they believe themselves to be over-exposed, thus bringing the prospect of a domino collapse of the banking system and the shaky framework of several countries at the same time. Could the United Kingdom survive this collapse unscathed? The structural weakness has several dimensions.

The situation in money terms is this. In 1980, OPEC oil surplus will be about 120 billion dollars. OPEC cannot absorb all this cash on development. OPEC countries have to deposit it with the banks. The banks pay such huge interest on the deposits that they, in turn, are forced to lend it out, but to whom?

Non-oil, less developed countries owed a total of 315 billion dollars in 1978, of which the total loaned by private banks in 1979 was 147 billion dollars. Of that amount, 20 countries account for 80%, and of those 20 countries, 5 account for 40%. Of those 5, Mexico and Brazil have absorbed private American bank loans equivalent to the total capital of the 5 American banks who have lent the cash. In 1980, Brazil alone requires 7 billion dollars to pay the interest of its foreign debt. Currently, it is earning 20 billion dollars per year, and paying out 7 billion on oil imports.

There is, of course, the perpetual problem of the poor nations, who find it more difficult to sell raw materials to rich ones on anything like terms attractive enough to enable them to pay for oil. Trade is being strangled by the inflated cost of industrial goods and energy.

The Arabs themselves (yesterday's poor) are now cock-a-hoop to find the shoe on the other foot, and are determined to keep it there. Since 1974, they have organised the most successful cartel, and have carried out the most spectacular transfer of paper wealth in the history of mankind. So far, they have carried it off without a shot being fired, but the question cannot long be deferred. If industrial nations as successful as Japan, Germany, the USA and the USSR now find themselves permanently in current account deficit, is it impossible to assume that matters will be allowed to rest? The cash position is illustrated with 3 examples. At 30 dollars per barrel, the most efficient exporting countries on earth, Germany and Japan, saw their respective surpluses of 9 million dollars and 17 million dollars in 1978 turn into deficits of 6 billion dollars and 18 billion dollars in 1980. Out of the most efficient developing countries, Brazil paid 600 million dollars in 1973 for just a little less oil than will cost 7 billion dollars a year in 1980.

Possible ways out are a deliberately induced hyper-inflating of all industrial based currencies (much as the Weimar Republic in 1926 debased its currency when faced with French reparations demands beyond German means of payment), which would have the effect of wiping out the Arab paper balances. This might be the occasion for a more sober Arab approach to oil tariffs. In the long term, this would solve nothing. Alternatively, a war could start among the Eastern and Western industrial nations to secure control of the oil fields. Capitalism could not survive either confrontation in its present form.

Hyper-inflation would destroy the political order, and a world war (if it did not destroy mankind) would pose other threats to capitalism —the most important being that the capitalist régimes might not win that war.

There are other dimensions to the crisis of capitalism, the scarcity of raw materials and foodstuffs. The world has dangerously thin margins. The cost of energy quadrupled in 1974, and had doubled by 1979, and doubled again between 1979 and 1980. Prices are symptomatic rather than a root cause. The crisis of capital revolves around people, not things.

There are too many people and everywhere their expectations are rising. This is the real cause of inflation. Ordinary people are no longer prepared to put up with the "share of the cake" or the role of passive acceptance which capitalism has assigned to them. There is a constant upward movement of wages wherever trade unions are strong enough to exert influence. In less developed countries there is impatience with the slow growth of prosperity over several generations. Change is required, expected, indeed demanded, within a lifetime. This "Revolution of Rising Expectations" is the real enemy of capitalism.

It is against the cloud banks of this gathering storm that we must once again raise the question of Welsh political freedom, and associate with it the challenges to capitalism within these islands.

There is no doubt of the sickness of English capitalism. The reasons for it are various, but their cumulative effect can be illustrated in simplified form in Figure 1.

The eclipse of English prosperity is due to moral bankruptcy and to a staggering complacency. The governing classes have been on the winning side in two world wars and had the ability to conduct "business as normal" after both. The forces of reform demanding a radical reconstruction of society and the economy have never been strong enough to overcome this inertia. Efforts for reform reached their climax in the General Strike in 1926 and in the career of Aneurin Bevan in his struggle with the Labour Party in 1953. Both events occurred about 7 years after the end of a war. The Establishment beat off both attacks skilfully. Business did continue as usual. It is the common people who are now paying with their own declining living standards for the complacency of the powerful.

It was not so elsewhere. Most countries in continental Europe, faced with the devastation of the Second World War, could not afford any but a most radical overhaul of their economies, and their thinking. This led to the birth of new forms of government —in particular the development, under one disguise or another, of some form of planned economy. In the United Kingdom, nationalisation was regarded as a substitute for planning. The skilful intellectual (as well as political)

13

Figure 1

THE CRISIS OF CAPITALISM IN THE UNITED KINGDOM LEADING TO THE COMPLETE DESTRUCTION OF THE WELSH COMMUNITY

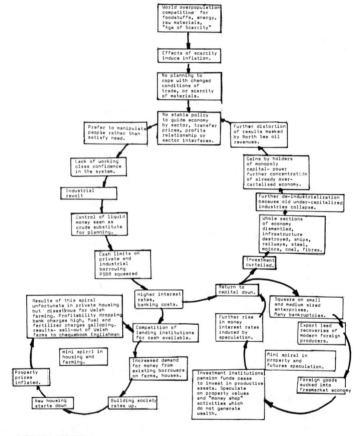

CONCLUSION:

1. Progressive collapse can only reversed by Fascist or Communist takeover or war.

2. Welsh economy shackled to a dying man by choice of Welsh electorate.

rearguard action fought by the owners of capital was responsible. Nationalised industries could be more easily manipulated than a "national" plan. Nationalisation presented less of a threat to the Establishment. For 30 years there has been a see-saw between the advocates of more nationalisation, and those who wanted less. This is the wrong debate in the wrong century. The real debate should have been conducted along different lines and should have revolved around the benefit to the community of any economic investment. This would have had dangerous implications for vested interests.

For 30 years, there has been no stable economic policy in these islands even for matters so fundamental as energy invest-ment, a unified transport policy, public housing, agriculture or prices and incomes. The economy has lurched wildly from one policy to another, harming communities, industries and lives of individuals as a consequence. The latest bout of Tory madness is only a more extreme oscillation which the deepening crisis was pre-destined to excite. Having inflicted the maximum possible damage, it will certainly be followed by another equally wild lurch in another direction.

The vortex of decline in the quality of government has set up satellite whirlpools, in the quality of private sector investment which is now effectively managed not by a government at all, but by insurance companies' fund managers and pension fund trustees. We have the paradoxical situation of an economy awash with funds, but starved of capital for productive invest-ment. Other whirlpools of decline have been induced in housing and land use, de-industrialisation, transport and monetary management.

The most serious effect has been away from the metropolitan heart of the English system. If the state of England is one of genteel decay, that of Wales is now one of acute crisis. The Welsh economy, always suffering from the existence of deliberately induced structural weakness, is now in collapse. 13% unemployment in Gwent, Gwynedd and Glamorgan will soon destroy the last shaky foundation of what we could once claim to have been the Welsh nation.

For Welsh nationalists, having suffered their most humiliating defeat in 50 years, now to watch the terminal collapse of the

Welsh economy, the prospects appear to be bleak.

This is not so.

To an extent, the Welsh people cannot accept all responsibility for the condition in which they now find themselves. There have been shortcomings in nationalist leadership for 25 years. While showing indomitable courage and the highest integrity at a personal level, the leadership Gwynfor Evans has given to Plaid Cymru has been lacking in boldness and intellectual honesty. The work done by Dr D J Davies in the 1940s laid the foundation for the success of nationalism in Wales. Gwynfor Evans could never capitalise on the achievement of *Towards an Economic Democracy* (1949), because he obviously could not bring himself to push the implications of Davies' insight into the psychology and economic circumstances of the Welsh people to the obvious conclusion. Gwynfor Evans wanted to be all things to all men. He fell into the trap that awaits all would-be revolutionary movements once they renounce the revolution. Instead, he concentrated his appeal on culture and political expediency. Culture is hardly a "turn-on" for the working class, and Plaid Cymru is now reaping the harvest of political expediency from all classes.

1. The régime of worker democracy advocated by Davies, and inherent in the Welsh folk political philosophy, is incapable of supporting itself except under the umbrella of a strong central state supported by an equally strong and self willed army. Federalism, internal or external, for the first decade of the Republic, is unworkable. Guided Democracy at the centre and small councils at the local level (for co-operating workers and townspeople) are the only possible solution that would fit the circumstances.

2. This régime requires strong organs of planning in order to nurse the infant economy through a difficult first decade of life. By its very nature, this would involve the total mobilisation of all means of production, distribution and manpower. It would offend many vested interests and would certainly require conscription of labour in compulsory para-military service to the economy.

3. It is inevitable that such a régime could not exist within a

United Kingdom, or indeed, within a United Europe, as now constituted. The policy of the Welsh Republic would be community directed. Indeed, the whole apparatus of raising revenue (monopolies —from where else would investment funds come?) and protecting nascent community industries would demand a stern tariff barrier. Separation from the English State's ideological, cultural and economic captivity would be complete. There can be no federal solution without betraying the revolution.

4. Gwynfor Evans could never accept the fact that leadership within the Party, the revolution, and the Republic is the leadership of a minority of dedicated, committed and absolutely uncompromising men and women. A Provisional Government needs at least 10 years of uninterrupted power in order to maintain stable government at central level and allow the ordinary people of Wales to acquire education in the art of genuine responsible government, at works and council level. They have never enjoyed these rights, therefore they need a period of apprenticeship in genuine responsibility.

Strange to say, the appeal of this simple policy, honestly put, with all the calls for sacrifice which it would entail would, in fact, have won for Plaid Cymru an unchallenged moral leadership of Welsh opinion. Cowardice in the face of the enemy was rewarded with a resounding vote of no confidence. And who, we may ask, is the enemy?

Welsh national ambitions are, and always have been, a loaded revolver pointed to the heart of the English State, and to capitalism, which is inexorably entwined with it. It is no surprise, then, that the monopolisation of the means of attitude formation have been most efficiently used against the Welsh national interest. The great migrations of the 1920s, the 1930s, and the constant haemorrhaging of the natural intellectual leaders of Welsh society after 1945 for want of adequate job prospects, have left the field wide open to the unrestricted manipulation of opinion of the remnant of the once proud Welsh nation. It is this rump which has now consented to its mass suicide.

It is precisely to this population that Plaid Cymru, under the leadership of Gwynfor Evans, has fed a rag-bag of self-contradictory political slogans which for 30 years has replaced the honest fare served up by an earlier generation of Plaid thinkers.

All other considerations aside, tactically this was the worst thing that Plaid Cymru could have done. The neglect of ideology in political affairs brings its own nemesis.

Plaid has found itself constantly catching after the shirt tails of other people's political campaigns, which have sometimes been trailed quite deliberately under the noses of the Plaid leadership. Had there been a firm ideological committment, it would have provided a yardstick by which to measure the true importance of any issue. All too often over the last 30 years, the Plaid has gone off at full cry after a red herring, and has overlooked the solid issue, which was precisely the intended effect.

In fact, a cool ideological analysis of the Welsh condition would have provided the answer to many problems which have clearly worried Plaid Cymru since the mid-60s. Figure 2 shows in simplified form some of the traditional guidelines of national-ist policy. This shows the dilemma in which the Plaid leadership has repeatedly found itself. Plaid had inherited a body of political thinking from D J Davies and other in the late 30s and 40s, which culminated in the publication of *Towards an Economic Democracy* in 1949. The core of these ideas is illustrated in Figure 2. But each element raised more questions than it answered until the English connection is obliterated.

Figure 3 shows the results of applying D J Davies' ideas (contained, for example, in *Plan for Electricity*, 1944; *The Welsh Coal Industry*, 1948) within a new environment which is totally Republican.

Yet this begs the big question for Welsh nationalism —the very one which it has always been afraid to pose, let alone answer.

"Can a régime of economic freedom be established in Wales by democratic means?"

The very question is enough to have sent the whole pack of "national" leaders off into a funk! To his great credit, we must record that Aneurin Bevan was never sure that Welshmen could bring it off by constitutional methods, and he said so, but he

Figure 2

TRADITIONAL PLAID CYMRU POLICIES ARE RIDDLED WITH UNANSWERED QUESTIONS ON EACH MAJOR POINT OF POLICY

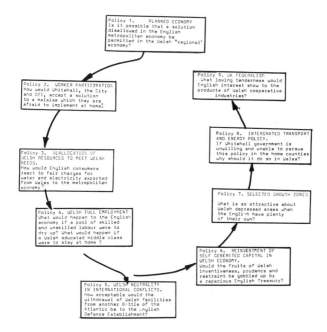

Policy 1.   PLANNED ECONOMY
Is it possible that a solution disallowed in the English metropolitan economy be permitted in the Welsh "regional" economy?

Policy 2.   WORKER PARTICIPATION
How would Whitehall, the City and CBI, accept a solution to a malaise which they are afraid to implement at home?

Policy 3.   REALLOCATION OF WELSH RESOURCES TO MEET WELSH NEEDS.
How would English consumers react to fair charges for water and electricity exported from Wales to the metropolitan economy?

Policy 4.   WELSH FULL EMPLOYMENT
What would happen to the English economy if a pool of skilled and unskilled labour were to dry up? What would happen if a Welsh educated middle class were to stay at home?

Policy 5.   WELSH NEUTRALITY IN INTERNATIONAL CONFLICTS.
How acceptable would the withdrawal of Welsh facilities from another Battle of the Atlantic be to the English Defence Establishment?

Policy 6.   REINVESTMENT OF SELF GENERATED CAPITAL IN WELSH ECONOMY.
Would the fruits of Welsh inventiveness, prudence and restraint be gobbled up by a rapacious English Treasury?

Policy 7.   SELECTED GROWTH ZONES
What is so attractive about Welsh depressed areas when the English have plenty of their own?

Policy 8.   INTERGRATED TRANSPORT AND ENERGY POLICY.
If Whitehall government is unwilling and unable to persue this policy in the home counties why should it do so in Wales?

Policy 9.   UK FEDERALISM
What loving tenderness would English interest show to the products of Welsh cooperative industries?

CONCLUSION:
1. Traditional Welsh Nationalist policies are fraudulent without a revolutionary will. "Non-violent Nationalism" is a nonsense. Self-help policies violate the principles of English government on all accounts.
2. It takes no great powers of persuasion by English controlled media to convince Welsh people that Plaid Cymru is a purveyor of humbug unless it commits itself to a fundamental change inconceivable within the English union.

also added that first, we must try to use them and only when the mass manipulation of pseudo-democracy had clearly demonstrated its overwhelming influence were men justified in seeking other methods. This has been proven beyond all possibility of doubt since his death, and the Referendum result has clinched the matter.

The common people of any nation are rarely able to judge what is to their advantage. That is why they remain the "common people". Yet they are not so unfeeling as not to be deeply dissatisfied with mass democracy. The people of Wales have every reason to feel a deep emotional alienation from the Whitehall régime. They recognise only too well that they are regarded as an expendable second-class people.

"There is nothing wrong with the Welsh: they make jolly good soldiers under white officers." (To quote a *Financial Times* gossip column.)

Their economy, their railways, their coal mines, their steel works, their branch factories, and their regional grants, are all expendable. The Welsh people fully know this. It is a measure of the failure of Plaid Cymru that they have not been able to turn this to their advantage over 50 years, and with so many dedicated party workers in their midst. (Whatever criticism can be levelled at the intellectual leadership, one must acknowledge that the quality of Plaid activists cannot be matched. The English parties cannot hold a candle to them.)

We have now come to the heart of the matter —to the "sacred cow" of Plaid Cymru thinking —parliamentary and non-violent change, enshrined in Gwynfor Evans' *Non-Violent Nationalism* (1973). This idea of change from WITHIN the system needs careful analysis.

* In fact, Welshmen 'enjoy' one of the most anti-democratic forms of government in Western Europe. It corresponds almost exactly with the government in the Italian South, where a coterie of criminals, clerics and aristocrats manipulate every government decision and the "mafiosi" collect their cut from every public works programme. (It is not for nothing that the vested interest in Wales is known as the "Taffia".) The apathy of the average Welshman to politics is akin to that of Sicily. It is as easy to manipulate a degraded proletariat from the pulpit

20

or the Con Club.

This is the system that Gwynfor Evans hopes to break with non-violent nationalism.

* The alternative is not necessarily violence. A cool re-appraisal of the way in which nationalist movements in Europe have come to power can be helpful. Of all the nation states to emerge since 1900, only one (Norway) did so as a result of a plebiscite. The others were the result of defeat. The wishes of the people, or the standard of education, or the state of the economy had nothing to do with the matter. The pre-occupation with head-counting constricts Plaid Cymru thinking, and results in a misdirection of energies along lines exactly pre-determined by the English Establishment and its Welsh puppets. DEMOCRACY IS NO LONGER THE PRIME-MOVER IN THE MARCH OF HISTORY.

Capitalism, as we have seen, is approaching a major crisis, which may precipitate war. It is unlikely that the Whitehall régime can escape unscathed from this crisis. Given the significant shift in the balance of power, it can no longer be assumed that the English state could emerge from the imminent struggle on the winning side. The successor governments to the old empires after 1919 emerged *not* because they had worried about their degree of representation in the Reichsrat or the Duma, but because they had bent their energies exclusively to ATTITUDE FORMATION.

Nationalists in Central, Baltic and Balkan Europe could see that the old régime was predestined to collapse. They went quietly, but determinedly, about their proper business — conditioning the minds of their peoples for the inevitable.

The intellectual energy spent in ideological study before 1917 must have been prodigious, but it was abundantly fruitful.

Any minority, tightly organised and subject to incessant ideological training, with an unswerving propaganda line, and a well-developed counter-espionage system, can impose its authority completely in any fluid situation caused during the disintegration of old political relationships. This is a vital lesson of European nationalism and Plaid Cymru has not learnt it, in the fifty years of its existence. The emotional preparation for

21

freedom has been neglected in Plaid propaganda lest it offend somebody. The mass democratic and big unit economic system is basically unsuited to the Welsh temperament, because it rides roughshod over Welsh individualism. This was D J Davies' central thesis, yet it is precisely this fact which Plaid Cymru have been unable to exploit.

If young people in Wales bear this in mind, it is clear that the cause of the Republic has not been defeated in our country. Quite the contrary, far from flogging a dead horse, the patriots may heave a sigh of relief at a near miss.

* Would not any state founded upon the half truths, contradictions and slogans of Plaid Cymru have fallen foul of the first squall that would have hit it? Did not the electorate sense as much and give Plaid a vote of no confidence as a consequence?

* If it is true that once the ship of state is launched into the cold and tossing sea, we will have no time to consult maps, then surely we must prepare the young people of Wales now with the most careful ideological training, so that they will be able to steer the Republic by instinct, lashed to the wheel?

In the terrible days of shortage, want and conflict into which we are now moving, the seas of disaster will beat again and again across the decks of the Republic.

The old Plaid could neither see, nor did it want to see, the true economic, political or emotional horizons. It was not an instrument fit to govern. It worked to the rules of others. A revolutionary party makes its own rules. That is why it eventually comes to power. The young people of Wales must build the new Plaid for themselves, out of the wreckage of the old. It will be built on this perception. There is much to cherish that was good and honest, honourable and wholesome in Plaid, before it fell foul of cowardice, expediency and intellectual dishonesty (and possibly manipulation from without). The core of what is good in Plaid is contained in the work of D J Davies. All that is good in this ABC is due to his inspiration, and any fault is my own.

There are three stages in the formation of new attitudes:

Figure 3

THE LOGIC OF THE WELSH REVOLUTION BROUGHT ABOUT UNDER PEOPLE'S RULE

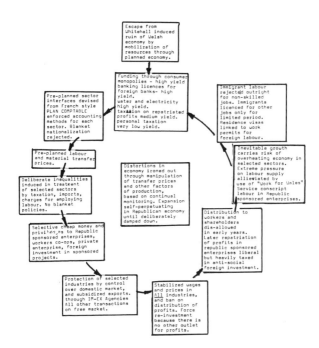

CONCLUSION:

1. Virtuous cycle of rehabilitation of Welsh economy conceivable only in terms of sovereign republic.

2. Every measure on this chart inconceivable under English rule.

3. These measures generate not merely finance capital for re-investment in people's enterprises but confidence that Wales can stand on her own feet. Release of a spirit of optimism and wonderful self-confidence.

* The destruction of old attitudes.

The most effective way to destroy them is to show that the society can be refashioned quite efficiently, using means considered beyond the bounds of respectability. *The Rise of the Welsh Republic* was an effort to do this. In its pages, I took a sledgehammer to some of the cherished myths of nationalism.

* The search for new parameters.

The Joy of Freedom pointed the way towards a new synthesis, by examining the emotional as well as the economic background which must affect the development of the ideology of the Welsh Revolution.

* This ABC is a conscious attempt to refashion cadre attitudes.

Those who have had the privilege of teaching young men and women at the peak of their perceptiveness, perhaps in the year before graduation, will recognise that they cannot be fed a catechism. They want to explore the reason behind the original premise. In politics, we must get behind the reasons to the emotive ground out of which those reasons sprang up. This is exactly the purpose of this ABC. In politics, it is attitudes, not reasons, which count.

This ABC is divided into a number of short essays which explore approaches to opinions which every activist is certain to encounter in day-to-day work. It is a matter of individual conscience (and eventually party programmes) to give a definitive solution to them, but the frame of mind in which that solution is conceived is of paramount importance. We must sometimes pick our way over old battle fields, to show the factors which created ideologies, but we need to take these, not at their face value, but re-evaluate them in the light of the needs of Welsh society as we can interpret them now.

It is really the battle fields of the next century which should concern us now. This leads to another point about this ABC. The struggle for Welsh freedom has gone on for 50 years. It may take 50 years more. The patriot will interpret his duty in a Christian manner —as duty— something which has to be done, because it is right, and for which no reward is to be expected. The struggle is one of unyielding persistence. In the perspective of history, a decade is little. What is important to the cadre is the fact that he has influenced the attitudes of others to such an extent that the climate of opinion within which another generation of nationalists will work is more favourable. It is within this context that the personal contribution of Gwynfor Evans to the well-being of his country will, in the long run, be assessed. It is massive —this must be acknowledged.

The other characteristic of this ABC are the apparent contradictions within it. The class war is an example.

Nowhere in Plaid literature over 50 years will you find any but a disavowal of the class struggle as a basis of political thought and action. You will not find it advocated in the ABC. Yet this is not the question. It is not the attitude of Welshmen to Whitehall that matters. On the contrary, it is the attitude of Whitehall to Welshmen. We may not believe in the class struggle. The mandarins do, and act on that belief. For them, this is a struggle of the possessors, the manipulators, against the dispossessed and the disinherited. They are few and we are many, but weak, undecided and soft as butter.

Indeed, in the oldest colony, the class struggle takes on its classic form. The struggle will run along familiar lines. Fudged ideas will have disastrous consequences for Wales. The battle ranks have already been drawn up as if history were running along tram lines.

What Welshmen decide when they have their own republic is another matter. They can organise their society along lines of class co-operation or conflict, if they have a mind to do so. For the time being, they are caught up in a class-war of classic dimension.

This illustrates the dichotomy, or contradictions, inherent in this ABC. The reader will be continually faced with a sort of "relativity" in Welsh revolutionary politics, an *inner* and an *outer* relationship. This will annoy him intensely, until he realises that inherited attitudes need constant re-evaluation if they are to make a worthwhile guide to our future. In particular, attitudes on the conflict between the political right or left are stood on their head. This is entirely correct. The Age of Scarcity introduces a set of economic realities quite outside the agenda of the old conflicts. It would be strange indeed if any primer on Welsh politics did not take account of this.

Let us now note other contradictions:

* While there is ample evidence of a detestation of monopoly capitalism and all its works, there is active encouragement for small scale capitalism (especially if it takes the form of worker co-operatives) or enterprises with substantial worker involvement.

* Indeed, the virtues of worker participation are not seen as a stepping-stone on the road to Utopian socialisation of the means of production and distribution. It is viewed primarily as the minimum *emotional* condition, which can maintain a national community of interest, strong enough to withstand the pressures that the Age of Scarcity will impose upon Welsh life.

* Similarly we advocate social control over the Welsh market, while at the same time rejecting solutions, such as nationalisation or uniform rates of corporate taxation, as a means to secure that control. We recommend more flexible expedients, such as direction of trade sectors, through the use of information (rather along the lines of the French *Plan Comptable Géneral*) which can, and should, lead to flexible taxation and investment incentives.

These contradictions are inherent in all nationalist literature put out by Plaid Cymru over the past 50 years.

However, there are other contradictions, which I have deliberately brought to the surface, which will not be welcomed by Plaid Cymru. We must now explore these, too.

* A distinctly ambiguous position with regard to Trade Unions in Wales. The unions, in their traditional bureaucratic form, are clearly frightened out of their wits at the prospect of worker control. They have made a compact with capitalism in return for a bigger share of the cake. Worker participation would clearly upset many union applecarts. On the other hand, a more flexible approach could revitalise Plaid Cymru and the unions, because neither are likely to gain their ends without each other. It is a high priority in Whitehall to wreck this marriage.

The final and most important contradiction is contained in

Figure 4

CRASH PROGRAMME TO RESCUE WELSH WORK PEOPLE FROM EFFECTS OF ENGLISH RULE

CRASH PROGRAMME TO RESUE WELSH WORK PEOPLE FROM EFFECTS OF ENGLISH RULE

WITHDRAW FROM THE UNION, WITHDRAW FROM E.E.C. CLOSE FRONTIERS TO FREE MOVEMENT OF GOODS AND CAPITAL. ALLOW FREE MOVEMENT OF PEOPLE OUT, BUT NO IMMIGRATION IN.

FREEZE PRICES, INCOMES, DISTRIBUTED PROFITS. STRIKES AND LOCKOUTS ILLEGAL IN ESSENTIAL INDUSTRIES.

50% OF CAPITAL IN ENTERPRISES OVER 30 WORKERS TURNED OVER TO WORKPEOPLE. MINES, STEEL, RAILWAYS BECOME COOPERATIVES.

IMPOSE COMMON CHART OF ACCOUNTS (FRENCH " PLAN COMPTABLE") ON ALL ENTERPRISES, REPORTING TO MINISTRY OF FINANCE.

ORGANIZED STATE WHOLESALING & RAW MATERIAL PURCHASE MONOPOLY. LICENCE MULTIPLE OUTLET CHAINS OPERATION ON STRICT CONDITIONS.

LICENCE OPERATION OF FOREIGN BANKS ON STRICT CONDITIONS AND HIGH FEES.

ESTABLISH STATE CONSUMER MONOPOLIES IN CERTAIN COMMON USE ITEMS.

CONSCRIPTS ARRIVE AT "WORK FOR WALES" CENTRES TO ENSURE SOURCE OF CHEAP LABOUR FOR INFRASTRUCTURE MAINTENANCE AND NEW WORKS.

FIRST FIVE YEAR PLAN INFRASTRUCTURE INVESTMENT IN:

* ELECTRONIC COMMUNICATIONS, VOICE, DATA , FASCIMILE.

* MOTOR RAIL NETWORK/ ROLL ON / ROLL OFF TERMINALS. ONLINE COMPUTER CONTROL SYSTEM.

* BEGIN DEEP PLOUHING AND REHABILITATION OF UPLANDS AND MARGINAL AGRICULTURAL LAND. PLANNING INDICATORS FOR FARM PRODUCTION, GUARANTEED MARKET ESTABLISHED FOR FARM PRODUCE.

* HYDROCARBON MONOPOLY VERTICAL INTERGRATION ENERGY INVESTMENT . COAL TO OIL REFINERY BEGUN.

* AUXILIARY INVESTMENT IN CEMENT, STEEL AND ALUMINIUM BUILDING PRODUCTS, PHARMACEUTICALS AND STATE MONOPOLY PLANTS.

* BEGIN RESEARCH INTO SELECTION OF HIGH TECHNOLOGY WORLD PATENTS FOR CORE ACTIVITY OF SECOND FIVE YEAR PLAN, FOLLOWING JAPANESE AND FRENCH EXAMPLES.

* ESTABLISH MICROPROCESSOR BASIC PRODUCE UNIT.

the Christian proposition that life is sacred. No individual or nation has the right to commit suicide. In the face of a declared intention to destroy the life of a nation, a minority has not only the right, but a Christian obligation, to seize control to prevent that life being snuffed out. Nationalists will find it hard to swallow this proposition. It implies two corollary opinions.

1. The national interest can be perceived by an élite who have the technical competence to do the job.

2. A nation, the individual and unique creation of God Himself, has, twice within a decade (the Common Market and the Devolution Referendum) demonstrated its determination to destroy itself. Let us suppose that at some time in the future, disenchanted with the English connection, the electors were to vote themselves a Welsh Republic, who knows, when the moon was in the right quarter, might they not vote themselves out of it?

References to democracy within this ABC must be continually weighed against these opinions.

Young people who read this book have effectively 20 years in which to take control of their nation. It is questionable whether there will be a Welsh "nation" by 2000 AD, unless a very different régime is established. The past neglect has brought us to this state.

The nature of the struggle may be judged from the March Dawn Swoop. This is an accurate indicator of what Welsh patriots have in store for them, and this is certainly merely the beginning.

It is a struggle which will require certain moral qualities. Young men and women who doubt their ability to measure up to this test of character had best view this book in the nature of a warning, and engage in a less demanding pastime such as rugby football. Those who cannot do so will have an awesome responsibility.

They have to answer these questions:

1. Are they able to analyse the crisis of capitalism as it affects Wales, within the limits of solutions traditionally advocated by Plaid Cymru?

2. Is Plaid Cymru synonymous with the Republican cause in Wales?

3. How do they view their own future political work for Wales? In particular, would violence be productive or counter-productive at this stage?

4. How real is the prospect of war? What effect would war have on their answers to these questions?

The purpose of this book is to suggest that the answer to question number one is "no". In more settled times, the answer to question number two would also be "no". Now let us jump to the last question. The prospect of war is real, and getting closer. In this case, what would be the role of Welsh nationalists, to fight for capitalism, or to fight for neutrality?

The whole rationale of this ABC suggests that this is not our war, and we should strain every muscle to keep out of it. It would not be a war fought about personal or political freedom (certainly not Welsh freedom). It would be a war of the super-powers to determine whether American business should have access to oil, or whether the reserves will be appropriated by the eastern bloc, whose economic system would be in peril without the cheap oil, upon which to base the hold of the USSR on its satellite states.

We can now answer question No. 3. If we accept the war scenario, then it is clear that time is fast running out for the Whitehall régime, and running out faster still for Welsh nationalism. The Whitehall régime could not survive another war, and any closely indoctrinated movement in Wales has a real prospect of coming to power —*if it can show a doctrine which is coherent and uncompromising.* Under these circumstances, dissipation of energy is useless and totally in-effective. A few acts of isolated violence would not be fruitful. There is fighting to be done, of a different sort. (In any case, technically, violence is only politically productive *after* a massive propaganda barrage, in a society where at least a third of the population offer assistance). Young people in Wales would also be quite wrong to set up any alternative to Plaid Cymru. There is not time. There is only time for the ideological renewal of nationalist policies. Ideological work has absolute priority over all other activities. This is the message of this ABC. If it is heeded, the young people of Wales who today find themselves unemployed and cast out of society, will govern this country within ten years. If not, they and their country will be burned up in a nuclear holocaust.

HOW TO USE THIS BOOK

This book was inspired by, and consciously modelled on, **The ABC of Communism,** *written by Bukharin and Preobrazhensky in 1919. That, however, is as far as any similarity goes, for while this ABC, too, has pretensions to become "an elementary text-book of Welsh Nationalist knowledge", both its form and the circumstances in which both books were written differ absolutely.*

Bukharin wrote the theoretical chapters of his ABC in the long hot summer of 1917 when the Russian Communist Party was working feverishly in preparation for the October Revolution.

This book will appear in the shadow of the most humiliating defeat ever suffered by Welsh Nationalism. It seeks to assist those young people who, in loyalty to their nation, have determined to nurture the roses of success from the ashes of defeat. It also accounts for the fact that there must necessarily be a certain amount of repetition. Each of the entries must stand on its own, as an essay in attitude formation. This will mean, for instance, that certain facts must be quoted, perhaps twice, once in one entry and again in another.

Wherever possible, I have tried to preface an essay with a quotation from the work of prominent nationalists, to whom we are indebted for laying the intellectual framework of Welsh Nationalism, 40 years ago. This contains the quintessence of the Welsh view of things. The principal source is, of course, Dr D J Davies.

The book itself was never intended to be read from cover to cover. It is designed to be read like a motor-car manual, as and when the need arises, as a text-book, which can assist in creating a proper attitude of mind with which to approach a subject of debate in the hurly-burly of day to day struggles.

This accounts for the peculiar construction of the book. The INTRODUCTION should be read first, as it provides an analysis of the political situation in which the effort to renew nationalist politics must be conducted.

Then, in ABC order, follow entries which cover the major subjects which young people would want to consult, before forming their own opinions. Like Bukharin and Preobrazhensky, I aim to place a work of reference in the hands of cadres, who I firmly believe will, within their lifetime, govern this country, despite present appearances to the contrary. They have bred into them one peculiar attribute of the Welshman, the doggedness and perseverance of the long distance swimmer whose stroke, slow and ungainly though it may be, will yet enable him, by sheer stamina and persistence, to reach his objective.

It is to these indomitable young men and women of Wales that I dedicate this book.

Age of Scarcity

This is a key to understanding the political struggles of the next half century. By this term, we mean the fundamental economic changes that began to show themselves in the early 70s. These were the growing shortage (and consequent high prices) of raw materials in the industrialised countries; the recurrent world-wide shortages (and artificial booms) in foodstuffs; the paradox of a scarcity of investment capital coupled with corporate treasuries with funds which are looking for investment opportunity; a continuing tug of war between price inflation and monetary means of creating an artificial financial stability. The large funds available from internal capital accumulation within the large corporations, and the vast quantities of "hot" money available in the Middle East will present a continual threat to financial stability, and will create cycles of dangerous speculative investment, particularly in currency, land and "non-productive" channels. These are the symptoms of the new economic order. The results we must now consider.

The obvious result is continual and worsening unemployment in the old industrialised countries. Prophets claim to see an improvement in the mid 80s. They are mistaken. We are at the end of the beginning, not at the beginning of the end.

This will lead to measures of protection, totally at variance with the policies of the last 30 years, particularly in steel, motor cars, textiles, shipbuilding and various branches of the electronics industry —particularly consumer goods. Free trade, now more honoured in the breach than in the observance, will become a thing of the past.

The cumulative political effects of the Age of Scarcity will be a "hardening of the political arteries", particularly in the United Kingdom, and in other countries where the last generation has succesfully avoided radical reform of its social structure and economy in the face of the opposition of the old vested interests. This will show itself in the intensification of tendencies already powerfully at work, principally the growing together of big business and government, the ossification of the trade union movement, and growing unwillingness to encourage any reform from within government itself. This will certainly make it even more unlikely that government, and the societies it represents, will be able to adapt to change, and the pace of change in the coming decades will be frightening.

The impasse between the forces calling for change and an unwillingness to change will certainly create in the population a growing feeling of alienation, frustration and resentment. This, in turn, will encourage the growing use of manipulative techniques in government and industry, upon an apathetic but increasingly sullen public. Among certain elements, this will encourage crime, vandalism, terrorism and growing irresponsibility.

The welfare state, once a great social benefit, will now become a political necessity, whatever the cost. Government will find themselves deeper and deeper in debt. Under these circumstances, it is unlikely that substantial oil revenues, already mortgaged, will result in significant new investment.

This, then, is the backdrop against which political struggles in Wales will be played out over the coming years. It behoves Welsh people to take a long, cool look at their prospects.

One thing is certain either with reform or without it. The common people of Wales are going to live through hard times. Without change, the next decade will certainly witness increasing unemployment and social dislocation, despite inadequate cosmetic attempts to mollify and mislead them. There will always be the prospect of improvement, but Westminster will have problems enough nearer home. There will neither be the wherewithall, or perhaps the political inclination, to make gifts to anyone. With change, this people must anticipate a painful and prolonged period of adjustment to high prices and low wages, with no immediate prospect of improvement.

Change requires a complete shift in the aims and priorities of the government —and much more painful— in the expectation of the people.

It is becoming crystal clear that the Age of Scarcity forces all societies in Western Europe (and our own colonial society in Wales in particular) to shift from an individual profit-oriented to a collective communal benefit way of life. We may not fancy the idea. Our whims and preferences have little to do with the çase. We have to pull together or we certainly go under, collectively and individually.

The community benefit state calls for costly investment in a completely new infrastructure of society, particularly in energy, transport, agriculture and land use. Our present way of life is totally geared to an extractive economy, based upon the systematic exploitation of labour and natural resources. The community benefit economy is based on catering for the needs of the community as far as possible within the limits of our own resources, and paying for what we cannot make for ourselves from the intensive exploitation of the intellectual and technical skill of our small working population.

The change is so fundamental that it can only be carried through with the genuine consent and participation of the whole people. In other words, the Age of Scarcity forces the Welsh people to institute a genuine people's democracy where it matters —in worker participation in industry and in local government. This is the cockpit of our struggle. Small units of government at work and at home (rarely more than one hundred people) are the chosen instrument whereby this people will pull itself up by its bootstraps. This implies a degree of self-help and individual effort not seen before in Wales.

At present, many are disinclined to recognise the gravity of the situation; more, perhaps, are disinclined after 30 years of Welfare pampering to make the effort. But it is an effort that will yield attractive reward, as much in the mind as in material satisfaction of our bodily needs.

Alienation

The characteristic attitude of the ordinary Welshman in the last quarter of this century is, and will continue to be, one of alienation. He does not belong, he does not feel wanted, he does not feel fulfilled, he is sure he is being manipulated, but he cannot prove it. He is sure he is cheated of the fruits of his labour (just as his fathers were before him), but he cannot do anything about it. They flatter him when they want his vote; afterwards he is very small beer. He just does not care any more. He "drops out". Why does the Welshman feel this way? There are three basic reasons. They are not peculiar to Welsh conditions, but for a variety of reasons, they are more keenly felt in Wales than elsewhere. Let us look at the burdens of the Welsh working class.

1. Despite beliefs to the contrary, the modern Welshman, when he has got any work at all, is expected to work much more intensely than his fathers. He certainly works shorter hours. Times have changed, he is no longer crudely exploited, but the modern industrial process *forces* both workman and manager to work in quite a different way from his ancestors. He has no choice. He is governed by standing orders, the demands of head office, the speed of the line, the productivity agreement, the requirement of the process. He cannot vary the routine: the thinking has been done for him, because the process, or the computer, or London, wants it done that way. This is particularly true in the case of the heavy capital-intensive industries of Wales:- coal, steel, oil, petrochemicals. In the old

38

batch steelworks or the "pillar and stall" mine, one could take a break, have a yarn. Now men are outcrops of machines. Now the Welshman is not by nature a precise animal. He is feckless and happy-go-lucky. Therefore, much of his working life is spent under stress. He cannot adjust to the monster to which he is harnessed.

2. This undercurrent of unrest can be brought off so long as wages are good. But wages are no longer good. It is becoming abundantly clear that the Welshman has become the "coolie of the Western world." Even in a population as parochial as ours, we are beginning to realise that wage rates for managers and men are among the lowest in Europe. Already by 1978, the *Economist* could publish a chart (4th February) which showed UK wages as the lowest in the 12 leading industrial nations. The World Bank Atlas measuring GNP in 1977 classed UK incomes in the lowest $2000-$4.999 bracket of per capita income, rubbing shoulders with Spain, Puerto Rico, USSR, Hong Kong and Yugoslavia (*Financial Times*, 2nd January 1980). The wages paid to women in the sweat shops of West Wales are a national disgrace. Where wages are good, the weight of taxation is keenly felt. Nobody tells the worker that he is paying a much higher *proportion* of his wage in taxation than even the landed aristocracy before the Lloyd George Budget of 1909.

Whereas the tax farmers two hundred years ago forced the taxpayer to pay up with much grumbling, the modern taxpayer is supposed to pay up with conviction. It is his civic duty. The wage earner has no choice in the matter, but the lucky ones who do not appear upon a payroll long ago concluded that "only fools pay taxes". Tax avoidance has become a national sport. The mismanagement of the Union economy over the past 30 years has resulted in vastly increased government spending which must be covered by taxation. Therefore the conviction that high taxes are unavoidable unless the public is prepared to put up with a substantial drop in public services has to be cultivated. Where there are doubts these must be stifled. The ordinary Welshman must be made to believe that the wealth, education and welfare services cannot be sustained without current levels of taxation. The man in the street suspects that this may not be so, but he cannot prove it. The Defence Estimates, for example, by their very nature, are not open to audit.

3. In the background, the unspoken thought among all Welshmen is that in the next war, they will be called to lay down their lives for the state —the English capitalist state. It is observed that no arms race in recorded history has lead to peace. The media is full of low key propaganda, but no-one can be in any doubt that, if the balloon went up, we should have to fight Russia. Is this anxiety necessary? Why should Welshmen endure all these stresses and discomforts? Why should they sacrifice themselves?

One cannot keep people in a state of intense effort without giving them good reason. One cannot be required to contribute a full third of one's income in taxes and be prepared to see oneself or one's children called up for the great capitalist-communist war without having good reasons.

What are these reasons? Are we convinced that we enjoy the good life? But the Welsh worker completely lacks personal fulfilment. He is a cog in a wheel, and he knows it. Life has no meaning. He works with tens of thousands of others. When the shift changes and the sheds and workshops empty, he is no more than an ant. He lives on an estate, or in a row of council houses or in a tower block. At home, he is not sure what the children have been up to when the wife has been at work. He is dissatisfied. He is unsure. He needs to be a somebody. He wants some self-respect, some fulfilment in his working life, he needs to belong, he wants security and stability.

What is the meaning of the grind and sacrifice? He wants answers, and is offered escape. He is offered distraction. He must be persuaded to live in a world of illusion. He must feel part of go-go, glamour, get on, something. The Welshman is offered the pub, the box and the match.

The mandarins know that our people want real satisfaction. The ordinary man wants to live as a real human being. They teach him in school about prosperity, liberty, freedom and democracy. Welshman, what does it taste like? The establishment is afraid that these discontents may one day become articulate. The seething cauldron may one day boil over. After all, the Welsh are a people, moody and unpredictable. The working class cannot then be permitted to have a society or a culture. In a real Welsh working class culture, men would air their discontents in common. They would begin to form a genuine working class opinion. Their society must be broken up, its bonds of comradeship must be undermined. All belongings, all roots, all things held in common must be destroyed, subverted or made to look ridiculous or old-fashioned. The Welshman must be turned into a consumer glued to a television set. He must accept the trivialised values, isolated, manipulated, helpless.

Perhaps human beings are not quite so malleable. They may be helpless, but they must react. They come to believe that the whole circus is not for them. They become alienated from "Society". Which society do they mean? The society in the club or village? No —they are disenchanted with "them"— the ones that sit in offices, in the halls of power, the marble halls, in the civic centres, in the Whitehall offices, the corporate headquarters. The people who write the rules and standing orders. What are the results of this alienation? Strikes in the workplace, vandalism outside it, the cult of the motor car (where a man can feel he is "somebody"), sex (because this is one of the few real "kicks" left to him), disillusion and disinterest in politics, falling election turnouts, and a complete distrust of any "official" statement. The minority turn to acts of crime. In view of what Welsh "society" has to offer, the wonder is that there is not more.

There may be those who insist that this is a caricature of tendencies in our society. Yet, if we want a projection of that state of Welsh society after another twenty years under English monopoly capitalist rule, we must look to America. In that country, the process of alienation has gone much further than in Wales.

It sometimes happens that a flash of lightning will illuminate a dark scene and reveal its features. The extent of the alienation of ordinary people in American society may be gauged from the power failure in New York City in 1977. There was no more restraint. There was no "civic virtue". Large sections of the

41

working class gave themselves over to uninhibited looting. This is the true measure of the alienation of the common man. Unless Welshmen determine to change the ground rules of their society, this is their fate also —total alienation from "the system".

It is a disease in society already far advanced. It affects, in one way or another, every attitude and every class of society to a greater or lesser extent. This is the sombre back-cloth against which the drama of the Welsh Revolution will be played out.

Army

This is one institution well calculated to raise the hackles in this country. The Army figures in the folk memory in association with violence and strike-breaking. It is remembered that machine-gun nests were installed at the pitheads in 1926. We refer, of course, to the English Army. It is a subject so distasteful that Welshmen can rarely be prevailed upon to speak on it.

Nationalism in its early days had a strong streak of Christian pacifism running through its ideas. Defence expenditure was, and still is, a favourite Aunt Sally. There is an inclination to discredit the idea of an army as anti-egalitarian, anti-democratic and anti-Welsh. The idea of a Welsh Army even appears to be faintly ridiculous.

It was not always so. Before the English conquest, the Welsh had a formidable reputation as soldiers throughout Europe. Indeed, it took the most efficient military machine in Europe to conquer them, and even after 1282, Welsh archers were often a decisive element in English victories. Welshmen have no mean military pedigree.

The time has come for a radical reappraisal. It is not a case of prestige, a manifest sign of sovereignty. It is a case of necessity. The more successful Welshmen become in setting up a true social democracy, the more vulnerable they will become, because success may provoke jealousy and distaste among our neighbours. Worn-out empires do not degenerate into democracy, they turn to fascism.

This would mean a soulless régime of bureaucrats and businessmen, kept in power by louts and backwoodsmen. One is given to wondering how sympathetic such a régime would be towards Welsh national aspirations. To those who believed that "this could not happen here", the Suez intervention of 1956 should be a reminder of the power reaction. Discounting this possibility, some means of defence is essential in the Age of Scarcity. The need to resist encroachment upon our fisheries, frontiers and food resources is now only an unpleasant idea. Circumstances could change this.

A nation of under 3 million souls, with a formidable programme of reconstruction can hardly view the prospect of armament expenditure with equanimity. All that is necessary would be the minimum needed for policing activity. Even this would be spent grudgingly, as it would appear that a standing defence establishment would be a heavy burden. If nationalists continue to view a Welsh army in the traditional role, this is true. The answer is not to imperil national security by going without an army, but to change its role in society. As it happens, a Welsh Army could perform work in rebuilding Wales which could not be done as well by any other institution. We envisage the New Welsh Army as being primarily a social service organisation, in these spheres:

* The organiser of full-time and part-time citizen conscription for labour service at a national level.
* As a helper of local labour citizen conscription, by providing a central pool of contractors' plant and specialist support services.
* As the superintendent of the survival features of the Welsh economy.
* As co-ordinator of all services of aid and succour, Mine Rescue, Ambulance and Fire Services, Air-Sea Rescue.
* As a helping hand in those community projects which are nationwide in application, and remain outside the bounds of traditional local government activity.
* As organiser of the workers' militia.

This last duty calls, perhaps, for some further explanation. It would be indefensible, initially on grounds of expense, and certainly on grounds of the scarcity of labour (which can be anticipated in a free Wales) to have an establishment of more than 10,000 men. This means that the Welsh Army is envisaged essentially as a Citizen Army.

Indeed there is a moral point at issue: we have promised ordinary people these last 50 years that they would be taken into active partnership in the workplace and in government. It follows, therefore, that when a worker is handed a share certificate in his company, under the worker share participation scheme, he is handed a rifle at the same time.

We are building a new sort of society here in Wales. Nationalism is offering genuine democracy, but its people must be prepared to defend what they have won.

A régime cannot bestow any greater compliment upon its people than to trust them with arms. It is a mark of a united, vigorous society. As long as each miner or steel worker knows that he has a weapon in the rifle locker at work, he feels that he is a free man.

If we nationalists say that we are genuine democrats, in work and in government, but yet appear to deny the means of defending the advances of Welsh democracy to those who are supposed to benefit from them, then our claims ring false. Nationalists will one day hold the reins of power in Wales. They will ask great sacrifices of our people for a whole generation, to begin to put right the neglect of 700 years of conquest and exploitation. You have to be very sure of your people to do that. Your people have to be very sure of their government. A rifle in the cupboard will bind people to government and government to people as fair words will not. It is the ultimate guarantor of people's rule.

A citizen army, then, in our view, is the cement which binds Welsh society together. It is the guarantee of freedom without and sobriety within.

Bureaucratic Harrassment

This is the technique of dissuasion, intended to discourage active political work by individuals whose views are unpopular with a power establishment. Unfortunately, it is necessary to have an appreciation of such activities, since they are likely to have increasing application in the closing years of this century. "Tinkerbell" disclosures should serve as a warning. (*New Statesman* – 1st February 1980).

Bureaucratic harassment is one of the tools used in a so-called "free society" in order to cripple its opponents. Its aim is to destroy the political effectiveness of a group of people in such a way that their fate serves as a reminder to others.

It is a cost-effective way of conducting activities against the opponents of any political establishment. For a small investment, great rewards may be expected.

De-stabilise the opposition middle management
This work is usually centred and staffed in an offshoot of a counter-espionage department, and one would normally expect it to be staffed by retired field officers. These men or women would be given a thorough training in the procedures of taxation, banking, bill collecting of the utilities (electricity, gas, telephone, water rates), and local authority and police procedures as they affect the motorist, taxation regulations and other specialist training as appropriate.

Each case officer will be responsible for between 6 and 20 cases. These are individuals "selected for treatment" on the basis of the criteria devised by the establishment concerned.

A file is created for each victim. This will contain particulars of his financial situation; his bank balance; his salary; copy debtors' ledger entires of his electricity, gas, telephone and local taxation accounts; his known commitments; and details of his family circumstances. This data can easily be obtained by a counter intelligence organisation. No great political muscle is required.

Ideally, this material is loaded to a computer file, and a case calendar is prepared for each individual, showing details of his contingent liability.

The case officer is now in business. From now on, his object-ive is to programme a series of events whose aim is to put pressure upon the victim by means of systematic harassment. Every administrative rule is exploited to establish a harassment situation. The objective is to induce a liquidity crisis. Adjusting entries are found necessary in the ledgers. The victim is request-ed to "discuss the situation of his account" with various officials. It is discovered that some aspect of his account is "irregular". This will call for a higher authority to rule on the matter. The inference made is that large sums of money may be owing. Once a pattern of this sort is established, the case can be programmed to produce an "event" about once every 2 weeks. This produces a background of low key harassment. The case officer has to engineer a crisis, possibly resulting in the dismissal of the man from his job. Unemployment is the greatest help to destabilisation. Alternately, he can be caught shoplifting.

Effects of destabilisation

This type of activity will be guaranteed to reduce the effective-ness of the man in a political context. A campaign can lead to a nervous breakdown or to disruption of the family. Those who work in espionage recognise that incessant harassment can play tricks with a man's normal behaviour patterns. The first response would be the bottle. Consumption of alcohol will rise. Nothing is more effective in destroying a man's personal-ity than strain, because strain will be immediately reflected in his marital relations. Anxiety destroys a satisfactory sex life. Under constant stress, a man will sometimes take a mistress. Once this has happened, the case officer is home and dry. The victim is now at his mercy, because arrangements can be made to blackmail him. Within a two-year period a man can be reduced to impotence. It is unlikely that he will ever again prove to be the threat he was before. He is a broken man —a pitiable human being, without a wife, without a job, and without any self-respect. What good is he going to be to any political party?

The advantages of harassment are considerable. Bureaucratically, it is cheap. It can be performed on a very simple budget. Using manual methods, one case officer can easily programme twenty cases at a time. With mechanisation on a very simple computer, he can handle up to 50. (The quality of the case officer's supervision would deteriorate sharply beyond that number). An average department can process up to 500 cases a year without difficulty. Another advantage is that bureaucratic harassment is absolutely legal. There are not going to be any "red faces" within the power establishment. It is a no-risk activity. Nothing illegal has been done, and ill-intent cannot be proven. No civil servant is putting the future of his career on the line. The whole matter is clandestine. It is protected by the Official Secrets Act.

This weapon is rarely used against the top people in the opposition. They are likely to have enough money to enable them to ask lawyers and accountants to look after their affairs. A more intelligent use of this instrument would be to direct harassment against the "second-line" personalities in a party, who look as if they might influence the course of events in campaign management. Effectively, this knocks out the "middle management" of the opposition. If the campaign is properly handled, an attack on the second-line can actually divide the opposition as well as frustrating it. Second-line people, suffering harassment, can develop resentment against the more prominent men, who are obviously under no such burden. Provocateurs can work up a useful conflict situation in these circumstances. Manipulation becomes easier. A mere decade ago, it would have been difficult to give credence to the notion of wide-scale surveillance of this type. The "Tinkerbell" revelations (*New Statesman*, Feb. 1980) have wiped out any lingering doubt on this score.

United we stand

There is little individuals can do to defend themselves. The bureaucratic state holds the whip hand. If a campaign is pressed home remorselessly, the moral character (as well as the political effectiveness) of its victims degenerates. This type of activity will eventually destroy the human personality.

However, while the isolated individual is defenceless, provided the party is alert to the damage a destabilisation campaign can cause, it is possible to neutralise it.

Early reporting of suspected harassment to the highest level of party organisation is beneficial in two respects:

* A definite pattern soon emerges in harassment situations. This is a useful piece of counter-intelligence information. It shows what activities threaten the enemy, and who shows promise in the organisation.
* The party can deploy a counter-harassment organisation. This is a panel of lawyers, accountants and "comfort" counsellors. These people should be volunteer workers who are prepared to work without fees. The team should swing into action as soon as a case is detected.

The position of the wife is crucial

Once the bureaucracy realise that they are faced with a professional and determined opposition, the game is no longer worth the candle. ("Cheap victories" are no longer possible). It is likely to result in a stalemate situation. The "comfort" counsellors are actually more important than the professionals. They bolster the morale of the victim, and more important still, they make it clear to the wife of the victim that the Party will back the family all the way. The women are really the vulnerable persons in this wretched business. Under harassment wives nag their husbands to relinquish their political activities. They "have their feet on the ground", and "cannot understand where all these 'good causes' are getting the family!" The wife is the key factor in the campaign. "What good is it doing you?" is a question that can break a man.

Conclusion

At first sight, it may appear that the bureaucratic state is omnipotent. It can inflict terrible mental suffering upon ordinary people. It can destroy men. It can do it legally, secretly and without fear of detection. The isolated individual is powerless against it. Yet, provided that the party can demonstrate that even the least significant of its members will immediately receive all the help the party can bring, it may come out of the campaign stronger than it went in. Persecution may steel the nerves and the resolve of its rank and file.

As the struggle for Welsh freedom intensifies, in the closing decades of the century, let us pray that nationalists will be alert and prepared for any contingency. We might do worse than adopt the motto:

In as much as you persecute the least of these our brethren, you persecute all, and all will resist.

Capitalism

1. Definition

Uses the instinct of greed within individuals as the basis governing their economic and political relationships. This involves the competition of one individual or one class with another, each bent on securing the maximum accumulation of riches at the expense of the other. Under capitalism, mankind exists in a state of permanent competition. Co-operation is practised only in as much as it contributes to prospects of greater returns within a group of entrepreneurs, acting together rather than separately.

The capitalist stage of development has superseded the feudal stage of human relationships which was organised upon the basis of co-operative life under the hierarchy of landowner and church. Commerce and industry were incompatible with feudalism, hence there were vested interests in the complete elimination of the old order of society. Let us follow Roger Garaudy's brilliant analysis of the implications of this movement in *L'Alternatif* (Paris 1972).

Between the 15th and 20th centuries, the market was transformed from a collection of nearly self-sufficient Local markets into a co-ordinated world market. Every political or moral obstacle to this extension of the market was eliminated. The market came to recognise no law but its own. It subjected all relationships to itself. Capitalism created an economy which within 300 years brought everything into open circulation on the market.

1st —money, by nullifying the religious prohibitions on usury.
2nd —land, freely transferable —which, after the dissolution of
the monasteries, struck a mortal blow at the church, feudalism
and the old community order.
3rd —human labour, men themselves were turned into a
commodity. "Once money, land and labour have been turned
into mere commodities governed by the laws of supply and
demand, they become so many cogs in the giant machine, run
by the jungle laws of private competition. In its purest form,
freedom of the market reflects the struggle among the various
possessors of wealth. Everything has its price in this blind battle
of everyone against everyone. Nothing escapes the meshes of
the devil's mill."

Capitalism is not merely an economic system. It necessarily
implies a social structure, a hierarchical social relationship, in
which the minority, who possess power and dominate those who
do not, owns the means of production. It implies a political
structure that reflects this social and economic dependency.
Finally, it is a model of culture and civilisation in which men
are moulded by market demands, competition and profit, and
all are manipulated by those who, along with capital, control
most of the communication media.

A society ruled by the blind law of competition among all,
and profit for a few, in which investment is not social, but
solely a private enterprise, is devoid of any conscious control
over its own destinies. This is precisely the point at which
western monopoly capitalism has now arrived "This is the first
society in history not built on any plan for civilisation."

2. The philosophy of capitalism

Adam Smith's *Wealth of Nations* was published at the end of
the eighteenth century, at a time when a comprehensive
philosophy of unfettered capitalist development was required
by the entrepreneurial class. Its ideas echoes down through the
nineteenth century, together with the Malthusian *Theory of
Population*, it provided the philosophical basis for the unfettered play of market forces, and in human terms, specifically
sanctioned the exploitation of the working class.

According to these philosophers, it was foolish and harmful

for society to try to interfere in any way with the free play of market forces. The market was the ultimate arbiter of human life. Artificial restraints due to misplaced sympathy would rebound on society. Eventually, the warfare (called "unfettered competition") between human beings would create optimum conditions for human advancement. The misery that would result was pre-ordained by the iron laws of population, which Malthus stated thus: the standard of living of the working class cannot rise substantially above subsistence level. Any rises are temporary, and population will re-adjust in order to cancel them out.

It can be imagined with what joy the entrepreneurs of the industrial revolution embraced these views. They offered *carte blanche* approval to any and every effort to maximise profit at whatever cost to individuals, communities or the human environment. This reflected what Marx called "the infinite capacity of human nature for remaining indifferent to the pains we inflict upon others, when we have a chance to get something out of them for ourselves."

As the first industrial revolution ran its course, the misery to which the greater part of the population was subjected provoked first an awakening of conscience as much as in the works of Dickens and Zola as Marx.

It is true to say that this awareness of the moral implications of capitalism, while it provided a new climate of opinion which enabled working men to begin to organise themselves, resulted in a very slow amelioration of the condition of the working class. It had to fight bitterly for every step of the way, and wartime gains could be reversed later. Boom and slump continued their cyclic pattern —until the crash of 1929.

We have seen elsewhere how Lord Keynes, the father of neo-capitalism, provided a formula to save capital from collapse:

* public works
* paid for by heavy taxation
* sometimes involving "industrial re-construction" (i.e., state intervention and cartelisation).
* social reform to ameliorate the condition of the poor.

The formula appeared to work well. What few noticed was

that not only did the internal core of capitalism remain practically untouched, but it actually came out of the crisis of the 30s stronger.

The internal core of capital in any economy is defined by Heilbronner in *Business Civilisation in Decline* as that strata of society protected by capital. In America, this stratum would have an annual income of one $100,000. In Sweden, 1% of the population own 16% of the nation's wealth. In the UK, 2% of the population owns 32%. In other countries, the internal core is more broadly based. In France, 10% own 36% of the national wealth. (*Financial Times* 4th Oct., 1977).

This core can make itself practically immune to taxation, however penal. While the core of the system has remained practically unchanged, capitalism has become institutionally stronger since the 1930s. It has expressed itself in new and unexpected ways, sometimes the result of policies of socialist legislation. The most powerful manipulators of capital in the UK are the pension funds. The NCB fund controls £½ billion worth of assets —more than those vested in the NCB itself. The Post Office fund *in a single year* handles a cash flow large enough to buy up P and O Navigation, Vickers and Pearl Assurance. All pension funds and insurance companies own together 50 billion. By 1985, this sector will be able to invest £20 billion —2½ times the Public Sector Borrowing Requirement in 1978 (*Economist,* Nov. 4th, 1978). These interests reinforce those at the inert core of monopoly capital.

The growing power of the multinationals add another dimension. They controlled ¼ of the world's marketable output in 1968, ⅓ by the end of the 70s, and are estimated to control ½ by 1990 (Heilbronner, *op. cit.*). So their success in dominating the market has been considerable while, in fact, the percentage value of their investments, in the case of US multinationals, has remained surprisingly stable, since 1914, at 7% of US gross national product. In 1929, it was constant at 7%, and only went up one % point by 1970.

The fundamental change since the 1930s has not been the shape or the size of monopoly capital. It has been the degree of government interference. It is Heilbronner's contention that this interference will increase in the next decade, due to acute instability, inflation and business concentration.

Inflation is now locked into capitalism due to several factors. (In the US, W Germany, France and the UK in 1979, all countries exceeded their target money-supply).

* in irresponsible tendency for wages to increase faster than profits.
* the vast OPEC oil surplus revenues chasing available goods and investment opportunities.
* the pressures of the arms race.
* the acute pressure of population on the environment.

These factors make it likely that capitalism will continue to develop serious local disorders and the trend to unprofitability in private enterprise will increase. "Non-interventionist" governments will be forced to organise bale-outs at an accelerating rate if capitalism is to survive. This will accelerate the "drift towards planning".

The era of planned capitalism, where the plan will no longer be the accumulation of private sector business plans, but an ordered market sharing, which no longer caters to the prerogatives of the corporate élite, will subordinate the needs of capital to the dictates of the state. The Heilbronner thesis is contained in the central proposition:

> The possibility that the very preservation of society may require changes that profoundly alter the social relationship of capitalism . . . that the government may detach itself from the economic base and assert control for the ultimate purpose of preserving a political system, is not part of the radical scheme of things.

This thesis forces one to recall the history of capital in Nazi Germany. Whereas Hitler originally made a compact with the industrialists in 1933 which appeared to protect their interests, 10 years later, the state had clearly subordinated capital to its own survival.

Despite Heilbronner's disclaimers, he appears to support the view that capitalism is drifting towards its penultimate stage of neofascism in the mass democratic corporate state.

The future of capital
Any reasonable assessment would not support the "Big Bang Theory". The end of the capitalist world —without a war —is

not yet in sight. A system which survived 70 million unemployed between 1929-1933 appears to be in better shape than ever to withstand the stress ahead.

* The institutional auxiliaries.
* The extremely well-managed multinationals.
* The powerful new tools of mass manipulation and computer forecasting.
* A docile working population (everywhere well supported from state funds).

All appear to carry capitalism over any crisis foreseeable in the immediate future. The only real threats to capital come from:

* war.
* unchecked speculation in the futures and currencies market.
* saturation of the banking system in the face of OPEC wealth.
* emotional discontent in the face of ideological and moral bankruptcy of the system.

It is against this picture, past, present and future, that Welsh nationalists have to re-think their attitudes to capitalism.

The nationalist view of capitalism

Wales has had a very bitter experience of capitalism. The "unfettered market forces" of capitalist philosophy have left scars on the Welsh countryside and on the Welsh outlook. Our population suffered the indignity of exploitation, both as a powerless class who had to accept any treatment that was meted out, and they had to accept it as a colonial society, Wales enjoyed all the disadvantages of capitalist exploitation and none of its advantages. Capitalist exploitation was purely extractive. Raw materials and semi-finished products were created in Wales. The distortions created over a century ago are with us to this day.

To a very large extent, Welsh nationalism itself is the direct consequence of extractive capitalism in Wales. It is inevitably anti-capitalist in sentiment. Yet time has not stood still. We can date the end of the *laissez-faire* exploitation of Wales at around 1914. There have been many changes. The growing forces of socialism resulted in changes in attitude which transformed Welsh society after 1945 into a predominantly state capitalist society. The result was disappointing, and predictable. "Even where nationalisation effectively shifts control to other hands, they are the hands of bureaucrats; and control remains centralised and therefore autocratic, whereas to be democratic, control must be distributed so that every worker has a real share in it". So wrote Dr D J Davies in 1949 in *Towards an Economic Democracy*.

The big difference was, of course, that while private capitalism paid handsome dividends, state capitalism did not. How could it, when "nationalisation" had attended only to the declining or unprofitable nineteenth-century infrastructure industries? Private capital enjoyed all the benefits of a subsidised infrastructure; state capitalism was carefully regulated so that it could *never* compete with private capitalism. It is no wonder nationalisation got a bad name.

Wales is now bewildered. Free enterprise is distrusted because of past association, while socialism (interpreted as nationalised industrial activity) has failed to live up to the promises imputed to it by two generations of Welshmen. Moreover, the power wielded by the English bureaucracy over Welsh nationalised enterprises has clearly been used to destroy productive assets, and put large sections of the work-force out of a job.

How does nationalism regard capital?

Ours is an empirical, not a doctrinaire position. It is dictated by current and anticipated needs of Welsh society. We believe:-

1. The development of the community economy needs to be planned and amenable to Welsh popular control, audit and decision.

State welfare capitalism is ameliorative. It is not revolutionary. *It does not change the ground rules.* The needs of our society force us, whether we like it or not, to change these rules. Instead of individual entrepreneurs making decisions, the English bureaucracy makes them. The Welsh Revolution is directed against the English bureaucracy.

The first impact of state capitalism on Wales was favourable. Working class conditions improved beyond recognition:

investment, neglected for twenty years, was accelerated. For twenty years after 1945, state welfare capitalism in Wales appeared a success. But it was an illusion. The English welfare state administered capitalism better, and rubbed off its sharp edges, but it remained capitalism. The welfare state was not transformed into the community benefit state.

"A small advance of money judiciously administered by the governing classes, always resourceful in avoiding crisis, would be enough to prevent their causing a scandal", commented Edmund Wilson in *The Finland Station*. "At the same time, it would keep them dependent, and make it possible for them to degenerate gradually."

The ground rules which governed the operation of the coal, steel, electricity, gas, railways and bus companies were much the same as those governing the international cartels.

2. Welsh nationalism is closer to continental syndicalism than socialism. English "socialism" has never seriously adopted planned economic development. It is too close to capitalism.

The commanding heights of the economy must be susceptible to direct manipulation by the community benefit state. These are not merely the commanding heights of the 19th century, but of the 21st century economy. "It is easy to say that the earth belongs to mankind" said D J Davies in *Towards an Economic Freedom*, "or that a nation's industries 'belong' to the people: the important thing is to ensure for each individual worker the right to work in a *particular place*, thus giving him in fact, not merely in name, the security of ownership."

"Direct manipulation" does not necessarily mean 100% government ownership, but it certainly means at least 33% worker ownership —which, as we shall see, may mean something entirely different.

3. The commanding heights of the economy, as defined by the nationalist, are not necessarily (or even primarily) the means of production of specific industries. That is a crude, inefficient and out-of-date definition. We do mean the commanding heights of the *market*.

4. This is a much more useful definition, because it includes the market for all factors of production and distribution, labour,

capital, land and commodities.

This community benefit demands a controlled market for labour and a controlled price. It means a controlled market for food at a controlled price. It means a controlled market for energy and transport. It does not necessarily mean that the production of these items is *nationalised*. It does mean that they are directly and speedily susceptible to manipulative action for the community benefit. One does not necessarily control the management directly. There are a whole battery of weapons which are just as effective.

5. This means that, providing a Welsh Senate can control very directly and very effectively the economic forces shaping Welsh lives, it can be very flexible indeed about the means it uses to achieve this end.

6. While it may de-nationalise certain portions of Welsh industry (perhaps vesting part of that control in Worker Co-operatives), it may decide to nationalise other sectors of the economy. It may thus declare it illegal for foreigners to own land in Wales. Note that the Welsh nationalist now begins to use the word "national-ise" in a completely different way to that of the English socialist.

7. It is not in the community interest that nationalisation always means a 100% state shareholding. Nationalisation, for the new generation of Welshmen, may mean effective control of the marketing organisation of economic activity inside and out-side the Welsh community. In practical terms, this may mean that while a Welsh Transport Authority controls the timetables of all rail and bus movements in Wales, some of the branch rail-ways and many of the buses can be better operated by private entrepreneurs. While the Authority insists that 70% of all freight movements use a motorail facility for journeys through Wales, private hauliers are more likely to manage their fleets profitably than nationalised (in this example) road haulage. Clearly, community benefit does not mean only the administrat-ive control over the issue of licences and registration of vehicles. It means the direction and dictation of freight and passenger movements in the interests of the community.

8. Control of the market is axiomatic for any community which

must transform itself from a warped colonial-style economy into a balanced economy. It is even more important for a community whose leaders are consciously anticipating the Age of Scarcity, and are feverishly relaying the foundations of Welsh life, so that the community may survive this crisis. When scarcity is keenly felt, the classic "free economy" will be swamped by the distortions of the market inevitable at the close of this century, when energy, food and industrial raw materials become scarce commodities. Capitalism has no answer to this situation. The free market (already more of a myth than a reality) will be quite incapable of handling it.

9. It is clear, then, that Welsh nationalism has a very direct measure for all economic enterprise. Does it benefit the community, or does it carry in it the seeds of a malevolent distortion of Welsh life?

* We do *not* say that all the means of production and distribution should be vested in a state —any state, Welsh or English. This unacceptable concentration of power is dangerous to efficiency and liberty.

* We do *not* say that capitalist enterprise is bad, but it is "tainted with original sin" as soon as "big organisation mentality" grips it.

* We *do* say that, provided the Welsh community can licence, audit and direct enterprise within the framework of our economic plans —and this can be done by disclosure on the part of the entrepreneur and steady policy guidelines on the part of the community —then we can live and let live. Where capital wants to play the game exclusively by its rules, there is no place for it in Wales.

* We *do* say that, within this framework, all that can be achieved by means of taxation policy will be done to liberate profits from excessive depredation because we anticipate a state which is financed by the profits from its own entrepreneurial activity, not primarily by siphoning off the profits of others. We expect direct corporate and personal taxation to decline.

* We *do* say that worker participation must be real, based on the ownership of part of the equity of any enterprise, state or private. Those who cannot (or will not) agree must leave Wales.

* We *do* say that where the new survival industries of Republican Wales cannot be set up by private capital, then the community must and will set them up itself. If these can be genuine joint ventures, so much the better. These enterprises are the means of the survival of this society in the next century. There can be no compromise in this matter. Economic effort, education policies and infrastructure networks are organised with this end in view —to make these survival industries viable.

Conclusion

Welsh nationalism, then, is feeling its way toward a middle road. Small scale capitalism is no threat to us. On the contrary, it is positively beneficial. Our attitude is not grudging acceptance, but enthusiastic support. The survival of capitalism in Wales depends upon flexibility. Provided that it can exist within the ground rules of Welsh democracy, there is every incentive to cultivate private capital. On the other hand, the community benefit criteria we seek to apply to economic activity derives its inspiration from Marxism (not from welfarism). It has teeth. English socialism has merely exhortation.

English welfare socialism is the great betrayer. It ameliorates the conditions and deformation of capitalism, without establishing any community benefit. It has colluded with international capital, to the extent that it is indistinguishable from it. Every organ of English socialism (including the trade unions) is an accepted adjunct of monopoly capital, a vested interest in its own right. It does not seek to change the rules of capitalist life. Welsh nationalism does. That is the difference. We must accept the implication —by its very nature, Welsh nationalism is a revolutionary movement.

Christianity

The Age of Scarcity is bringing with it a sharp deflation of expectation, all the sharper because of the short time between the halcyon days when it seemed that nothing could stop wealth increasing exponentially, and the present stringency. In purely material terms, the United States, the most powerful industrial nation on earth, was practically self-sufficient in food and raw materials in 1945. By 2,000 AD, it will have to import 80% of all materials needed in industry to maintain existing levels of prosperity.

The prospect provokes soul-searching in the temples of Mammon. Material values have imposed the absolutism of the market on Western society for 500 years. The materialist interpretation of history finally threw out God in the last century. The crisis of self-confidence which accompanies the collapse of materialism will, perhaps, open the door once again for God.

It is against this background that young people in Wales will re-evaluate the Christian faith. For the most part, one suspects, this will take place outside rather than within the Church. It has a lot to live down. One should pity young people who fumble and stumble over the obstacles that traditional Church attitudes have put in their way, exemplified in traditional "Christian" attitudes to sex. It will be a long pilgrimage back to faith. Perhaps the republic cannot survive without it.

Christianity provides its title deeds. Our community benefit state has no philosophy and no legitimacy outside it. To understand this, one has to go back to the words of Jesus Himself.

The Christian faith is essentially an intense inner struggle —it is hard work. Unlike Judaism or Islam, where external observance to rules can bring individual salvation, Jesus Himself repeatedly emphasised the internal nature of Christian life.

God is a spirit, and those who worship Him do so in spirit.
or
Beware of the doctors of law . . . these are the men who eat up the property of widows, while they say long prayers for appearances' sake; and they will receive the severest sentence. Luke 20[45]

This may not make it easy to follow. Standards of thought and conduct enjoined on wayward men are rigorous, but each man must "run the good race" and persevere in the faith.

These doctrines, taught for 2,000 years, would have a profound effect on human society. Whatever the spiritual excellence produced in individual souls, Christianity became the dynamo of Western civilisation, and the more rigorous the Church's teaching, the more efficient did Christianity become in creating the thought patterns which are basic to philosophical and scientific enquiry.

Another aspect of the Faith that had a deep influence was the way in which Jesus taught, through the use of parables.

In all this teaching to the crowds, Jesus spoke in parables: in fact he never spoke to them without a parable. Mathew 13[34]

These stories often ended by Jesus turning to His hearers and asking them, "Now, what do you think?"

In Christian terms, the Son of God sanctified human reason by forcing ordinary men to think out each situation afresh in terms of the love of God.

In political terms, the Son of God invited men to use their judgement, in stark contrast to the faiths of revelation where salvation flows from authority. The effect was immediate. As soon as Christians began to organise themselves into communities, these were self-governing. This much is clear from the Acts of the Apostles and the correspondence of the early church. However twisted the tradition of Christianity became afterwards, due to secular influence, pockets of democracy would always reappear within the Church, because it was endemic to the faith. The closer the church came to the Bible, the more democratic did church government become.

The balance between the acceptance of secular authority and wrathful disapproval is a feature of the gospels. While Jesus would tell men to give to Caesar those things which belong to Caesar, He could also lash out at authority in uncompromising terms when it was Godless. He took a whip to the money-changers. Whatever else the real Jesus may have been, He was certainly not "meek and mild".

An explosive quality within Christianity has always made secular rulers uneasy. They felt uncomfortable until the church had been cowed. Its integrity has been under constant attack, since it could encourage a breed of men who asked the reason why.

Can one really say that Christianity fits the Welsh character like a glove? It might have done so from time to time, when its influence was strongest.

If it has sometimes given our community a moral basis, which has given it an irrepressible energy and the confidence to push great things through, it has done so when Welsh life was free of outside interference. Under strong English domination, religious energy has often fractured and splintered into myriad pieces. Fragmentation and individualisation of Protestant Christianity has often been the prelude to its decline. The older, healthier forms of the faith were concerned equally with the communal and the individual aspects of religious life. Nationalists look to the reconstruction of church and state together.

Christianity is the ultimate sanction of real democracy —not the pseudo-democracy practised in the UK, whereby power is delegated and alienated from one group to another. Genuine decision-making within a congregation is an inalienable process. Re-fashioning of church and state fuse within the congregation. Roger Garaudy in his *Alternative* expresses it as follows:

> *God exists whenever something new is coming to life . . . a new faith has taken over . . . we are united, not only to our common task, but by belonging to a common flux, to a rising of the sap.*

Christianity gives us an absolute measure not to be found in the tawdry standards of materialism. Competition, between individuals, enterprises or nations, capitalist or communist, reaches the point where no-one is competent to reach decisions about an ultimate purpose —to maximise the rate of return. Ultimately, materialism leads to nihilism. There can be no disembodied politics any more than there can be "materialist" art or science. All, in the last analysis, demand value judgements.

Pius XII saw in this materialism the ultimate degeneration:

> They boasted of progress when they were, in fact, relapsing into decadence. They conceived they were reaching heights of achievement, when they were miserably forfeiting their human dignity.

Christianity may, in fact, hold up a stern rod by which man may measure himself, but for the republic, this is our best foundation. It breeds a degree of "combat-readiness" which can hardly be obtained otherwise. John Mills, in his little essay on Gerald the Welshman, put it this way:

> He (Henry II) knew that convictions rooted in religion were very deep rooted indeed. He knew, too, that patriotic fervour all too easily became a fanaticism that erupted in defiance and confrontation and set a whole people flying to arms in support of some national cause. His personal regard . . . was easily outweighed by his knowledge that men of principle and conscience can be far more dangerous and difficult than the unmitigated rogue and political adventurer.

Common Market

This was one of the worst bargains 67% of the Welsh electorate ever made. It was a bargain struck in ignorance of the outcome, as the result of intense propaganda. It was no accident that pro-marketeers could command ten times the campaign funds raised by the anti-marketeers. The results of membership were carefully covered up for several years. In 1978, when an Ashridge Management College study was made, researchers were appalled to find that no summary of EEC accounts was available. The best summary they were able to compile was published in a letter to the *Financial Times* on 3rd January 1979. The study concluded that the UK taxpayer contributed £320,000,000 in 1977, a sum likely to rise to £1 billion in 1980, (Treasury calculations suggest the real figure will be around £1.3 billion —*Economist*, 1.3.80) which is £19 per head of population, from £6.7 per head in 1977. Germany paid in £9.7 per head —£601 million— but received payments of £1,312 million against £657 million received by the UK. This memorable letter forced subsequent Treasury disclosures in the same vein. The EEC 1980 budget is not optimistic about the rate regional funds will be paid out. Very little will come to Wales.

The EEC Referendum was symptomatic of the condition of "democracy" in these islands. The EEC and the Devolution campaigns are case studies in population manipulation. Consequently, it is no surprise that in ideology and practice, the EEC is detrimental to nationalism. Membership handcuffs our economy by stealth.

One cannot reconcile EEC membership with any condition

that a free Wales could anticipate. The republic would need a protected market for sectors controlled by state monopolies for the purposes of raising revenue. Wales has been taxed to the limits of its ability to pay. Proceeds of general taxation are unlikely to rise, so funds must be raised from monopolies without EEC hindrance.

We would need to erect tariff walls around a few carefully selected survival industries. These would be the best long-term prospect of stable employment. If the initial choice is good, and research, development and marketing are effective, their products will sell over any trade barriers. However, it is unthinkable that they should be subject to interference from Brussels.

A free Welsh economy would need an open market in warm climate foodstuffs, clothing and consumer durables. It would increase choice and bring down prices from artificial EEC levels to those we could expect from the Third World markets. Free trade in these commodities is an essential element in a campaign against inflation.

The EEC was set up to revive a shattered European economy, to tie Germany into Europe, and to create trading units large enough to compete with the Americans. In practice, the German economy dominates Europe, and German monopoly capital calls the tune on most matters. Meanwhile, the EEC has failed to make significant inroads against American competition in aircraft, computers, chemicals and oil. There are also fears that American auto-makers will use their small cars to invade the European market. Set up by reformist socialist politicians, the EEC has become the big business club. There is no place for it in a small community benefit state. Is it completely accidental that European states with strong social consciences —Austria, Switzerland, Sweden— have remained outside the EEC?

Communication

Welsh nationalism views communication from two points of view. How it affects the individual within the context of his community, and its constitutional significance in the way in which the means and techniques of communication affect the way in which Welshmen can govern themselves.

Communication under monopoly capital

Mass media require large outlays of capital to function. Behind it stand the economic or political interest of those who supply it, who, indeed, have ends of their own. If they do spread information, they do so in a way which suits their own ends, to protect some vested interest or to smother some opinion potentially a threat to them, or to give power to national rivalry.

Commercial radio and TV —the opium of the people

Communication, gradually degraded from anything that makes the ordinary man think to everything that doesn't, became an end in itself under the guise of the endless record request shows and quizzes. The rise of the transistor, now the personalised tape recorder, march hand in hand with drug-taking. Both express a deliberately engineered dependency, by those who make money out of exploitation. Many cannot get through the day without their "shot".

The media, so far from drawing our attention to the issues that people are in danger of ignoring (because they lack the necessary information) end up by distracting the common people from the very things on which they should keep a firm hold. Television does so in such a way as to isolate the individual, to make him apathetic, subject to uncritical suggestion, frivolous, stupid.

Divide, isolate, fanaticise, then manipulate

Communication as we know it in Wales is designed to feed into the people an identity of interest with the English, a fear of withdrawal of English mass stimuli, and to provide a poor opinion of Welsh identity. Above all, it must *divide*, it cannot afford to allow the population to *unite*. The seeds of division and conflict within the community must be sown and watered. That is the function of the media. The TV will show the sad position of our young and old people begging, in indignity, for work, in a country where there is manifestly so much work to do. This may infuriate the viewer, but can he react? Can you turn around and answer back? These gadgets do not put us in touch with real people, but only with ghosts. Common people cannot share their terrible private burdens with them. They are creatures of illusion. At a turn of a knob, they disappear, and they are alone with their eternal problems again. Isolation produces warped judgement of what really is possible, what should be expected of life; what to expect out of a wage rise; what to expect as satisfaction from our sex life; what to expect of democracy. There is an image, but fulfilment is withheld.

Nationalism and communication

For us, communication is not a matter of gadgets: it is a matter of coming together. That is the only true communication. By uniting we find ourselves, our purpose and our contentment. The tools of Welsh nationalism are the small group with a purpose, the works or ward council. We expect to find something through them.

* We all share the same emotional need. This is more fundamental than our physical need.
* We need to belong, to shape our fate in common with others, within the visible limits of what we can see to be practical.

The media of communication must serve these objectives. In fact, the main problem of communication is not of the state to the people, but the people to the state.

   (i) If we are to break down our people's activities into manageable units, how can they make their needs known? By direct, or only by traditional indirect means (representative needs and delegation)?

  (ii) How can each of these units be co-ordinated into the planned progress of the whole economy?

 (iii) How can extreme democratisation at the periphery be integrated with strong guided democracy of the revolution at the centre?

 (iv) If we were to give free expression to our people's fears on the day after liberation, would they not be afraid of a revolutionary Welsh state, which counter-revolutionary propaganda will tell them will thrust a Welsh language régime down their throats?

These are the problems of communication for the nationalist.

The Presidential circuit

In *The Rise of the Welsh Republic*, I suggested that all state organisations be headed by a president, from Electricity Boards to Ministries. The presidential system should also cover the local government units. Some presidents would be elected, some would be appointed. All presidents, however, would have one duty in common. They would be required to go in circuit around their parish, great or small. They would set up office in a specially fitted railway car, complete with computer enquiry terminal and tele-conferencing facilities to speak with their executive officers. The object of the presidential circuit is to make government visible and approachable. It is a twenty-first century throwback to the old custom of holding open court under the great oak, where the citizen with a grievance could go right to the top of the government without intermediary. Emotionally, the Welsh people need to be able to see and speak to the head of the executive's departments of government. The microprocessor revolution makes this practical. These tiny devices, plugged into data lines at each railhead can turn the presidential office waggon into an extension of his headquarter building.

    Travelling to ex-colonial territories, and speaking with people who knew the colonial régime, it is indisputable that the District Officer's Circuit was the principal means of holding the entire government system together. Many ex-colonials (now in high position in government in the successor republics) look back wistfully to the District Officer's Circuit. Things got done as a result of that visit, and that was important. Even more important was the fact that men and women of any station could take up a case with the only man that really counted in the administration. The presidential circuit is a direct copy of this procedure.

The place of the five year rolling planning mechanism in Welsh government, in conjunction with the "Carte Comptable"

The breakdown of Welsh life into very small units is only viable provided the activities of every ward and works council are co-ordinated into one computer library of maintainance programmes and development projects, so that consolidated cross-economy and cross-programme elements can be abstracted and evaluated.

In real life, no plan can remain intact for long. Reality over-takes it. The impact of that reality in a myriad of small units can only be assessed centrally by a national computer grid, linked to micro-computers at each ward and works office, which record all transactions. This is the logic of the French "Carte Comptable" taken to a new dimension. This develop-ment requires a word of explanation.

By 1942 in the Second World War, the Nazi occupation régime in France was creaming off one third of the French GDP (Gross Domestic Product). After Stalingrad, the Germans had to squeeze the last drop out of the French economy. They did so with typical Teutonic thoroughness. Every enterprise was forced to report its accounting activities in a stereotyped fashion for each industrial sector. It was soon possible, using a unified chart of accounts in that sector, to identify areas of surplus or deficit. The Germans did manage to squeeze the lemon dry.

When France was liberated in 1944, the economy was in ruins. The French Ministry of Finance and the new "Bureau de Planification" did, however, inherit a magnificent tool from the

Germans. The Carte Comptable was used "in reverse" by a free France. It was elaborated and extended in the scope of its operation. Today, there are specialised charts of accounts for over 170 industrial and agricultural sectors, incorporating state and private enterprise. This mechanism of communication in large measure became the architect and tool of French economic recovery. Used in conjunction with development plans which are formally updated at least once a year, upon a national Welsh computer grid, it will provide a finely tuned mechanism to integrate the small work unit which Welshmen must have in order to perform at their best. The aspirations of Welsh nationalism are not a pipe dream. They are within our grasp. The tools are at hand, the computer package programmes are specified, the hardware is available —very cheaply indeed. What is required is the will to employ them in our great national adventure.

In place of fear —proof of freedom

If Wales were to be militarily liberated, the day after the last English soldier was sent packing back over the frontier, many Welshmen would mourn their going. They have been taught by the media over at least a century, that victory of the Welsh revolution is equivalent to language dictatorship by an intransigent minority. Protestations to the contrary by the successor government would be received in stony silence.

This is the most real of all fears in Wales, and it was certainly responsible for the "no" referendum result. The monopoly control exercised by the English media and Welsh traitors was only too effective.

The Welsh Revolution is only viable upon one premise: that the Republic shall embrace at least two self-governing palatinates —The Bro Gymraeg on the one hand, and the Palatinate of the Marches on the other. Within them, communication, controlled by local worker co-operatives, is entirely free. The local community radio station is controlled from within the Palatinate, not from the Republican Government, so that by demonstrating good faith in communication, education and civil service appointments within the Palatinate, all the poison of English lies and Welsh malice is drawn.

Guided democracy and the Welsh revolution

This phrase has occurred several times in this ABC. Certainly it will frighten some, and delight those who want to prove that Welsh nationalism, all along, is an intolerant, dictatorial movement with sinister overtones of one-party rule —Welsh-speaking one-party rule, at that.

In one sense, of course, the ultimate legitimacy of the whole process of Revolutionary Welsh Government resides in the consent given by the whole nation to the particular form of Five Year Plan chosen by our people. It will be the basis of their hopes, their taxes and their customs duties. It will circumscribe their freedom to spend and to move (literally, in the case of conscript labour). It will be the basis of much of their legislation and administration. Therefore, each must consent to that level of burden he or she feels able to bear. The whole process of government is guided by their consent. Once taken, the executive may rule with a rod of iron during a period of revolutionary change, and is to be judged not on any basis but the ability to produce results. In a very real sense, then, the *ultima causa* of any action is the result of the will of the people, which literally guides all processes of government.

The whole pattern of communication in the revolutionary successor state must service these needs disclosed above. We may draw several conclusions from this analysis.

1. Under People's Rule, the role of communication in the life of the community is directly contrary to that under the rule of monoply capital.

2. The prime role of communication is to draw the community together, to educate it in the possible options open to it, and to give each individual the absolute emotional certainty that, within the limits of what is possible in Wales, it is all up to him.

3. Its role then is to educate and motivate. Entertainment is within a national context, but distraction has no place whatsoever in the new revolutionary order.

4. It is inconceivable that private press barons, however well-intentioned, can be permitted to influence attitude formation. None may presume to touch the sceptre. Co-operators may

take over the communications industry in exactly the same way as any other, but they must operate within the same community benefit disciplines. Revenue generation by advertising is not acceptable. Capital can be provided by the state, on exactly the same terms as for any other industry.

5. The national optical fibre telecommunications net is not a personal or business convenience, but a tool of democratic control, as both the Presidential Circuit and the work and ward computer system hooks into it.

Communism

Looking at Capitalist production in its details . . . we find it is very economical with materialised labour incorporated into commodities. But it is, more than any other mode of production, prodigal with human lives, with living labour, wasting not only flesh and labour, but also nerves and brains. *Indeed, it is only by dint of the most extravagant waste of individual development that human development itself is safeguarded*, and advances into that era of history which immediately precedes the conscious reorganisation of society.

Karl Marx. DAS KAPITAL. Book 1

All our inventions and progress seem to result in endowing material forces with intellectual life, and in stultifying human life in a material force.

Karl Marx in an 1856 speech

These two quotations account at once for the strength and weakness of communism. Its strength is self-evident 150 years after these words were uttered. The basic appeal of communism is moral. Neither the blandishments of monoploy capitalism nor the brutality of communist governments has completely erased it. Capitalism, certainly, has never had an apologist who has come near to generating the fervour engendered by Marx. His protest against the inhumanity of capitalism as he knew it, and the diagnosis of its working, is quite as fresh in the era of the paternalist multinational as it was in the day of the callous, hard-driving coal-owner. Capitalism now has perpetually to be looking over its shoulder.

Let us take one example of Marx's insight, not primarily as an example of economic, but rather of his moral, attack on capital —the Theory of Surplus Value.

"The worker", so the theory goes, "has nothing to sell except his labour. This is sold like any other commodity on the market. Its value is determined by the minimum amount to keep him alive and capable of procreating a fresh generation of workers. He is hired for this minimum amount which, let us say, represents six hours labour. His firm then compels him to work eight hours. Either he does so, or goes without. In effect, the employer robs him of two hours work a day. The firm incorporates his labour into a product which is sold at market value. This constitutes "profit on labour", "surplus value", or "stolen work".

This doctrine made a powerful appeal in Wales until 1945. We experienced, as a nation, the crudest form of exploitation. Steel workers cosseted in a nationalised industry believed themselves immune to the old conditions. With 68,000 out of work in Wales, they are due to learn again the truths which so angered Marx. Having once experienced exploitation by hand or brain, the appeal of the communist analysis will become irresistible. This is the tide which has carried the fortunes of communism to their present state. It is of no consequence that economists have made many telling criticisms of Marx. They may be true. Yet all is as nothing compared to the emotional diagnosis of his situation by a man thrown on capitalism's scrap-heap. There are certainly other factors important in communist doctrine, but it is the moral indignation generated by the communist view that has been its locomotive. Some of these doctrines are the work of Marx and Engels. Others are ideas grafted on to the original theoretical base by their successors.

The class struggle is fundamental to Marxist thinking. Propertied classes have always waged war on the masses in order to exploit their productive capacity and maintain their own privilege.

The class struggle is sharpened as the contradictions of capital first in the hands of individuals, then in those of companies, and finally through international concentration into the massive accumulations of monopoly capital. These contradictions take two forms, between the masses and monopoly capital within the state, and between advanced capitalist states and developing nations. According to the World Bank Atlas, the richest 15% of the world's population continues to enjoy 60% of the world's income, and the poorest 20% make do with less than 2%. At a purely national level, according to the *Financial Times* commentary of 4th October, 1979, it is supposed that 1% of the UK population own 32% of its wealth. According to communist ideology, these contradictions result in a perpetual class war which can be won by the masses overthrowing the power of capital and instituting a dictatorship of the proletariat.

This dictatorship must monopolise the means of production and distribution. Capital can never be permitted to accumulate in the hands of private individuals. Human nature is such that men will revert to a condition of exploiters of labour in an effort to further enrich themselves.

Since 1917, procedures have evolved which amplify and direct Marxist thinking. The monopoly of production and distribution is expressed through the planned economy which promotes enterprises and activities upon the basis of communal need rather than individual or corporate profit.

It is impossible to create a planned economy unless it takes place within the environment of the dictatorship of the communist party, because the indiscriminate competition of rival groups would distort the economy by creating artificial needs which contribute to corporate profits, and leave genuine communal needs unsatisfied, because they do not contribute to profit. It is impossible to permit any alternative government because it would not truly represent working class interests.

The results of the application of these doctrines in communist countries have been:

1. A spectacular advance in activities which are associated with rapid industrialisation, transport rationalisation and improvement, town planning, health and education. These advances have brought peasant economies to the standard of old industrialised nations in a very short time. They are played down in the capitalist media.

2. In those activities which demand individual dedication, e.g., farming or women's fashion wear, performance has been abysmal. Even where it is clear that private enterprise could have improved communal service, such as catering, the state has

been doctrinally unable to create centres of private initiative and permit accumulation of enough working capital to run effective private enterprises.

3. Communist countries have concentrated upon the establishment of state power at the expense of satisfying individual needs. Occasionally, they had good justification for doing so. The intervention of 14 foreign armies in Russia from 1918 to 1920, and the trauma of Nazi invasion from 1941 to 1945, were powerful incentives to create a state capable of repelling attack. Eventually, the fact that individual human beings and the satisfaction of their humdrum needs were neglected had its roots in the environment in which communist ideas matured. However, this environment was created by non-communist influences. It is necessary to go back to March 1869 to trace the most powerful of them to source, to a pair of anarchist theorists, who have done as much to shape the development of Communist practice as Marx, and very much more than Lenin. These were Bakunin and Nechaev. In 1869, they published *The Chatechism of a Revolutionary*. They laid down ten commandments for the behaviour of those who opposed the régime. The precepts, despite their origin, became the principal influence over they way in which communist ideas were applied in the real world.

* The revolutionary is a doomed man, with no personal feelings of his own.
* He is absolutely single-minded.
* He has broken with the moral code of his society.
* He may pretend to be a part of it, to destroy it more surely.
* He may have to experience torture and death, therefore he must kill human sentiment within himself the moment it interferes with his purpose.
* Accordingly, he has no honour to his own colleagues within the revolutionary movement, apart from their utility. Comrades of inferior calibre are expendable.
* A comrade in trouble will be judged by his potential contribution to the cause. This contribution will be carefully balanced against the expenditure of resources which

would have to be spent to save him.

* The utility of members of established society is to be measured by their potential for harm which they can inflict on the revolution.
* Liberals are to be exploited by making them believe that one falls in with their programmes. Then the revolutionary must compromise them by involving them in his own.
* Radicals must be persuaded to do things which destroy them completely, or convert them into true revolutionaries.

These doctrines became part of the thinking, first of the Bolshevik party and subsequently of the Soviet state. One can now understand the theory behind the low priority accorded to the satisfaction of the ordinary man in communist societies.

Individual freedom is not only inessential, it is positively counter-productive. Communist government were born of a state of siege, hence the dictatorship of the proletariat must needs be crudely and brutally enforced. How crudely we may judge from Lenin's remarks upon hearing Beethoven's *Appassionata*:

"I know nothing that is greater than the *Appassionata*: I'd like to listen to it every day", Lenin commented to Maxim Gorky, "It is marvellous and superhuman music. I always think with pride," he added, "what marvellous things human beings can do, but I can't listen to music too often. It affects your nerves, makes you want to say stupid things and stroke the heads of people who could create such beauty while living in this vile hell. And now you mustn't stroke anyone's head —you might get your hand bitten off. You have to hit them on the head without mercy, although our ideal is not to use force against anyone."

Lenin was by no means a cruel man. One knows only too well the nature of those who succeeded him. The cynicism of his heirs has so alienated ordinary people that the oligarchy has found itself drawn into a spiral of repression and further alienation.

Contrary to what some would have us believe, however, this does not mean that all populations of socialist bloc countries yearn for a return to capitalism. They long for freedom to travel and to speak their mind. They may express grave dissatisfaction with the ruling clique, whom they privately regard as scoundrels, but they are proud of their economic advance. This is secondary, however, to the self-confidence they have acquired during the years of sacrifice when the foundations of their economy were being re-laid. Despite their backwardness, despite the hostility of the rest of the world, despite the continual need to improvise, they have built industrial states whereas previously they made a miserable living as tomato pickers. These achievements are marred by lack of freedom. They have gained a world and lost their souls. The predominant characteristic, then, of ordinary people in communist countries is exactly the same as those of the capitalist world —alienation.

In communist countries, this expresses itself as a lack of inventiveness, the need to keep one's head down, to dodge responsibility, the "ohne miche" mentality. Lack of freedom is positively tangible. It can be smelt in the air. There is no joy in communism.

In one respect, however, communist societies are better placed than the West to face the Age of Scarcity. Their régimes were born to want and their populations are able to cope with it. Industry, communication and distribution systems have been geared to it. Their governments are practised in imposing priorities to deal with it. Their institutions and popular attitudes are attuned to it. In the conditions anticipated at the close of this century, these states are more likely to withstand the blizzard. Societies dominated by monopoly capital will have difficulty responding to conditions which capitalist free market operations will themselves aggravate. Western societies will become less free, as monopolies collude with government, integrate completely with it, and impose their own priorities upon a manipulated population.

Nationalist evaluation of communist experience

A superficial comparison of nationalist attitudes to monopoly capital, extractive colonialism, community benefit, or the human waste associated with capitalism might suggest that we are fellow travellers. Such a comparison discounts the fountain from which all nationalist ideas spring.

1. The quotations at the beginning of this essay have shown the source of communism's strength, but they also give the secret of its weakness. These were the words of a prophet. Marx was to create a "substitute" religion built around the predestined destruction of capitalism. Like all substitutes, it cannot satisfy when it encounters the genuine article. Communism cannot cope with two fundamental human emotions —religion and nationalism. When the two can be kept apart, communism can find an accommodation. When, as in Poland or Afghanistan, they combine, there is trouble.

Communist theory or practice can find no room for God. God deals with absolute values and absolute truth. He is the ultimate point of reference —above even the expediency of the communist party.

There is no room, either, for nationalism, since the class struggle knows no frontier. Actually, people do not work this way. Strange to relate, ordinary human being need both God and a nation. However many betrayals of Christian principles may have taken place in history, it is a fact that whenever God's law is overthrown, freedom, truth, justice, tolerance and kindness soon fly out of the window. Human beings and human institutions cannot function without an absolute standard of belief and conduct. Communism cannot acknowledge this, so government is reduced to a series of variables. Truth is variable according to the effect it might have on the supremacy of the party. Freedom is variable, because tomorrow it may be expedient to disallow it. Justice is variable, according to the view the party might have on the case under judgement. So in the view of Welsh nationalism, communism is a fraud. It offers the prospect of the emancipation of mankind, political, emotional and economic —and it cannot deliver the goods.

2. Welsh nationalism, then, has no place for the godlessness of communism. We see no freedom without Christian order. If a man fears God, ultimately he will respect his neighbour. Every man is infinitely precious because God gave His Son for him. That is his absolute value.

3. We see the dictatorship of the party as a dangerous fraud. It

is impersonal and inaccessible, quite apart from inviting the corruption of power. There can be no emotional satisfaction outside the self-government of small groups of men and women bound together as a works council, a ward council, or a small nation.

4. Consequently, the grand international struggle of the labouring masses is also a fraud —emotionally and historically. The proletariat of the world is too big for any man's imagination. In times of stress, loyalties revert to the nation. This is a fact of life. Any political philosophy which ignores it is humbug.

5. The desire to enrich oneself by one's own hard work is an indestructible human instinct. Welsh nationalism does not seek to eliminate but to channel it. Even with the crudest methods, communism cannot supress it. Yet it does not hesitate to use the most violent dictatorship to try to do so.

6. Communism is an obsolete political creed, no longer in practical or emotional accord with the condition of our people. Wherever it has been applied, it has failed to synthesise the political, economic and emotional needs of ordinary people. This is exactly what we set out to do. That, in a nutshell, is the essence of Welsh nationalism.

Community Benefit

The power which causes the several portions of a plant to help each other, we call life. Intensity of life is also intensity of helpfulness. The ceasing of this help is what we call corruption.

Ruskin

Community benefit determines the extent and limitations of what nationalists believe that government can and cannot do for the happiness of our people. It is the highest good to be pursued by the republic. It is in direct antithesis to the theory and practice of capitalism and communism.

Let us first say what it is *not*!

* We do not equate community benefit with welfarism. We do not seek to mollify the ill-effects of monopoly capitalism upon Welsh society. We seek to devise a completely new order. It may have socialist implications, on the other hand it may also foster genuine private enterprise, but the Welsh community will be supreme judge and beneficiary.

* We do *not* equate community benefit with a high growth rate. We believe that the effect of nationalist policies in a free state will be rapid growth, but this will be incidental to our form of government.

* Community benefit has little to do with the search for monopoly power of a state machine. We certainly need a strong state, behind which our people can shelter. The power of the English state has gone far in destroying our society. We do not now seek to replace one tyranny with another.

We can now make a positive definition.

* Community benefit looks at everything from one point of view —"Does it contribute to the good of the born and the un-born community?" It it does, whether it is inspired by communist or capitalist practice, we shall adopt it.
* It seeks to offer the individual the opportunity to fulfil his personality, but it does so within the embrace of society. It cannot be a régime of unfettered individualism. Even a collect-ive society will be barely able to withstand the terrible stresses of the Age of Scarcity.
* It lives within the limitations of the Welsh environment, emotional and physical. It seeks to preserve, rehabilitate and enrich our countryside, because the land is itself a priceless possession to be cherished, but so are its people. People have got emotional limitations to the sort of environment they can live in, and these are every bit as important.

Nationalism is strictly empirical, because it does not start out on the process of government with a set of doctrinaire ideas about its purpose. Little people are disenchanted with grand ideas. We seek only to re-order society to live in a reasonable comfort, with reasonable security, and in reasonable liberty. At the threshold of the Age of Scarcity, this is no small ambition. The Republic is the protector of our society, but it does not claim to make men happy. There are limits to what it can do, its powers and pretensions. It cannot be *total* to a Welshman's life. It is a framework within which ordinary people make or destroy their own happiness by the exercise of their own responsibility. Seen in this light, welfarism is anathema to nationalism, because the greatest benefit the republic can confer upon any individual is the exercise of his own responsibility. A free society is degraded by state welfare into a dependent mass, incapable of freedom. If the state is the great provider, it is also the complete master. We aim to rebuild from a passive mass consumer society, a people who will take part in an active, participating producer society.

Another limit imposed by community benefit ideas is our belief in flexibility of means. Since we have no total solutions,

84

we do not seek to take over total control of the means of production and distribution. This has resulted in the totality of state intervention, too much administration, too much bureaucracy, too much expense. We certainly mean to dominate the market, to intervene, to lay down guidelines, and to inflict severe penalties on those who stray across them, but within these lines, individuals and institutions are free to do their own things in their own way.

Competition

The theory and practice of competition are completely divorced in the Union régime. In theory, the Tories claim to be the champions of free competition. We are told that it is the essence of "capitalism with a human face".

In practice, monopoly capital goes to great efforts to eliminate competition. Profits are made by reducing risk, not encouraging it. This is true in the competition market for insurance, clothing, consumer durables and foodstuffs. Even professional services are governed by associations whose principal aim is to prevent competition. The restrictive practices written into the Royal Institute of British Architects' standard conditions of service would be vilified in every English newspaper if a trade union were to attempt to write them into a labour agreement. Indeed, the only area in which free competition works in the UK is in the labour market. Welshmen are free to compete with each other over scarce jobs in order to fatten profits.

On an international level, monopoly capital consistently pursues a policy of eliminating international competition. One of the most blatant cases has been the 1967 General Electric Company of America cartel with several other firms to destroy the Brazilian domestic heavy-electrical industry. In 1967, importers had under 50% of the market. By 1972, this had risen to over 70%, due to systematic price-cutting and "dirty tricks". One year, for example, the cartel bought up all the entire domestic production of copper wire to force native Brazilian enterprises to import foreign, expensive, wire and so put the price of their own goods up.

In Republican Wales, we are dedicated to establishing a protected domestic market in certain designated trade sectors. This automatically rules out EEC membership. In consumer affairs, we are interested in breaking down English market agreements to share out the Welsh market, by deliberately introducing selected foreign products to force consumer prices down and increase the variety of goods in the shops. The comfortable professional restrictive practices characteristic of the Union régime will be curtailed in the public interest. The shoe will then be on the other foot —not before time!

Conquest

On 12th December, 1982, the Welsh nation is called upon to observe the seventh hundred anniversary of the final conquest of this people with the slaughter of Llywelyn ap Gruffydd, the last legitimate Prince of Wales.

This is no ordinary observance. It brings home to us what we would often, perhaps, prefer not to face —the illegitimacy and illegality of this present régime.

It was born of conquest, and nurtured on exploitation. It was established by force, and maintained by force, however veiled this circumstance might be, and whatever form this force might take. Neither time nor appeal to hallowed custom can alter this basic reality of this people. Even today, Wales is a principality subordinate to the Crown of England, in prosperity as well as in point of law. This is a fact fundamental to the present condition of this people, and fundamental to the way they think.

Conscription

In an undated Plaid Cymru pamphlet, *Wales Against Conscription* (probably written around 1956), Gwynfor Evans and three other leading nationalists wrote an impassioned case against conscription into the English Army.

This was an important pamphlet, not on account of its place in the politics of the day, but in terms of its basic philosophy. This is worth quoting at length. Mr Evans asks:

> Why must military conscription be abolished utterly? Because it is the worst social evil of our time: for Wales an unmitigated evil . . . be it for a day or for a lifetime, no person or institution has a right to seize and use the life of another. Therefore it is not against conscription for 2 years rather than 18 months that we take our stand, but against the principle and practice, whether it be for days or for years.

Again,

> Welsh nationalists have . . . consistently and continuously stood for the limitation of the state's powers. Their nationalism has always been of the liberal and democratic kind, rather than of the totalitarian brand which has elevated the state to a place of complete domination. The state's powers must be limited, and in conscripting the lives of persons, it goes beyond its lawful limit.

Mr Evans then goes on to give his historical justification for his position:

> There have been two clearly distinct streams of nationalist thought in Europe and elsewhere, and the difference between them has centred mainly on their conception of the place of the State. One line of thinkers has held that the State is the supreme power to which all persons, institutions and powers are subordinate. These thinkers have had great influence in England, though not as great as in Germany, Italy and Russia. The other lines of thinkers insisted upon the supremacy of

human personality and held the state essentially the servant, rather than the master, of the community.

Most of the evils fathered on nationalism are attributable to the first of these doctrines of the State. It is this which is practised by the totalitarians of the left and the right. Its adherents have been Statists rather than nationalists . . . Since they are free from totalitarian tendencies and from imperialist commitments, Welsh nationalists can, and do, stand for the freedom and dignity of the human person and against conscription in all its forms. In this, they are near the heart of the Welsh tradition as exemplified in the religion, literature and ancient law of their land.

These sentiments must be examined in some detail.

As conscription is a modern institution, dating from the Napoleonic practice in revolutionary France, we have no ancient law in pre-conquest Wales which refers specifically to it. We have to rely on the temper and customs of the community as they are recorded in literature. In fact, one of the principal witnesses we have for the state of the people in pre-conquest Wales, Gerald the Welshman, does not appear to support Mr Gwynfor Evans' views. Listen to Gerald in his *Description of Wales* (written around 1160).

> This people is light and active, hardy rather than strong, and *entirely bred up to the use of arms*; for not only the nobles, *but all the people are trained to war*, and when the trumpet sounds the alarm, the husbandman rushes as eagerly from his plough as the courtier from his court. (**Book I, Chapter 8.**)

> For the Welsh (who are neither worn out by laborious burdens, nor molested by the exactions of their lords) are ever prompt to avenge an injury. Hence arise their distinguished bravery in the defence of their country: hence their readiness to take up arms and rebel. Nothing so much excites, encourages and invites the hearts of men to probity as the cheerfulness of liberty; nothing so much dejects and dispirits them as the oppression of servitude. (**Book II, Chapter 8.**)

Gerald was, in fact, quite specific about the temper of our young men:

> In time of peace, the young men, by penetrating the deep recesses of the woods, learn by practice to endure fatigue through day and night; and as they meditate on war during peace, they acquire the art of fighting by accustoming themselves to the use of the lance, and by inuring themselves to hard exercise.

It would appear, then, that our ancestors willingly conscripted themselves in order to remain a free people.

However, we are not now concerned, in the last quarter of this century, with academic arguments on what has been, but on what will be. Conscription has to be viewed in the future not so much as a military but as an economic expedient. Its principal beneficiary is not the state, but the community, to which the state is but a servant.

Let us examine the circumstances in which the Republic will inherit.

* An ageing population with not more than 600,000 males of working age, after accounting for sickness and the congenitally unemployable.
* An economy with a chronic inbuilt tendency to inflation, due to the enormous demands soon to be made upon it by the need to build a national economic infrastructure.
* A serious shortage of skilled managers, tradesmen, and a bursting demand for unskilled labour for construction projects of all types.
* A chronic shortage of capital. What funds exist must be poured into infrastructure and permanent job creation projects. We simply will not be able to afford a "Dutch auction" for labour.
* A skilled workforce who will want high wages for the intensive work they will be called on to perform. These men and women will have a strong moral and economic justification to claim high differentials and high wages after tax. They will be building the co-operating society with their own hands.

If we open our frontiers to the free movement of labour, we will be flooded with immigrants. The free market would push up wages, particularly for unskilled labour, and we would experience what England has already experienced. The less attractive jobs, particularly in the service industries, are filled with immigrants. On cultural and social grounds, is this what we really want? The less attractive jobs in our community will be done by our own young people. It will do them no harm, and our society a power of good. It would seem that Welsh freedom is economically and culturally impossible without conscription. We may just as well kick against a gorse bush as attempt to ignore this. There is only one way in which cheap labour can be forthcoming. There is only one way in which trade unionists can guarantee high real wages for their adult members. There is only one way in which the rudiments of the Welsh language can be quickly re-introduced into the communal life of our young people. There is only one way in which the whole of the child-bearing population can be deliberately and systematically conditioned to Welsh loyalties. Finally, there is only one way to force a rampant and malicious fascism beyond our borders to hesitate before intervening to nip the co-operative society in the bud. The price of freedom is vigilance. That way is universal military conscription.

* Conscription into the Army of the Republic of all young men and women *full time* between 18-20 years.
* Conscription of 14 free labour days every year from all able-bodied citizens up to the age of 60, to be directed by the neighbourhood council (the Rhanbarth).

The tasks of the full time conscript army would be:

   * care of the countryside and beaches.
   * preparation of road bed for the North-South railway.
   * maintainance of the roads and railways under professional supervision.
   * drainage and rehabilitation of farm and marginal land.
   * planting and tending of hedges and windbreaks, restoration of old stone walls on highlands.
   * harvest and farm labour.
   * cleaning of streets, buses and railway coaches.
   * collection of rubbish.
   * rehabilitation of rivers and canals as pleasure amenities.
   * hospital cleaning.
   * trench digging for communal heating schemes.

The ward conscription could provide labour for communal projects.

   * clean-up operations in the neighbourhood.
   * building and maintenance of community centres.
   * damming of streams to create small head-waters capable of running small generators.
   * cleaning of water-courses and disposal of rubbish.

* demolition of eyesore derelict buildings and sheds.
* tree planting and maintainance of grass and parkland.
* site work in preparation for communal and self-help
  housing projects.
* pavement and road works undertaken with plant and
  materials supplied by the local authority.

The assumption behind these proposals is that drastic cuts in
local government expenditure will be forced upon us to enable
productive investment to be channelled into investment which
create jobs. (Irish experience records a minimum capital cost of
£stg. 2,000 per job created). The infrastructure of the co-
operating society will be built on a shoe-string. There would
appear to be no other way out of this predicament other than
conscription. Let those who disagree show good cause.

If we need conscription, in the first place, as an expedient to
correct the damage inflicted upon our society by colonial
exploitation, we need it more as a tool to build a healthy
community spirit —a spirit which English monopoly capitalism
has done its best to eradicate. Rebuilding is a process which
goes on in the mind. Our people, young men and maidens, old
men and housewives, can rediscover their emotional roots in
service to a purpose outside themselves. This is precisely what
capitalism seeks to destroy. "Culturalists" within the national
movement cannot speak of the "Welsh community" and at the
same time oppose conscription, because conscription equals
community. It is a non-sequitur to deny it —unless they are
capitalists in disguise. Conscription is a tool in the re-creation of
a spirit of community. This is a state of mind brought about by
working together. It is particularly desirable for the mental
health of Welsh women whose record of disturbance is among
the worst in these islands. The housewife (particularly with
young children) is isolated. Nationalism offers young women
with children and older women whose children have left home a
part in a wider family, that of the Welsh nation, where they are
wanted, they have a part to play, and their own laughter will
infect their neighbour.

Conscription service becomes a propaganda high school of the
nation. The Republic will have a tremendous job of re-

conditioning to do. The attitudes bred by English monopoly capitalism (and remorselessly ground into our minds by the media) are in need of replacement. We are not thinking in terms of crude political propaganda, but of healthy Christian attitudes about such basic concepts as equality of the sexes, the social value of work, and neighbourly self-help. These attitudes are experienced, not taught. Conscription will become the last and most important link in the chain of public education. It is the basic qualification for Welsh citizenship.

Contentment

Nationalism cannot be organised on the basis of a movement that promises all things to all men. It is quite impossible to make glib promises of an easy future. They would be disproved by the evidence before our eyes.

Nationalists can say with assurance that it will take a decade of hard work merely to put in the foundations of a community benefit society. These will be legal and psychological as well as physical. We do not believe it right to compete with English parties in making claims to "catch up" with the living standards of this or that nation. After the foundation investments of the new society have been laid, however, rapid advances can be made.

Nationalism has never made a case purely upon a high standard of living. We believe that this will be a by-product of a community benefit state. The immediate advantages freedom makes possible are the assurance that a new society is being built before our eyes. Indeed, because it will be built largely by our own hands, we will know exactly what is being done and what has not been done. It will be difficult for politicians to lie, as they have done for the last 30 years. For all the difficulties, we believe that the active involvement of the whole working population in rebuilding our country will give a reassurance and contentment that they have never before experienced. They will realise that they are not being cheated. When, at last, we feel able to relax, we will find that we have changed ourselves in the process. This is the real basis of the contentment that Welsh freedom offers this people.

Courts

The court system advocated for the Republic is composed of three elements.

* ward courts
* normal criminal and civil courts
* military courts

Ward courts consist of the elected ward councillors sitting in a judicial capacity to settle neighbourhood matters; for example, breach of the peace, vandalism, enforcement of standards of hygiene, price control regulations, problem family matters, non-payment of rent, failure to comply with conscription notices for ward conscription.

The object of the ward court is to take justice to the people at the level at which it affects them most. It is also an attempt to produce faster and cheaper settlements without resort to higher courts. Alienation of the individual from his society starts when "they" take him for processing in a bureaucratic machine.

If the ward is small enough (not more than 100 souls), the government and the court are one and the same group of men and women. They are accessible. They live at the bottom of the road. Many bureaucrats (and, perhaps, not a few solicitors) may be horrified at this idea. They will speak of local victimisation, inconsistent standards, the need to separate the executive from the judiciary. No doubt there will be cases of abuse, but weighted against the gain to the community in terms of the growth of responsibility, and the sheer economy in speed and cost, is the balance likely to be unfavourable?

Normal civil and criminal courts will be relieved of a burden of petty offences, but otherwise no great change is recommended.

Military courts. Welsh society has always had a certain feckless, happy-go-lucky attitude to "the rules". Where their enforcement was in local hands, provided no serious crime was committed, it was often a society which would wink at their infringement, unless matters got out of hand. Who is to say that this is wrong? When we become a free people, we could do a lot worse. However, in one area, the consequences of these easy attitudes cannot be accepted.

We have bitter testimony of the effect of treasonable dealings with the English government upon the Welsh community. This is not all a matter of ancient history. We are still faced with many years of painful struggle to set this people free, but once free, how then shall we regard those who would harm it? There are certain categories of offences which destroy our society. This is no mere injury, but wilful destruction, of the born and unborn community.

Let us resolve, then, so to govern our community that every child will recognise that his pathway is free and broad, and upon it he may do much as he pleases, but there are certain bold lines painted on either side of the road. Provided any man's activities keep him within these lines, he will rejoice, make merry, he will marry, and give in marriage. Once let him cross them, and he will come face to face with some insignificant gentleman with expressionless eyes. When a man confronts them, let him know that there will be no extenuating circumstances, no arguments, and no mercy in this life. These offences are activities on behalf of foreign powers prejudicial to the integrity of the Welsh commonwealth. Our history teaches us that treason in the English cause can enslave a nation for centuries, and has, and still enslaves us. What shall be the penalty for this treason?

Democracy

Democracy is the tip
The rich and the well born give
for your homage.
R S Thomas. *His condescensions are short lived*

Democracy is the most emotive word in the political vocabulary. Like God, mother and socialism, everyone is for it. Once an idea, person or instititon is labelled anti-democratic, there is no more to be said. Political democracy is barely a hundred years old. In the perspective of human activity it is a system "whose true potentialities have barely been scratched" as Aneurin Bevan believed. Just four generations ago, men were striving like fighting cocks to bring it to birth. Today, general election turnouts hover around 40% and local elections often attract no more than 20% of the electorate. Why has this change taken place? Why has democracy become the sacred cow of this century?

The high hopes placed upon universal suffrage have been disappointed. It would arrange, it was hoped, the peaceful transfer of power from the possessing to the labouring classes. Between 1870 and 1950 the democratic process certainly re-formed the harsher effects of capitalism, yet, in the last 30 years, the character of democracy in the industrialised west has undergone a sea-change. It has become a technique for organising central authority and manipulating the masses. It is now a process sanctifying the authority of the oligarchy. This process to some extent is common to all the old industrial nations. Nowhere has it gone further than in the United

Kingdom. It is bound to lead to a difference in sympathy between government and the masses. It is a principal factor in the alienation of ordinary people.

Policy is decided exclusively within the higher echelons of the oligarchy. Just how thoroughly members of democratically elected government in the UK administration are excluded from the decision-making process was illustrated in a remarkable address given by Mr Anthony Wedgewood-Benn (Labour, Bristol South-East) to the Royal Institute of Public Administration, and published in the *Guardian Weekly* of February 10th, 1980. Mr Benn, an ex-cabinet minister, illustrated methods by which the civil service manipulated ministerial decisions by a variety of methods used in concert.

1. By setting the framework within which policy decisions are made, i.e., determining the alternatives within which decisions can be permitted.

2. By briefing ministers on central policy matters at a time when the individual minister is expected to make simultaneously a series of decisions merely to keep the administration going —at the beginning of his term of office.

3. By control over information.

4. By mobilising the Whitehall machine to block an initiative disliked by the Civil Service, sometimes by securing the intervention of a fellow-minister.

5. By mobilising external pressures from business, NATO, the EEC or the State Department.

6. By the use of expertise —"blinding with science".

7. By the use of the "think-tank" as a preliminary to framing policy options (a powerful personal lobby of the cabinet secretary).

8. By the use of patronage to draw up lists of safe candidates for quangos.

9. By the use of "national security" as the long stop to block any unwanted policy.

Not only have democratic hopes been disappointed, there has

been a vast change in the nature of so-called democratic régimes since 1919. There has been a sleight of hand. Democracy — freedom —capitalism have been associated together in the mind of ordinary man.

The watershed in this development was the crash of 1929. For some years, there was a real danger that capitalism would not survive. Until 1929, the cry of big business was "hands off business". Monopoly capital and the oligarchies in control of the state discovered their common interest. Either they co-operated, or communism would put an end to both of them. It was not unnoticed that at a time when 70,000,000 men were unemployed in the West, there was an acute labour shortage in the USSR due to the implementation of the first five-year plan.

Consequently, the state put itself unreservedly at the service of the economy. Keynes introduced the era of neo-capitalism. His policy had two aims: high employment and growth at any cost —or else the system would collapse. These aims were achieved through the use of three expedients.

   * High government expenditure to generate demand.
   * High taxation to pay for this expenditure.
   * The fight against inflation.

What is the connection between neo-capitalism and democracy? It started a course of events which led to the inte-gration of interests and the development of the new totalitarian state, we now enjoy not a democracy, but a fake democracy. We live under a new absolutism, the absolutism of the market. Ordinary people realise this, and stay away from the polling stations.

This integration has now proceeded very far indeed. For half a century, intense psychological warfare has been waged against the common people through the media to convince them that they were genuinely able to influence the course of their own lives. The Second World War interrupted the psychological war, but only temporarily, because the cold war became primarily a struggle for the loyalty of the masses.

The west is now in the middle of another crisis. This is not a crisis of the capitalist market, as in the thirties. The crisis of the eighties is a crisis of the political state, because the state, the bureaucracy, the armed forces and monopoly capital are effectively part and parcel of the same thing. The parliamentary régime fits into this pattern as a remarkable piece of deceit. It appears to authorise decisions already made elsewhere, as the will of the majority. The masses, misled by managed information (the Official Secrets Act permits less circulation of government information than in any of the other principal "democratic" régimes of the western world), are sadly ignorant of basic political and economic facts. They are blisfully unconscious of the way their own value-judgements are determined. They suspect they are used as pawns and so they opt out, or turn to vandalism, crime, strikes, or absenteeism. The alienation of the masses is practically complete. Under these circumstances, the totalitarian state as conceived in Nazi Germany is obsolete.

What is the nationalist definition of democracy?
Plaid Cymru attitudes have been consistent for 50 years. We seek to re-interpret democracy in our native fashion.

* For the nationalist, there is no democracy without responsibility in the workplace and in the community. Democracy begins locally and is a continuous state of responsibility for and control over decisions affecting one's working and social life. The Welsh State would educate its citizens for this responsibility. Democracy thus integrates the citizen with society, making him a living part of it.
* It is a means of organising the education of citizens in responsibility —a task deliberately neglected by the English system.
* The means of education is the direct participation in decision-making.

In Welsh conditions, this definition appears to be incomplete. We are forced to amplify traditional Plaid views, as follows:

* Where direct participation involves direct labour, the citizen must give that labour. This is the logical consequence of participating democracy. Labour is the principal means of creating wealth for community and private benefit. Money raised through taxation is strictly secondary.
* Participation involves choice of aims to be pursued. In

101

particular, investment is a social function, too important to be left to private finance, pension fund managers and bureaucrats. Investment policies should be put before the nation together with costs and benefits for the direct choice of the people.

* Powers of audit of any public investment involve access to information, ability to force an interrogation of state servants, and a means of unravelling by whom and by what process decisions were made.

* The fundamental characteristic of nationalist democracy is that by achievement in common, the individual will fulfil himself more than could possibly be the case under any other system. "Being" is more important than "having".

These characteristics differ in every way from those of English mass democracy. Since Henry Tudor launched an avalanche of greed with his sale of church lands after 1535, our society has been dominated by growth, wealth and material benefit to the exclusion of all else. Welsh nationalism looks for a new direction.

Discipline

If political organisation cuts across the will to co-operate . . . its stability
and effectiveness are endangered . . . The mutual understanding and the
readiness for mutual sacrifice which patriotism implies are slow and
precious growths not to be cast lightly aside.
Towards an Economic Democracy. **D J Davies**

This is the nearest Plaid Cymru has been in 50 years to its own
definition of discipline. The Age of Scarcity will force
governments to impose a discipline on their populations if it is
not forthcoming from below. Enforced discipline can take
several forms: wages and prices policies, strict anti-terrorist
measures, anti-strike legislation, tapping of telephones, close
computer record-keeping on the affairs of the individual, and a
great deal of "inspired" attitudes generated by the government
propaganda machine. Such measures have a noticeable effect
on the public mood. Those with close working experience of
disciplined societies of the communist or fascist varieties detect
a distinctive flavour in popular outlook —apathy, laced with
intense cynicism, fear of the authorities, and reluctance to
accept any kind of responsibility. (Decision-making can be a
very dangerous pursuit). In private, there is a "dog-eat-dog"
approach to one's neighbour. The discipline imposed by these
régimes is sometimes a consequence of fear of opposition, but
sometimes for motives misunderstood in the West. Governments of backward countries have sought to impose change at
great speed —faster than the subject population is willing to
absorb. Were they free, they would revolt.

This is precisely the sort of change we can expect in the West

—a very rapid adjustment to a new economic order. This would be particularly true of a free Wales. The transition from a colonial economy to a free economy is difficult for any people. We could expect to superimpose a period of feverish reconstruction of our economy on top of adjustments brought about by the Age of Scarcity. Foodstuffs, housing, energy, the cost of services, transport and raw materials of every kind will become expensive. The need for change will be great, its acceptance by Welsh society small.

The reaction of government will depend upon social discipline. Small homogeneous states are likely to adjust better than large ones. The attitude of the average Scandinavian, Austrian or Swiss to his government is significantly different from that of the Britisher or American. He is prepared to accept burdens because he sees the need to accept them. He believes he reaps the fruit of his forebearance, which he certainly does. The comparative wages paid to working people in these small nations reflect voluntary acceptance, for a time, of what has been occasionally, a harsh self-imposed discipline. In a table of comparative labour costs, published in the *Economist* on the 4th of February 1978, while UK cash wages per hour stood at 31 points, Austrian stood at 33 (with almost 25 more points for fringe benefits), Holland and Belgium stood at 55, Sweden stood at 63 and Denmark stood at 71.

These communities have to a great extent retained their social virtues which have been seriously eroded in other capitalist economies where the fruit of any forebearance is syphoned off to end up as the profit of large corporations.

Conscription, worker participation and ward democracy are recommended in Welsh society not merely for their intrinsic merits; they are the only way in which our society can remain free, governable and successful in an age of change. They are expedients designed to force people to establish their own discipline, without interference. It is an open question whether government could otherwise impose the level of discipline required without resort to deception and perhaps worse.

Education

There are two distinct ways of looking at education; from the point of view of the state (any state), and from that of the individual. Sometimes they conflict, and it is the individual who suffers.

"Educated for what?" is the question that divides the one interest from the other. The state sees education as the most important basic industry after agriculture (and in some countries, before agriculture). It is the foundation of the power of the state and the means through which it exerts power.

The education reforms in Wales one hundred years ago were occasioned in part by the rapid growth of the German economy, attributed to the Prussian education system and held to be responsible for the quality of the German challenge, and the desire of the English government to stamp our "regionalism". Education has been statist in outlook ever since. Today, it is considered dangerous to have more than 20% of the undergraduate intake of the Welsh university of Welsh origin.

The individual has other standards of values. The statist view of the world to such a population is rigorously conditioned in its formative years, and is found to be sadly deficient in helping to live a complete life.

Education for exploitation

* It spurs individual achievement in a narrow band of academic pursuits, really suitable for absorption by a mere 2% of the population. It does not educate for contentment and integration within a community, but for translation to some "higher existence" outside it. The accent is on competition

rather than co-operation. The teaching of binding or integrating skills is therefore deficient. A young person is catapulted into life with no real preparation for a trade under the state system or, much more important, for the community relationship within a working group. In a word, he is educated for *exploitation*.

Socialist environmentalism in opposition to reality

Mass socialism applied to education has led to the comprehensive system; whereby it is assumed that since environment (rather than innate ability) is predominant in shaping attitudes, the provision of the old academic curriculum of the nineteenth century public school to the council house tenants of this century must necessarily be to the public good. When a young person drops out of this doctrinaire system, he is treated as a delinquent, rather than unhappy with an education which he believes irrelevant.

Tasks of nationalist education

Nationalism is faced with a fundamental reappraisal of fashionable policies in the light of its own view of society, which revolves around several questions.

*   How can we integrate young people into a co-operative society?
*   How can we give them emotional satisfaction within that society?
*   How can we make their training relevant by the age of 16 to themselves and to their community?
*   What vehicle can we provide which, above all else, locks them into a system of social values which will give them an identity?
*   How can we train that tiny minority of all children who will become the servants of the Republic and the effective masters of Welsh society?

The emotional needs of the majority

The needs of the Welsh state, as a state, and of the poor-to-average ability child have more in common than one might assume, but not under a régime of capitalism.

The state, as a state, needs a dependable supply of skilled craftsmen at the age of 18, when young people begin conscript service for the community. The average child wants relevance, belonging and certainty. All these add up to self-respect, a commodity that capitalism has not developed in Welsh education.

The solution is abandonment of the ideals of the comprehensive in favour of an early craft training which can turn average (or below average) youngsters into competent workpeople by 16 years of age. The objective of craft education is to prepare them to enter conscript service at 18, fully productive in socially useful skills, the old usual skills and the new "republican" skills demanded by an economy not exclusively oriented to growth —e.g., the skills associated with land reclamation, intensive care of the land, and the environment of the community —in a word, the "beautification" of Wales in a way not conceivable under capitalism.

Their integration into a co-operating society is achieved by:

* Christian instruction to give a moral base.
* Welsh language instruction to develop identity and to "lock" young people into a set of values, Christian, Welsh and communal.
* Sandwich instruction in craft and technical high schools, working in conjunction with community labour brigades, whose objectives are set by the State Planning Authority (and who, in consequence, will have a vested interest in the quality of instruction and performance).

Let us examine a few illustrations of this new way of instruction.

Learning by doing

* Basic curriculum subjects leading to work in soil science, hedging, dry stone walling, care of rivers and damming of streams, associated with land rehabilitation, drainage, auxiliary production of electricity for farming and creation of refuges for game and wild-life. This work has no place or reason under capitalism.
* Subjects leading to a revival of skills in breeding of horses, mountain ponies and draught animals, to provide auxiliary power to Welsh farms, not oil-dependent.
* Subjects leading to smallholding, and auxiliary support skills

to encourage young people to take over marginal land to produce food and recreational parks, breaking up large farming units (particularly when they are owned and exploited by foreigners).

* Subjects leading to building skills, so that every ruined abbey in Wales can be rebuilt by the labour of young people, to put right the old wrongs inflicted upon the nation. Every abbey and every castle to be restored, decorated and catered for by "sandwich" and conscript labour, to provide places of retreat and recreation.

In every illustration, the focus of education has been imperceptibly shifted from that leading to a competitive, acquisitive society —a consumer society— to a co-operative contributing producer society, caring about land, creatures and Welsh tradition. We have come a long way from the preparation to act as cheap, acquiescent labour to be exploited on the industrial estate. The product of education stays at home, it is not converted into superprofits for export.

Preparation of the super-producers

Lest it be assumed that nationalism is purely an offshoot of the Ruskin school of Romanticism, let it be noticed that the benefits of education have to be paid for by exceptionally high productivity from that small minority of young people biologic- ally endowed with the ability to excel in scholastic subjects.

These become the élite stream in the Republican educational system, no longer held back by the pace of the slowest in the comprehensive, but coached and pampered in up-to-date versions of the Welsh Grammar School. The education of the super-producers presents a complete contrast to that of the below-average student.

* Whereas the average stream specialises very early in life, the élite stream specialises very late, so that instead of 3 subject at A level, 6 subjects are studied to Baccalaureate standard, of which two, compulsorily, would be Welsh and mathematics, with at least two foreign languages (English will *not* be taught), one chosen from History, Economics or politics, and one experimental science, and computer science.

* Wherever possible, 6th forms would be residential and would combine education with intensive outdoor skills, such as seamanship, navigation, gliding, windsurfing and compulsory military and weapons training.

* All Grammar School pupils would study at the Welsh university for first degrees.

Conclusion

The inescapable purpose of a nationalist system of education is to work with the realities of biology, and not against them, as mass socialism tried to do. Our purpose can be put in one word —*integration*, while capitalist education aims to *dis*integrate, isolate and divide, as a preparation for exploitation. Nationalism need not fear accusations of double standards or élitism, since while it clearly has two paths, and is indisputably élitist, nevertheless, it has an overriding purpose, whose strength binds both halves of the community together. That purpose is nation-building.

Energy

The life principle of democratic planning, . . . is an awakening in the whole people of a sense of common moral purpose. Not one goal, but a direction. Not one plan, once and for all, but the conscious selection by the people of successive plans.

T.V.A. for Wales. **Plaid Cymru, 1944**

Energy is politics and politics is energy. In the Age of Scarcity, there will be cause enough to remember it. Under a régime of monopoly capital, it is not surprising to observe that not one single question of energy politics has ever been put to an electorate in the English state. The massive conversion of power stations to burn oil to replace coal in the 1960s had far-reaching economic and political implications which were keenly felt in Wales. On what occasion was the Welsh people inform-ed of the options, or asked to contribute their opinion, let alone their assent? All over the world, energy in mass democratic states is too important to be left to the people: it is too import-ant even to be left to their parliaments. It is handled by their civil servants, who have links with other, and less disinterested, organisations. Wales presents a classic example of the effects of *laissez-faire* in energy politics.

In a summary, *Welsh Coal Mines* by Dr W Gerwyn Thomas (National Museum of Wales), we find that the pattern of coal production in Wales is as follows:

SOUTH WALES		NORTH WALES	
year	millions of tons	year	millions of tons
1855	8½	1870	2¼
1913	57	1906	3
1930	45	1913	3½
1945	20	1940	2½
1975	8½	1974	½

Coal was the chief source of industrial and naval energy in the last century. South Wales alone accounted for one-fifth of all energy in the United Kingdom in 1913. Apart from broken bones, and a subsistence economy, what did the creation of this wealth do for the Welsh people?

This ABC is concerned more with the future than the past, yet we will not understand the future unless we are aware both of the present and the past. We have to develop distinct Welsh attitudes. In order to do so, we might like to start by asking six questions.

1. *How much energy do we produce within Wales, in respect of coal, electricity, oil and nuclear power?*
2. *How much do we consume as a percentage of that production? How much is exported? Does any benefit accrue to the Welsh community thereby?*
3. *How much will be produced and needed in 1990 and 2000?*
4. *Where is it going to come from, and at what price?*
5. *How much energy would we need to drive a free Welsh economy —using as a minimum yardstick the amount needed to satisfy current demand and the level of economic activity envisaged, say, if Plaid Cymru's economic plan of 1970 were to be implemented?*
6. *What factors really relate to energy production and consumption in Wales? What political attitudes should be generated by nationalist perspectives of the energy question? What information or perspectives are witheld because they would give too clear a picture of our position?*

These are not straightforward questions to answer, and I am certainly not able to answer all of them. As we shall see, what statistics are available need careful evaluation according to national criteria about which nothing is published in the economic press. I have to beg the indulgence of the reader, and set out to provide the most complete answers possible.

Let us start with the last question, and see how this perspective enables us to interpret the answers to the others. Several factors govern the Welsh view of the energy crisis.

Transport —no substitute for a million tonnes of petrol per year
Despite the break-through of the Gulf and Western Zinc Chlorine Battery, and the determination of the General Motors Corporation, it is unlikely that more than 120,000 electric cars will be on American roads by 1985, 1.3 million by 1990, and 6.6 million by 2,000. By the turn of the century, even in America, only 2 out of 5 new motor cars will be electrically driven. (*Economist*, June 14th, 1980).

Petrol is now, and will remain for the forseeable future, the best way of storing power for motor transport. If methane gas were liquified at $-163°$ C, it would be feasible to use it to propel a passenger car, but 1 gallon of petrol would contain twice as much power. The expense of refrigeration apparatus would add at least one thousand pounds to the cost of the vehicle.

Hydrogen contains only $\frac{1}{3}$ of the power of petrol, and presents other problems of storage. The gas has to be dissolved in the hydride of a rare metal (lanthanum, titanium or zirconium) in order to store it, and should be kept at $-253°$ C. A 10 gallon tank would add 200 lbs of weight to store it. The rare metals cost not less than $10 per pound. (*Economist*, October 20th, 1979 —'Could Coal be King of the Road?').

20% alcohol can be added to make the petrol go further, and this can be distilled from material grown in the Welsh climate, but the distillation process is very inefficient. To distil 1 gallon of ethyl alcohol from home-grown corn, which would yield energy in a motor spirit of 85,000 BTUs equivalent, 140,000 BTUs of energy would have to be burnt to fire the still. The net energy loss on the process would be 44%.

Quantifying the oil from coal option in Welsh conditions
Whether we like it or not, we must live with the internal combustion engine for at least 20 years, and the machine must

be run on petrol, made available from some source inside Wales, unless we are to import 967,000 tonnes of petroleum spirit per year (at 1977 figures) or crude oil to produce a total of 3.7 million tonnes of petroleum products in Welsh refineries. These were the amounts consumed in 1977 (source —*Welsh economic trends*— Welsh Office, p.61).

It is sometimes suggested that Welsh mines could produce coal for feeding an oil-from-coal process, such as that currently employed at SASOL in South Africa.

In South Africa, the Fischer-Tropsch process will produce only 20 US gallons of petrol for each tonne of coal. To satisfy the needs of our motorists alone, this would demand a production of 5.6 million tonnes of coal, at the present state of efficiency of the process. There are, indeed, hopes to treble the yield within 3 years. At present, Welsh pits produce about 8 million tonnes from 37 pits. We need to return to levels of production of the 1930s to mine this amount. These figures, of course, refer only to coal which has to be processed into motor spirit. This excludes amounts required for electricity generation, gas and steel works needs.

Imported coal and imported technology for oil substitution
If we had to import coal, the necessary quantities might be available from South Africa, Poland, Australia or the United States —at a price. European coal tends to sell at about $55 per tonne, and American coal sells at $20 per tonne —if it can be obtained.

The large American oil companies quietly bought out many American coalfields in the 1960s (just at the time when they were successfully convincing many South Wales industrial managers to change over to oil. Many pits closed in Wales as a result of their persuasion).

American oil companies have been pioneering better forms of the coal-to-oil process, which promise to be more efficient than the Fischer-Tropsch process. The best patents appear to be owned by Exxon, Mobil or Texaco.

Underground gasification —the hope that failed
The alternative to mining coal is to gasify it underground and produce methane gas. This is of poor quality. While pure

natural gas yields 1,000 BTUs per cubic foot, methane produced by deep burning yields only 150 BTUs per cubic foot, which with expensive oxygen enrichment can yield a gas of about 350 BTUs per cubic foot. (see Science and Technology section of the *Economist*, January 26th, 1980).

This is technically feasible in America in sub-bituminous coal seams which shrink when fired (allowing more air to rush through the coal seams to hasten the process). It is not easy in Welsh bituminous seams which expand when fired, and choke off the air supply.

Back to the pits
In other words, if we want to use the 300 million tons of coal under our feet in Wales, men will have to go down and get it.

If and when we have it on the surface, the coal-to-oil conversion plant currently costs five times as much as a conventional oil refinery.

Estimation of total demand in millions of tonnes of coal equivalent
Having examined the current state of the art of oil substitution, one must add normal non-oil equivalent consumption taken from the 1979 edition of *Welsh Economic Trends* published by the Welsh Office, and information made available by the South Wales area of the NCB. The results are shown in Figure No. 5.

The energy gap —implications of the "coal-equivalent" equation
We now have some measure of the predicament into which our country has been driven by the policies of the English state. We may draw the following conclusions.

1. If the Welsh people were to find themselves free tomorrow, the government would face an energy problem of serious dimensions. Wales would have to import oil and coal on a large scale to keep its refinery and generating capacity operating at existing levels. However, Wales produces twice as much electricity as it needs for current uses, and contains 28% of the UK crude oil distillation capacity —all of which it does not need for its own consumption, since, for its own uses, it needs only 3.7 million tons of oil product (out of a total UK requirement of 56.3 million tons). This level of oil imports would have to be

Figure 5

THE ENERGY GAP IN WALES

ILLUSTRATED FROM 1977 ENERGY CONSUMPTION CONVERTED INTO TONNES OF
COAL EQUIVALENT (TCE) FOR APPROXIMATION AND COMPARISON ONLY. (FOR
COAL EQUIVALENT RATES, SEE PAGE 101 ECONOMIST MEASUREMENT GUIDE 1975).

ENERGY ELEMENT	QUANTITY CONSUMED/ PRODUCED	CONSUMPTION MEASURED IN TONNES OF COAL EQUIVALENT	SOURCE DATA AND/OR CALCULATION REMARKS
1 Electricity generated	22,950 gigawatts/hrs	2,868,750	22,950,000,000 x 0.125 　　　　1000 Welsh economic trends (1979) Caution! Only 12,920 giga-watts actually sold to Welsh consumers.
2 Natural gas consumed	650 million cubic feet	865,800	650,000,000 x 1.332 　　　1000 No gas produced in Wales in significant quantities outside steelworks own production and consumption
3 Oil products delivered	3,760,000 tonnes	5,640,000	3,760,000 x 1.5
4 Coal delivered for electricity generation	2,370,000 UK tons		
5 Steelworks consumption	3,027,000		
6 Add coal imports from UK or abroad	1,101,000		
7 House coal	730,000		
* Coal longtons sub-total	7,228,000	8,095,360	Factorized by 1.2
Total short tonnes consumption		17,469,910	
8 Less coal produced	7,988,000	8,946,560	
WELSH ENERGY GAP		8,523,350	

CONCLUSION:
In round figures Wales needs to double its production of coal in
order to be self-sufficient at home and produce an exportable
surplus of electricity.

paid for with export earnings, or by selling off surplus energy to English consumers.

2. Assuming that we were to decide upon a greater measure of self-reliance by using deep-mined coal as a refinery raw material, we would have difficulty in producing it. Of the 37 Welsh pits working in 1977, how many will be left in 20 years' time?

3. The costs, at internationally prevailing prices, of reconstructing our energy base around home-produced coal would be between $12-20 capital cost per tonne produced. This would amount to an investment of between $444 million and $740 million at 1979 prices —assuming that all motor spirit used in Wales was to be produced from oil-from-coal conversion, and new pits were to be sunk solely for this purpose. (Refer to *Coal – Bridge to the Future*. World Coal Study, Balinger Publishing Co., Cambridge, Mass.)

4. It is in the context of these figures that we can appreciate the implications of English energy policy in Wales twenty years ago. One wonders to what extent the damage wrought at that time was purely co-incidental. The destruction of our pits and their feeder railway lines (costing £50 million for a single stretch of 8-kilometre track capable of handling 300 tons per day) present a barrier to the emergence of a Welsh nation state —formidable, but not insuperable.

5. It must already be clear that some rethinking must take place within Wales. We may arrive at conclusions which are political rather than purely technical or economic.

The gravity of the energy crisis facing the Welsh people is masked by the flow of North Sea oil. This will peak and decline within 20 years. At that time, Englishmen as well as Welshmen, will begin to ponder on the implication of the tonnes of coal equivalent figures of their transport system.

Do the Welsh people want to continue to tag on to the shirt-tails of English decision-making, as they have in the past, without any form of consultation? What benefit accrued to Wales thereby?

Need we remain complacent just as long as we can drive into a garage and fill up our petrol tanks? Cannot we recognise that the time taken to plan, approve, finance and construct all the elements of a national energy system will take 20 years? Looked at in the context of the tonnes of coal equivalent figures, can we see any alternative for the Whitehall régime except nuclear power, if monopoly capital is to survive intact in these islands? Is this not the picture around which the class struggle in these islands will swing? For once, there are grounds for believing that it is not the influence of the industrial lobby that is so important, but the determination of the régime itself to survive that provides the driving force in this campaign. The French have already committed themselves to a nuclear solution —whatever the risks.

What are the implications of this policy for Wales? Closer dependence on a centralised English power structure? As a dumping-ground for waste products, which the English common people are already determined shall not contaminate their own land at almost any cost?

Welshmen must seriously ask themselves whether they did not pay too high a price for their lack of resistance to the closures of mines and railways in the 1960s. Can they afford to repeat their errors twenty years after? In the energy equations which we have studied, it is clear that in a free state, some adjustments would be needed. It would be impossible to return to 1913 levels of production. It would take too long to sink the pits and the seams are not easy to tap. All the easily workable coal would appear to have been taken already. (In this context, one notes with dismay the drop in open cast production from 2.9 million to 2.5 million tons within the 5 years after 1971). What would have to give way in a free Wales? Gas supply for the central heating systems? Electricity, or the convenience provided by unregulated private motoring? In each case, the sacrifice would be so painful that the people, *as a whole* —not the civil servants —would have to sanction any action. What alternatives are possible?

Do we really favour a nuclear alternative in Wales? Do we need an alternative to conventional fuels, other than tidal barrages in the estuaries of the Severn, Loughor, Tywi, Mawddach and Dee? In a carefully planned economy, would it be possible to maintain standards of service without a catastrophic drop in living standards?

There are alternatives provided by a strictly Welsh national approach to these problems:

1. Provided power station capacity and their feeder mines are not destroyed, Wales produces a useful surplus of electricity. This could provide the key to a solution of our problems.

2. If this surplus were used for large-scale railway electrification, building quite a new type of railway —a roll-on, roll-off ferry service within Wales and the border crossing points— our people could continue to enjoy the use of their motor cars. The private motor truck would need to use the ferry service within Wales for as much of its journey as possible. This would require regulation.

3. Despite the diversion of 9000 gigawatt hours of electric power consumption to our own use, the Welsh Republic would be unwise to follow a "beggar-my-neighbour" energy policy. These islands are too small. An intelligent relocation of resources would benefit all within them. It would be profitable to sell surplus energy at realistic transfer prices. This would contribute towards the costs of building a new energy base in Wales.

4. The correctness of the Plaid Cymru policy over the last 40 years is established beyond question. The energy gap which is opening up before us vindicates the philosophy of *TVA for Wales*, 1944, *An Electricity Board for Wales*, 1956 and *Towards an Economic Democracy*, 1949. This recommended a single Hydro-Carbon Trust taking in all energy-related matters, and turning over the pits to Miners' Co-operatives. This is certainly an obvious way of increasing production as fast as new pits can be sunk, and existing and derelict pits can be rehabilitated.

5. The whole nation is involved in the choice of an energy policy. It is fundamental that the continuing life of the community, to its living standards and to the sacrifices that must be borne in common for many years to come. It is a subject, fit and proper, for the consultation and the assent of the whole Welsh people, particularly with regard to such matters as nuclear energy. The choice of policies and the exact questions to be put to the people cannot be left to the Whitehall

régime. No referendum would be valued if administered by an English government. Only a national government can be trusted to observe the best interest of the Welsh, rather than the English, people —a best interest accurately percieved by Plaid Cymru many years ago and advocated, in season and out, in the face of the Labour Party mass bureaucratic solutions, which have played into the hands of monopoly capital.

6. We may conclude, that as there is no incentive for the English state to look to our best interests, we had better do so ourselves. Energy is no longer a technical or an economic matter. It is not even a political matter —as that has been understood in Wales. It is now a matter of revolutionary politics.

Equality

Our approach to this matter makes one of the fundamental differences between nationalism and socialism.

We draw our faith in the equality of man from Christian teaching of our equality before God. We interpret this to mean that all Welsh citizens have an equal right to health, education, process of justice, and the right to practice their own craft or profession in their own country rather than in somebody else's.

We do not interpret this to mean that the Republic must force all men to have an equal standard of living. This is an assumption running through much Labour Party legislation. "It is morally wrong to be in different circumstances to your neighbour." We will try to make our medical services and our schools as good as any in Europe. If some would prefer to accept alternative services, we will do nothing to stop them, provided that these services are not financed by public money. We are simply unable to offer open or hidden subsidies to alternative services. The available resources must be concentrated on the services available to the whole community.

The community benefit state is not prepared to adopt rigorously egalitarian principles in taxation, health or education, because we cannot introduce workers' shareholding, and then deny incentives to make their shareholding profitable, and to spend their extra income as they see fit. Nationalism does not seek to force all men into a mould —this is the essence of totalitarianism. The Republic will actively encourage difference, whether in the exploitation of personal talent, income incentive or the consumption of luxury services. Variety makes for a more lively society.

Fascism

A mass electorate . . . is irrational, and politicians learned to appeal not to mind but to emotion, seeking less to persuade than to manipulate.
J S Mill

Fascism . . . is the future refusing to be born.
Aneurin Bevan

Since the horrors of fascism were revealed at the Nuremburg trials, it has been a taboo subject. Little scholarly research was done into the social origins of fascism until the 1960s. It was a creed written off as mere opportunism, without serious intellectual foundations.

The horrors are real enough, but it is impossible to write off fascism. Its importance to the Welsh nationalist at this time is significant, and growing. Fascism always appears in a particular combination of social and economic circumstances, and these account for its importance for Welshmen of all persuasions.

These are:

* a sense of national defeat of disillusion (particularly in an ex-imperial power).
* concentration of industry and commerce into the hands of powerful cartels.
* emancipation of the bureaucracy from all effective control by a parliament or by the laws of the land.
* increasing co-ordination of the bureaucratic and industrial élites.
* perfection of existing means of mass manipulation of opinion or the development of new ones.

121

* the classic overture to fascism is a sudden shift of opinion from the far left to the far right, particularly in the lower middle class.

These portents are signs of the times, and it is their appearance in these islands that make a re-estimation of the intellectual foundations of fascism a priority.

Whenever a Labour politician has a particular fit of spleen he will label Welsh nationalists as "fascists". The Plaid has been sensitive to thses charges, and this is well known to Labour politicians. In fact, all nationalist movements do have certain common ground with fascism. It is likely that the intellectual climate of opinion in Continental Europe between 1890 and 1925 had much more to do with the moulding of early Plaid doctrine, than party members either know or would care to admit. All the more reason to make a careful exploration of the similarities between fascism and all nationalist movements and their points of divergerence.

Let us, firstly, trace the history of fascism in the early period, usually ignored by political writers.

While the word fascism was not used widely until Mussolini's "March on Rome" in 1922, the principal beliefs of what became known as fascism had been common property in Europe since the turn of the century.

By 1880, while universal suffrage was still a novelty in the more advanced countries of Western Europe, a profound disillusion had begun to spread among the intellectuals over the results it was having on society and the practice of politics. It was clear that parliamentary liberalism had become a mask for capitalism. Crude capitalist exploitation drove the workers to Marxism. The intellectuals went in another direction. Many were aghast at the ease with which the electorate could be manipulated by monopoly capital. They saw the trivialisation of European culture, to the vulgar commercialism of capital. They believed (quite correctly, as it turned out) that Marxist materialism would produce an even greater deformity of European culture because of its opposition to, or denial of many of the forces that had made Europe great —particularly religion, and the contribution of distinctly national traditions to the richness of the European way of life.

There was a total reaction against the idea of the individual as the centre of all activity and a re-emphasis of the organic Community. Quite suddenly nationalism and socialism coalesced. In May 1898, Maurice Barrès, standing as a nationalist candidate for Nancy, first used the term "nationalist socialist". "Yellow" socialism advocated national solidarity, in place of the class struggle, and advocated the virtues of wide distribution of property among the people, rather than the exploration of that of capitalists. Workers should participate in profits. Workers' and managers' unions should exist side by side. An assembly of national and regional representatives should assist a strong government which would not bow to the pressure of commercial lobbies, but consider solely the community benefit.

Many years later, Sir Oswald Mosley, (who, it might be remembered, was for several years a close associate of Aneurin Bevan) summed it all up in one phrase.

> If you love our country, you are nationalist,
> and if you love our people you are socialist.

The new mood swept through all the countries of continental Europe like a bush fire. By 1913, popular opinion among the politically *avant-garde* young men, was anti-socialist and anti-capitalist at the same time. It was often anti-parliament, because that was where the "interests" stopped things being done. This mood was in some measure responsible for the zeal with which all classes of young men welcomed the war in August 1914. The Marxist class war dissolved at its first encounter with national feeling.

By 1922 *Das Dritte Reich* had been written by Arthur Moeller van den Bruck in Germany, Mussolini had marched on Rome and fascist parties were springing up all over Europe. Adolf Hitler did not invent fascism. Its main ideas had a long and respectable currency in the European middle classes from Ostende to Bucharest.

It is against this background that we must re-examine Saunders Lewis' early writings. We must never forget the fact that Saunders Lewis was a French scholar and was intimately aware of developments in French thought. From 1880 to 1925, there is reason to plead that France, not Germany or Italy, was the intellectual home of European nationalist ideas. Saunders Lewis was a lieutenant in France during the great war.

It should not surprise us, then, that there was a certain similarity between nationalist and fascist ideas all over Europe. While these movements were to develop in quite different directions, their similarities up to the mid 1920s are striking:

1. There is an absolute refutation of the "social contract", which was the basis of nineteenth century political emancipation and was to be the basis of twentieth century economic emancipation —socialism.

> In so far as man is outside the organization of society he has no freedom. Outside society man would be the subject of nature, not its master. He would be the enemy of all, and the friend of none. He would be threatened by things and persons, in a state of abject dependence. There would be no freedom, and no security. Each man would be exposed to the open wrongs of every enemy. There would be no assurance of life, much less of liberty. The freedom man is supposed to barter away in order to enter society (in order to secure the enjoyment of the remainder) has no real existence. An imaginary transfer —it could not have been a real one. Ultimately man has existence only in so far as he is sustained and determined by the community. At the root of 'I' there is 'WE'.
> *The Philosophic Basis of Fascism.* **Gentile**

2. Super-imposed on this intellectual foundation, the crisis of European Capitalism in the immediate post-war world of 1919-1929 produced a keen sense of urgency, which was channelled in fascist thinking into a national reconstruction plan (well before the USSR adopted the first five year plan in 1928). This pragmatism began to attract life-long socialists throughout Europe who rejected the sterility of classic Marxism on the one hand, and bourgeois democracy on the other. (After all, had the solidarity of international working men prevented the war?) The Plan had to be given priority in the crisis. This was no time to squabble about the exact definition of the private and the public sector. What was required was to get idle capacity back into use, and workmen back in jobs. De Man, the Leader of the Belgian Socialist workers party pointed out how unrealistic were the attitudes of communists in calls for immediate

programmes of expropriation and nationalisation which would further disrupt a fragile economy. Control, not direct ownership, over the means of production and distribution were needed, and a strong central state could provide it. The liberal parliament could not since it was merely a reflection of the political lobbies of capitalism.

3. Fascism, (like Welsh nationalism) made a point of stressing that it was a new way of life. It was not a movement in the old political sense dedicated to the parties of the right or the left. It was a synthesis of many empirical ideas derived from both, but it specifically rejected the materialist concept that wellbeing equals happiness. Men are not animals content to be fed and fattened. Men were spiritual creatures and the rejection of their spiritual being would debase society. The fascist state could not enter into the usual political auction. It was above that level of activity. On the contrary, it called for sacrifice and self denial for the benefit of the community born and unborn.

4. Again Welsh nationalism and early Italian manifestations of fascism have strong affinities in their development of syndicalist socialist ideas. Both were convinced that the liberal mass democratic state was a swindle. It was a cockpit for struggle between two fundamentally similar social groups struggling for the fruits of office, each advancing a sustaining myth.

The masses had neither the foresight, the will, nor the ability to shape their destiny, and the net effect of universal suffrage was to relegate the true revolution of the people to the Greek Kalends. Arturo Labriola, head of the Italian Socialist Party referred to socialism as a "piece of parliamentary machinery put at the disposal of the politicians". On the contrary, the proletariat and the new professional middle classes had a common interest. Socialist class war notions merely kept politicians in safe seats. The common fate and common interest of the Italian and the Welsh middle and working classes over the eighty years that separates Labriola's speech in Paris from the Wales of today was and remains an exclusion from ownership. The common enemy was finance capitalism.

5. Viewed in this light, the insistence of nationalists like D J Davies, that workers' participation was the minimum emotional

as well as the minimum economic condition which would be required to keep industrial society together, may not be as novel as nationalists believe. This is as far as these comparisons can be taken, because there is a sharp divergence on other matters.

6. In the fascist view, the dangers of manipulation of the masses forced an élite in the nation to impose their authority through the state, which embodies the ultimate character and virtue of the nation. The nation and the state became one and the same thing. It is treasonable to oppose the state, because thereby the nation is undermined. It is precisely this line of thinking that Saunders Lewis was at such pains to refute in his first memorable summer school lecture in 1925. Indeed, his over-emphasis of this particular point suggests that already in 1925, he recognized that European nationalism could develop in directions which would find little sympathy in Wales.

7. Welsh nationalism has, indeed, gone in diametrically the opposite direction in the face of the failure of parliamentarianism. The Welsh response has been to attack the representative principle. Nationalists want to control the administration of civic and economic affairs through direct participation of the citizen through the Rhanbarth and Works Council. They believe that the smaller scale of such operations make them comprehensible to ordinary people who can identify with them. They cannot identify with a bureaucratic party organisation which has questionable associations with big business.

8. The ultimate conflict is, of course, over the concept of the authority of the totalitarian state. This implies no external higher standard of values. It condones any action provided it is expedient for the state. Christian belief cannot sustain this doctrine. There is one authority and one truth. That truth is a continuing revelation in the spirit of man in his search for God. This involves the individual in continual discussion and continual challenge, particularly when the values enshrined in the way people traditionally live in their communities can be at variance with the values of the state.

The Welsh struggle against fascism

1. The writing is already on the wall. If we judge the events in

these islands by the criteria mentioned in this essay then the Whitehall government is already crypto-fascist. All the pre-conditions exist for the mask of parliamentarianism to be thrown off. This is not the English way. The substance of the fascist state already exists. What real need is there for any action which might galvanize the opposition?

In Wales, the most proletarian part of the United Kingdom, has not the electorate freely joined the international capitalist cartel at Brussels and the ascendancy of English national capital over Welsh affairs?

Welsh nationalism is the most consistent opponent of fascism in these islands. Communists take their orders from Moscow, which may find it expedient to sell its own supporters down the river at any time. Any form of socialism cannot be relied upon.

2. There is much to be learnt from fascist techniques as well as from fascist ideas. The most brilliant propaganda campaigns in European history have been conducted by the fascists, with spectacular success. Nationalism in Wales would do well to take a few tips.

3. The most important lesson to be learned from fascist experience is the universal failure, after they came to power, to organize a genuine régime of people's rule. Had they been able, within 24 months of attaining power, to force through their syndicalist ideas for worker participation in large scale industry, the history of Europe might have been very different. They would have created a genuine non-communist alternative to finance capital. It was precisely upon this point that Gregor Strasser (who was certainly no martyr to the cause of the common people) came into conflict with Hitler in 1934. He paid with his life for his attitudes during the "Night of the Long Knives" in 1934. Europe paid the price in 1945 when Communism advanced to the Elbe. In the last analysis, work-ers' power is the touchstone of a wholesome Christian alternat-ive to communism.

Foundation Occupations

Foundation occupations are those whose services are essential to the smooth operation of civilised society as we know it. Traditionally, these services are taken for granted. Each of them is under pressure, which will become more severe as the Age of Scarcity advances. The community benefit state would be more vulnerable to deteriorating standards of service than the mass democratic state. The signal for the collapse of any weak régime is a general strike in the foundation industries. Nationalists are well rewarded to ponder the implications. While the main body of the population is coming to grips with the realities of a participating society, the régime will be at risk. Foundation occupations as listed below do not lend themselves to easy experiments in social control. As special cases they have a high political priority. There are several questions which we might ask before formulating policy.

1. What percentage of the male workforce is involved? What is the relationship of these groups to the "productive groups" in the economy in terms of direct wages, fringe benefits and age distribution?

2. Can the Republic reduce the size of the problem by hiving off some services to private contractors? What would be the likely effect of this on prices?

3. In what areas may conscript service be used as a substitute for privatisation?

4. Which areas of activity could safely be contracted out by a

weak revolutionary government faced with a strong counter-revolutionary neighbour?

Foundation occupations might be classified as follows:

Class 1: Occupations calling for the exercise of considerable professional skill —*unalienable.*
* state and local government servants.
* regular army (a small professional cadre)
* police (criminal police only)
* medical services
(public sector core services only —possibility of parallel private sectors —unsubsidised.)
* public education —as above.

Class 2: Occupations with duties where incentives are impractical —capable of some conscript substitution.
* traffic police
* post
* fire service
* garbage disposal
* prison services
* ambulance service
* other para-medical and support services

Class 3: Occupations with specialist technical skills —where precipitate alienation may be unwise.
* electricity generation and distribution
* telephone and telegraph
* water and sewerage

Class 4: Occupations where productivity can be affected by the worker, and where worker co-operatives can be organised (with or without conscript labour contribution).
* transport operation
* transport maintainance
* mining

Class 5: Delivery services now in private hands which contribute to a good standard of living —whose maintainance is now in doubt —where conscript labour could be used.
* delivery of bread, milk and newspapers
* delivery and distribution of foodstuffs, fuel, building

materials

The danger for present-day nationalists is that current prejudices make it impossible to contemplate future solutions. The object of a thorough review of popular attitudes in the light of the ideology of the Republic is to clear the road for fresh ideas. One fact may be taken as fundamental —it is unlikely that the free state would be able to support the cost of essential services without radical departure from traditional habits.

Free Collective Bargaining

Free collective bargaining is as dead as the dodo. Many are not prepared to recognise this fact, or to draw the necessary inferences from it. The decay and demise of *laissez-faire* wage negotiation is inevitable in the Age of Scarcity.

Free collective bargaining was a natural product of the capitalist system. In practice, it means that the entrepreneur tries to get away with as mean a wage as possible, while the function of the union of working men was to negotiate collectively to prevent this. In the Age of Scarcity, raw material cost and financial charges will rise. There will be constant pressure on wage levels. Currencies will be liable to fluctuation. Since wages are such an important element in inflationary pressure, the state has been driven more and more to restrict bargaining. This is an international phenomenon. The English state has not taken the necessary corollary action.

* to keep a rigorous control over prices by taking an active part in the market, intervening by releasing stocks of commodities to counteract profiteering or high import prices. The English state is doctrinally unable to accept this degree of market intervention.
* to develop a state wages scale to raise (*and lower*) wages in certain industries to encourage or actively discourage over-consumption of skilled labour, or to encourage men and women to retrain for a job in another industrial sector.

In Wales, most people (including nationalists) have not yet appreciated that a free state would mean very heavy pressure on wage levels. In round figures, this workforce is composed of a mere half million working people. This is manifestly not enough to service the enormous appetites of the economy for labour in a period of frantic reconstruction of the community benefit economy. Hence, the pressure on wage levels will be particularly severe. A whole battery of ameliorative expedients are necessary to combat inflationary pressures. Conscription is essential to provide unskilled labour and the state wages scale indispensable to keep the cost of labour in hand, otherwise soaring labour charges will start up a severe inflationary cycle.

Under the Republic, we will have the paradox of a reversal of roles in a labour situation. In England, high and persistent unemployment is inevitable under monopoly capitalism in the Age of Scarcity. In Wales, we will have to endure over-full employment.

In the community benefit state, direct wages will come to represent only a part of family income. We believe that the profits from workers' shareholding will become as important, or perhaps more important, than the wage. The wage buys the necessities. Workers' profits provide discretionary spending power. While the State Scale would have a restrictive influence on earnings, workers' shareholding will provide a non-inflationary method of increasing wages, because these profits will be linked to dramatic rises in productivity.

If inflationary pressures will be a constant threat to price stability, hence the monopoly capitalist economy will be forced, willy-nilly, to intervene repeatedly in the labour market. Has the Trade Union movement fully digested the implications of this long-term trend? Surely, workers' share participation, linking take-home pay to profits and ownership, is an inevitable development.

This, in turn, means that the workers themselves will be the first to throw out restrictive practices and over-manning. They themselves will come to prefer to work in a small scale plant, where they can appreciate the problems.

This leaves the trade unions looking very hard at their own role in society. They can slide into the corporate state solution, and ally with the monopoly capitalist state, thus becoming (like the medieval guild) a reactionary element in society, in an unacknowledged but comfortable alliance with the corporations, or they can respond to new circumstances in a constructive manner to support the worker share participation, and support development of the community benefit society by a willing acceptance of conscription and the State Wages Scale: vital measures in the early days of our Republic, to dampen inflationary tendencies and protect the wage levels of skilled workers.

The Age of Scarcity, then, will stand accepted alliances and enmities on their heads, sometimes reversing the traditional roles of worker, union and management. The very existence of the Republic may be conditional upon appreciation and acceptance of the new realities.

Government

It is possible to look over any bookseller's shelves, and be over-whelmed with the number of books on government.

This is symptomatic of a condition. There is a lot too much of it. Unfortunately, the problems of allocation of resources in the Age of Scarcity make it certain that there is going to be much more.

We have theses and comparisons of every different type of government structure, in nauseating detail. Schools of political science fill their students' heads with this stuff, and send them out to staff the civil services of the world. They believe them-selves to be "qualified to govern". The one question which these august academic bodies seem slow to ask is "Why?" This is not so naïve as might first appear.

If a community has developed layer upon layer of govern-ment, it ought to be clear that there is something radically wrong with that society. Too much government is a symptom of a sick society. A healthy community does not need much by way of government. It governs itself. It does not do so through officials sitting at desks. It does not do so by delegates voting measures in assembly. A "normal" community does so by what goes on in the minds of its people. The majority would not entertain doing this or that, and their reaction would be auto-matic. This is a matter of imprinted civic virtue.

Surely a minority will always try to break the rules, but they will soon be sat upon, because the second characteristic of a healthy community is that the rules of behaviour are well understood. There are no soul-searching questions about the "morality" of forcing people to obey.

The community is so sure of its own values that the civic virtues of the majority are outraged by delinquency. The transgressors are soon brought back into line. The minimun of machinery is necessary —certainly not all the razmatazz of government in the welfare state.

The healthy community, then, is self-regulating. Our own society in Wales, unfortunately, is not in this happy condition. On the contrary, it is moving away from it. Our communities are breaking down, sometimes deliberately destroyed. It is becoming a dependent society —dependent, that is, upon a bureaucracy to be doing for it what it should be doing for itself. The result is more and more regulation by more and more civil servants, (all, you may be sure, with inflation-proof and index-linked pensions).

Are the results satisfactory? On the contrary, the emotional sterility of a regulated society is the principal factor in the alienation of the community. Delinquency is the result. This is not confined to a few louts vandalising telephone kiosks. The fact that tax evasion is now a multi-million pound industry patronised by perfectly respectable people is a more telling manifestation. These people are not scoundrels. They are fighting desperately to keep hold of what they have worked hard to gain. "Society" has become their enemy, because ordinary people are robbed and regimented in its name.

The pioneers of Plaid Cymru were well aware of the ill effects of too much government 40 years ago. They were able to predict with perfect accuracy its effects both upon the state and upon the mind of the individual.

Insistence upon the break-up of the mass democratic state into a "community of communities" is the direct result of this psychological perception. When they first put out their views, they were mocked. The ridicule is muted today. Socialists are not so sure of themselves. Overriding emotional dissatisfaction with the quality of life under welfare capitalism has become widespread over the last twenty years.

The paradox of the nationalist philosophy of government, of course, is this. By breaking government down into small human units, you thereby increase the need for a strong central government. Small units need to be defended. There needs to be an umbrella under which the experiment in genuine social democracy can be tried out. This experiment could not be started at a less auspicious time. The chill winds of the Age of Scarcity are going to force the best-intentioned government to the centralised allocation of resources and a very careful selection of priorities. This is the key role of the community benefit state. It is a moral role. It is not the role of satisfying consumption appetites.

Therefore, the community benefit state cannot accommodate monopoly capitalism, for capitalism, like Satan, roves abroad seeking whom it may devour.

To a very large extent, the destruction of the homogenous society may be directly attributed to the workings of capitalism. (And by capitalism, we do *not* mean the activities of the sole trader, the professional man or the small factory owner — we mean the large conglomerates of cartelised capital whose *raison d'etre* is the complete control of the market and the elimination of risks).

Monopoly capital is the arch-enemy of the community, because every necessity of its existence can, and will, be exploited for gain. The labour of its hands, the land under its feet, the trees and the sands and the common land where it plays. Only money values count.

Everything is negotiable for a "fast buck". The division of swollen government and industrial bodies into self-governing units would open the sluice gates and Wales would soon be swarming with sharks, hungry for quick pickings. It is possible, in theory, to outlaw capitalism in any form. But this edict goes against human nature, and could only be maintained, as in the communist countries, by continual repression.

Nationalism in Wales has turned its face firmly against this course, so we are left with the Welsh state as the supreme patron and protector of the communities within our frontiers. This state will not wink at the rape of the community; neither will it stand sentinel over every commercial transaction, lest by chance the citizen makes a profit. Instead, it will establish itself as the strong trellis-work upon which the new community institutions may anchor themselves.

Government, for the nationalist then, takes on a different meaning. It is no longer the means of transmitting the will of the oligarchy downwards. It becomes the means of regulating and co-ordinating activity across many communities, each of which will certainly be mobilising and conscripting itself to pull itself up by its bootstraps.

This calls for a very strong commitment to government by all. Each citizen will want to know what the choices facing the nation are, and the cost and benefit involved in each. He will want to be consulted locally and nationally about the means and ends of government in Wales. In this case he assents both to the hopes and the burdens. He is knit closely into his society. This is a very different understanding of government from that accepted by the English régime. It is also quite different from the notions of British socialism. Once the citizen has cast his vote, all the rest should be left to a benevolent bureaucracy. From its earliest days, nationalism has parted company with this view. We do not rest content with a given opinion. Nationalism now turns around to the individual and asks him to do it —not only at a desk or at a lathe, but also with his bare hands, in common with his next-door neighbour. "They" have become "us". We have redefined democracy. Nationalism has shared the power of the state with the individual. It has given him an effective partnership in civil and economic affairs, but it expects the citizen to live with that responsibility. He is answerable for it in his own standard and quality of life. This is something no English government has ever dared to do, nor would it ever contemplate doing so.

It is upon these principles that we shall govern the Republic.

Government by Committee

This is a style in vogue in Wales. It has several variations.

* It can mean that members are appointed in recognition of services rendered to the régime. It is a reward. It is intended to boost the ego of its members. One thing is understood — whoever takes the decisions, the committee does not. Its members sit in an advisory capacity.
* It can be a means of spreading the guilt for a course of action known to be against the interests of the community. This type of committee is packed with "wise men".
* It can even be a means of producing a committee solution to a problem, technical or political. Such solutions are recognisable at sight.

Government by committee is felt to be "safe" in Wales. It has all the respectability of being democratic. It is a damnable heresy. The methods of making appointments do not stand up to close investigation. They are in the hands of a régime which, as a rule, is only prepared to appoint pliant toadies. Every one of the seventy-odd committees in Welsh government has questionable claims to democratic legitimacy.

In the days of our national freedom, there can be little room for committee government, as it has been practised in this country. It is safe to assume that there will be a movement towards a new style of government: decision-making by the responsible man, accompanied by powers of popular audit. In fact, there will be a very real need for committee government in Wales, but of quite a different sort. Effective use of this system is determined by questions:

Is the committe composed of people empowered to negotiate and empowered to decide?

Is the work of the committee subject to detailed and regular audit by an elected body?

This implies that each member is a power in his/her own right, with a definite expertise to contribute and with results of a definite programme to report, and that programme is legitimate.

The English régime does not encourage this style in Wales. Under nationalist rule, there will be the need for close co-ordination. There will be the need for intense committee work at the top of policy-making, so that the top men will have an excellent grasp of the implications of technical detail.

The only other type of committee that can serve us is the tribunal of enquiry to hold government officers responsible for their decisions and to search out how those decisions came to be made in the first place.

Both types of committee are unknown in Welsh government. The word has been so debased that it is, at best, a synonym for gerrymandering. At worst, nationalists suspect every committee as an instrument set up to subvert the interests of the Welsh nation, and packed with men liberally paid to do so.

Gwerin

A uniquely Welsh body of ordinary men and women working with their hands for a living, yet who managed to educate themselves in a wide range of matters. They were truly educated, in that their learning was the key to fuller living. In a sense, if we may borrow English class-bound terminology, the Gwerin was an "educated working-class phenomenon".

To say this distorts the reality, because the Welsh consciousness did not recognise English class conventions. The gwerin, then, was how Welsh society in the last century saw itself. What of the present condition of the Welsh working class? There are two quite distinct points of view, each of which leads to a totally different style of propaganda. No 1, the Romantic View, and No 2, the Organic Society View.

No 1. The romantic view

According to this view, the Gwerin was the body of opinion that taxed itself to support the foundation of the Welsh University College at Aberystwyth in 1863. Its consciousness was intensely Welsh. William Morgan's Bible was the foundation of its thought and expression. It gave rise to the cultural explosion in the mid-years of the last century. This cultural sensitivity was bound to be translated into a new type of political consciousness, for 40 years Liberal and vaguely pacifist, then, at the turn of the century, increasingly socialist and internationalist.

Gwynfor Evans is able to record that it was still possible in the early twenties for a coal miner to teach the rules of *cynghanedd* to his workmates with a piece of chalk on the back of a spade. In fact, the gwerin was in fast decline after 1919. This was due to several factors.

* The language of the working class had become predominantly English by 1930.
* The recurrent economic slumps and savage industrial warfare in the coalfield drove out many thousands. The intellectually adventurous were the first to go.
* The temper of the times became Marxist and socialist. Men looked for salvation through the international class struggle, rather than through Christianity. Workmen began to belittle their fathers' values: they appeared to have no relevance to modern conditions. The ministers had no economic doctrine to compete with Marxism.
* The influence of the radio, the cartelisation of the English press (and the difficulties faced by Welsh language newspapers) were slowly eroding the strength of a distinctively Welsh working class.
* The new educational opportunities in the Grammar Schools finally destroyed the old gwerin. It was no longer necessary to study in a Welsh home environment to acquire learning. It could be had for nothing in an English environment.

The gwerin is by now no more than an historical curiosity, but it is a curiosity which exercises great influence upon the way nationalist propaganda is presented. Let us ask ourselves the question: *"In our propaganda activity, do we approach the ordinary people of Wales as we would approach the self-educated, self-respecting workman, or do we speak to our people treating them realistically as the human refuse of exploitation and manipulation?"*

This is a question which one would choose to avoid. If we say that we speak to our people as if they were still a people seasoned with splendid self-taught men, then we expose ourselves as romantic fools. We are unrealistic to enter into a life and death struggle for the minds of this people with a set of false assumptions. Our opponents have no qualms. They appeal to the lowest common denominator.

If, on the other hand, we say that ordinary people have been so meanly treated in Wales that most intelligent working class children have both left Wales and the working class, leaving only a proletarian rump, then we should employ the same sort of manipulative tactics as our political opponents. But does this not imply that we, who set ourselves up as champions of ordinary people in Wales, have the same low opinion of them as do our clever manipulators in Whitehall?

This is the sort of private agonising engendered by the Gwerin myth. It is a fatal barrier to effective propaganda.

It is no betrayal of working class people to recognise the condition to which they have been brought by sorry history of conquest, neglect and manipulation. You cannot take a diseased body and, observing one condition, treat it as another simply because one cannot bring oneself to overcome the revulsion occasioned by the truth.

In the Anti-Romantic view of the Welsh people, the style, tone and methods which can profitably be adopted in propaganda to liberate this people are those which fit their true condition, a conclusion which profoundly agitates many nationalists.

No 2. The organic view of the gwerin

According to this view, the previous interpretation is in error, since *y werin* are not just a body of people who suddenly appeared in the last century, finished and then disappeared. They were the indigenous Welsh population left leaderless by the old *uchelwyr*, who were constantly attracted to English society. Part of this population were themselves descended from the old noble families and thrown off their lands during the English conquest, and after the rebellions that followed.

According to this view, the men who amused themselves writing *englynion* on the backs of their spades were the direct in-line-of-descent heirs to 1,500 years of literary tradition. Accordingly, while they have been proletarianised, anglicised and pulverised by the economic blizzards of Welsh life, were they really a proletariat in the English sense? Should national-ist propaganda tune in to the deepest social instincts of the Welsh community? Will it be counter-productive to treat the Welsh worker as the ungovernable, irresponsible and debased rabble to which monopoly capital has reduced much of the English working class?

Nationalists had better get their answers right. While one method of propaganda might serve West Wales, would it necessarily serve South Wales?

Ideology

This is a fancy word for something simple. It is a standard of values, a yardstick by which ordinary people may judge events or proposals and class them as negative or positive to their interest. But it is also something more than that. It is a set of ideas about our community, about the way we think of ourselves as a living society, and where we ought to be going. Ideology explains our past, analyses our present, and sets goals for the future. It is fundamental in the formation of men's attitudes. It gives us a set of value judgements. These are a great comfort to common men.

The very word ideology has received a bad press in the United Kingdom. Whenever it is used it is accompanied by snide comments which suggest that ideology is a pursuit of cruel, ruthless, and narrow men, who probably wear thick pebble glasses, and have never been known to take a drink; men who are stubbornly doctrinaire, devoid of humour or humanity. It is implied that such men are dangerous. They are "too clever by half", and divorced from the real world. Ideology is clearly "un-British".

There are cogent reasons to cultivate this impression. Ideology *is* dangerous. It is dangerous to those who would seek to exploit people, and seek to divide and confuse public opinion, since this is the best way to continue their manipulation of them. While they are distracted and bemused, someone has already got the loot and have got clean away. It is not an accident that ideology is consistently played down. It is subversive to monopoly capital.

People who hold carefully reasoned views about society are immune to the elaborate conditioning process to which the general public is subjected. They are a nuisance, better to paint them as cranks on the fringe of "normal" society, lest they spread their mischief.

In Wales, the ideology of nationalism is in fact, extremely dangerous to the Establishment. It takes the folk ideas which have been passed down from generation to generation. These are ideas about natural justice, the standards of value of the community, tales of the degradation heaped upon it, the humour of the people caught up in the struggles and pleasures of Welsh society. On the basis of this inheritance, locked into the subconscious, it is building a vision of the alternative Welsh society. There is no place for the Establishment in that society, and not much by way of profit.

Two pioneers of nationalism, Saunders Lewis and D J Davies in particular, seized upon the aspirations of the community and developed them. These are very simple ideas:

* Wales wants to be left alone to work out its own future according to our ideas of what is good, and these are very different from what is good for the English governing classes. Internationally Wales is pacifist and neutralist. We don't want to be involved in other men's quarrels. We have no grand ambitions and no great "civilizing mission".

* We want to work to our own goals and resent having other peoples' goals imposed on us. They do not profit us. Therefore we want a say in running our own factories, mines and workshops. The consensus in Wales is that life is to be enjoyed. It is more than a vehicle for the profit of others. If we must work for others then, at least, let us be very sure that we have a fair share of the rewards.

* We want to see clearly who is running our local community. We want to make sure it is run according to our aspirations. To do this we must run it ourselves *directly*. We have learnt *never* to trust others to do for us what we should be doing ourselves.

* More significant than any of these notions, these men let out a cry of conscience. No nation has the right to degrade and profit themselves from the weakness of another. For this cry,

they were punished. Such thoughts cannot be allowed to go abroad.

These *are* dangerous ideas. They imply the end of English rule in Wales, the loss of face that this would imply and the end of exploitation.

There are many influential interests who believe they stood to lose. Is it any wonder that the ideology of Welsh nationalism is unacceptable?

Let us have crystal clarity on this matter. The struggle of Plaid Cymru is an ideological struggle. This is no ordinary political circus. With every hand turned against the common people, with every avenue of mass communication barricaded lest they be "infected" with ideas that will illuminate their miserable future under English government, nationalism has only one weapon at its disposal, its ideology.

The Welsh are a people forced into a corner. Ideology is a sharp cutting edge to hack our way out, before the Age of Scarcity engulfs us. We need not fear that any other "party" can "up-wind" us. They may have powers to divide and distract, but they can only offer shoddy substitute satisfaction. Nationalism is offering the real thing.

Individualism

Thoughtful people may view the collectivist approach to the
problems of the Age of Scarcity with distaste. Is this a return
to feudalism? Will it fit the realities of the Welsh character as
we know it? What of those who do not want to be too closely
involved with the affairs of the Ward? What about those who
would prefer to opt out?

These questions beg another. "Do we really have a choice?"
As in so many other matters in a United Kingdom, the choice is
more apparent than real. There are, in fact, more insidious
pressures at work to sap individualism. The dangers of the
community approach are, at least, clear. In the corporate state,
they are not. High personal taxation, welfarism, bureaucrat-
isation and incessant propaganda harassment are more destruct-
ive of self-esteem than having, occasionally, to do one's stint
for the community.

The advantage of the community benefit society is that the
citizen can see a beginning and an end to his obligation to his
group. Within that obligation, relationships tend to be at a
personal level, at the factory or in the ward. Conscript labour is
for a definite number of days.

Relationships to the state are less a matter of memos and
files. For the nationalist, cash is strictly a secondary consideration. We require the citizen's involvement, his labour and his
interest. The state, which is already taking shape in our minds,
does not need to consume the citizen. We know that while he
is working for the community, the community is subtly
changing him. We do not seek to hedge him about with restrict-

ions to wring the last penny out of him. We can coax more out of him by cultivating him than by taxing him. The corporate state has no time for the individual. He is a consumer, a tax-payer, a wage earner. It is suspicious of community institutions. It fears that community consciousness bred of them would ultimately be levelled against itself.

The British state, then, transacts all its business on a cash basis through a bureaucracy. Will the Age of Scarcity humanize that bureaucracy? As the screws tighten the individual becomes first a matter of impatience, a nuisance, and finally expendable.

Let us ask the question once again: Will the individual be more satisfied by Welsh collectivism or so-called British individualism?

Intelligence

Intelligence is the work of clandestine information-gathering concerning the activities and ambitions of enemies (or potential enemies) of the state. Originally an activity associated primarily with warfare, it now embraces very much more, namely, information-gathering on commercial matters associated with stockpiling, trade union and irredentist activities.

The intelligence community has become in many régimes, (including, one suspects, the UK) almost a crypto-government. It has acquired great influence in the preparation of policy briefings and news digests for politicians. This influence has often been unwelcomed by the more conventional departments of government, who might find themselves "short-circuited" by a department, able to withold, edit, or "doctor" information. This over-mighty influence has been exposed in America by the Watergate publicity, but it is unlikely that the intelligence establishment in other régimes act differently.

Public opinion has generally been tolerant of these activities, because enemies (or potential enemies) were real. The intelligence function was legitimate.

It is likely that the tensions brought about by the Age of Scarcity will accelerate the trend of governments to spy upon their own people. Frequently this will be to gather information on public attitudes to government activity, but there is a growing unease that this may not always be the case. As mass democratic government comes to feel itself isolated and beseiged by an alienated society, the urge to misinform, divide, frustrate (or at least, slow down) activities that it does not like must become irresistible. Everyone, for example, will want to "dish the nationalists".

When they came to power, the members of the first Labour government in the twenties were astonished at the degree of surveillance over Trade Union and working class activities generally. This wealth of background information was clearly decisive in Davidson's handling of the General Strike. This Scottish Civil Servant probably did more to disorganise the anti-government forces and mobilize middle class opinion against the strikers than either Baldwin or Churchill. These clandestine activities are hardly likely to have subsided in intervening years.

There are several factors which prompt a revaluation of the intelligence function in relation to Welsh nationalism.

* It is a characteristic of contracting empires that the organis-ations and instruments used to coerce subject races are re-patriated. Once at home, they use exactly the same thinking, apparatus and methods of operation. Wales is the oldest colony. Its retention is a matter of prestige. Nationalist activities of any nature are a target for infiltration, disorganisation and de-stabilisation.
* Invariably the Intelligence Establishment is firmly right-wing in its political loyalties and affiliations, and devoted to the maintenance of the unitary state within its existing frontiers.

The targets for covert activity are usually:
   * Translation activities.
   * Clerical and accounting functions within a political HQ —
     particularly the mail room.
   * Membership activities and rôle preparation. Lists of sub-
     scribers and donors.
   * Interface or liason functions between branches and the
     centre.
   * Secretarial functions of policy-making committees (or
     typing associated with their work).
   * Matters associated with ideological debate.
   * Telephones and mail.

Generally, the golden rule of this work is to intercept, delay or confuse by controlling the interfaces. "Tip-offs" to the press to blow up certain activities and play down others are a derivative of this function.

Unless one has a great deal of money to buy-in counter-espionage expertise, and rigorous discipline to enforce the procedures specified by these professionals, this type of surveillance is a fact of political life.

Intelligensia

This was originally a Russian word for a Russian phenomenon, a body of educated opinion independent of the court bureaucracy and the merchants, in the early years of the last century. From its inception, the intelligensia had political overtones. From the first, it was vaguely Liberal and against the establishment. This type of intellectual opposition moved westwards to the Dual Monarchy, and by the close of the last century was firmly associated with the national movement in the submerged nations. The café society of the larger towns in Central Europe provided its clubs, and the free press contributed to the growth of its numbers and the spread of its predominantly middle class ideas.

In fact, it was a distinctively European phenomenon, and Central European at that. English society could never show a parallel, because the English middle classes attained political maturity with the Civil War, and their inference was consolidated by the "Glorious Revolution" of 1688.

On the face of it, Welsh society provided the classic conditions for the growth of a native intelligensia. It was a society with limited access to the charmed circle of court and government, it arose from a distinct racial background (more distinct than now) and it spoke a different language. The opening of the Welsh university in Aberystwyth in 1863 should have provided the stimulus for the creation of a truly national bourgeoisie, led by a distinctly Welsh intelligensia. It didn't happen. Apart from a very few individuals (generally nonconformist ministers), by the time Saunders Lewis and his friends founded Plaid Cymru in 1925, the Welsh middle class were thoroughly British in outlook. Effectively, there was no Welsh intelligensia. Why was this?

Partly, this was a result of the "Treason of the Blue Books". Six hundred years in subject status seems to have knocked the stuffing out of the Welsh middle class. So mesmerised had they become with the patent advantages of the English connection that they could cheerfully concur in the opinion of the commissioners that all things Welsh were "a barrier to progress". In fact, what was happening in Wales was directly contrary to what was happening in the Hapsburg Empire. The cause of this capitulation is clearly accounted for by the "psychological rape of the country" (to use Gwynfor Evans' phrase). The Welsh were at the nadir of their self-confidence.

To this, one must add the undoubted prosperity of the middle class in the last half of the century. Clearly, it *paid* to be British, just as now it clearly does *not* pay to be British.

This is an appealing but incomplete explanation for the failure to develop a national intelligensia. It would be wrong to overlook the effect of calculated subversion, particularly in the matter of university appointments. There appears to have been a policy initiated from the founding of the college that anything resembling articulate political nationalism was a barrier to promotion. This was powerfully reinforced when the prosperity of industrial Wales vanished after the First World War. It was necessary to bend the knee; provided one had the safe ground of culturalism, one could prosper and take one's place at the high table; but let there be a hint of suspicion that one's views went further, and doors were quietly shut. One's work was "not quite convincing". The fate of Saunders Lewis left the whole academic establishment in no doubt as to the consequences of political nationalist activity. After 1945, the deliberate dilution of student intakes successfully headed off the formation of any solid body of Welsh student opinion —the indispensable foundation in the development of a national intelligensia. At every point, the English government has done its thinking and planning well in advance. One must admit to a certain admiration of their thoroughness.

It is only now that we are witnessing the development of a

truly Welsh *national* intelligensia, in the classic continental sense of the word. Unfortunately, it is growing upon a soil now much depleted in nourishment. It is essentially centred around the self-help institutions which have developed since the 1960s. These are the Welsh Language Society and the Welsh Schools movement. These have arisen in the teeth of the obstacles strewn in their way. The "national intelligensia", therefore, is weak in numbers, positions, and influence. Poor employment prospects hold this country more effectively in bondage than bayonets. Impoverishment of Wales must remain, then, a deliberate and permanent Whitehall policy. This is the rationale behind the destruction of the Welsh economy.

The clever policy of Whitehall has, then, been a notable success. It has certainly delayed the formation of an intelligent body of Welsh opinion for many decades. Welsh education has been subverted. It was not to become the vehicle for the development of a national middle-class opinion. Yet the signs are that is has been a policy which backfired.

The success of Whitehall in frustrating the development of a strong middle-class oriented intelligensia has undoubtedly held back the development of political nationalism. It has done great harm to Plaid Cymru, but it has also forced nationalism to become the concern of the common people. The intelligensia has, in fact, a very limited influence on policy-making. Nationalism in Wales has skipped a whole era in the development of continental nationalism. It is not a middle class movement, and its policies are definitely worker-oriented. The fact that many of its leading personalities would appear to prefer a more moderate policy has been significant. They could *not* force these policies on the Plaid. The rank and file would not buy them. Clever Whitehall policy-makers have yet to digest the implications of this fact. They are now delighting in their own abilities. It is so deliciously easy to manipulate nationalism, but it is manipulation at a price.

The intellectual level of debate within nationalist circles may occasionally be at a very low level, but there is another side to the coin. Nationalism is not riven with the devastating arguments that wrought havoc with continental nationalist movements before 1914. Indeed, it is a surprisingly homogeneous movement because, very early on, it *had* to develop a working class consensus. In its early days, this was a definite disadvantage, but now it is becoming increasingly important. Whereas continental nationalism has always been a "top down" movement, Welsh nationalism has been a "bottom up" movement. The writing is on the wall. Whitehall has succeeded very well in delaying nationalism, but it has not been able to stop it. Meanwhile, it has ensured that the eventual triumph of Welsh nationalism must be radical to an extent far greater than any middle-class nationalism would have permitted. It would be well for the "clever" gentlemen to ponder the implications of their handiwork. Chickens are coming home to roost.

When all this is accounted for, one cannot ignore the weakness in the national movement due to the dis-association of intellectual opinion from the grass roots movement. The ill-effects will become more noticeable with every step taken nearer to the Republic. Working-class nationalism and the Welsh middle class need each other. One central circumstance rivets them together —they are both excluded from ownership, in a country which is being deliberately destroyed. All are dispossessed equally of a means of livelihood. This is the breeding-ground not just for an alliance but for a revolution.

Interrogation

The Amman Valley was honeycombed with sedition. Christianity itself
was challenged: the anthracite area was now confronted not even with
true communism, but with a bastard form of it, which stood for the
disruption of the British Empire and the end of constitutional government."

**Chief Constable's report to
Standing Joint Committee, 1921**

Can wicked rulers be allied with you,
Who frame mischief by statute?
    Psalm 94^{20}

Legal structures can be violent. The legal structure binding
Wales to the English state is by its nature violent. It was based
upon brutal conquest, maintained by confiscation and
sequestration, and the deliberate impoverishment of the Welsh
people. The means change. The ends do not change.
Withholding balanced economic development in Wales is the
contemporary version of policies put in train by the Angevins
and Tudors.

From a Christian point of view, there are two types of sin:
personal sin and structural sin. Religion is tolerated by the state
only so long as it confines itself to personal sin. When Christian
teaching is turned against the state, the Church is told to keep
out of politics. Structural sin is any evil, or inequality
deliberately enshrined with the protection of state violence
under the gloss of legality. Poverty, degradation of human
beings through unemployment, the indignity of wage capitalism
—these are all structural sins given the full blessing of the law of

the English. Revolution against this established order is, then, a criterion of a living Christian faith, in addition to being the patriotic duty of a Welshman.

Sharpening of distress, as the Welsh community is deliberately destroyed by the English established order, must sooner or later call forth a violent reaction. "Where has this come from?" the commentators will ask. Where indeed? On the one hand, it is a response to Welsh history and the appalling misrule of the Welsh people, but on the other, it is the rebirth of a system of new values and the re-emergence of old ones. Essentially, it is a matter of belief.

We can already envisage conditions, then, when the nationalist cadre is subject to spasmodic violence at the hands of the organs of English state power. He will be held up as the cause of that violence.

Interrogation is the means of harassing the patriot, breaking him, and "turning him", that is, recruiting him as an informer. All police and intelligence procedures revolve around the interrogation procedure. Very many hours of instruction are devoted at staff college and intelligence schools to techniques of breaking down the will to resist in the victim. Evidence has emerged of what appear to be very substantial sums of money paid to research institutes to devise effective methods. We are indebted to the American Freedom of Information Acts for throwing most interesting sidelights upon English practice in this area.

Let us examine some of the techniques of the interrogator.

Behaviour of the interrogator

1. The interrogation is stage-managed to a degree not imaginable by the ordinary man. The interrogator is cast in the role of the *messenger of the inevitable*. The object is to convince the target that he is an all-time loser —a natural bungler, he must be made to feel personally inadequate. This softens him up for the main business at hand.

2. The manner of the interrogator is leaden to the point of indifference; he acts the low-key official time server. His best weapon is silence. Pen and form at the ready, the target feels almost obliged to say something. He is acutely embarrassed,

frightened, and unsure of himself. He has to blurt out something, if it only abuse or lies.

3. The victim's behaviour and beliefs are portrayed in monosyllabic hints to be an orchestrated series of disasters. His whole life is a disaster. This is to be his turning point.

4. The clever interrogator will never allow the target a choice: he has only one possible course of action —to collaborate. Choice will promote obstinacy, and the Welsh penchant for self-destruction.

5. In every successful interrogation, there is one slip which cannot be recovered:

* a gesture, tacit or direct, of self-concern, reveals weakness, lack of inner strength, uncertainty. A man lacking in inner self-esteem, lacking in faith and personal integrity.
* the acceptance of a "kindness", a cigarette, a cup of tea.
* acknowledgement of the "reasonableness" of the interrogator.

The eyes of the interrogator are alert for these signs. They mark the crumbling of the will to resist, and they signal the willingness to collaborate.

6. Contrary to popular belief, the experienced interrogator will *never*

* menace
* raise his voice
* resort to histrionics.

The will of the state directed at the hapless victim

The Welsh nationalist cadre is young, inexperienced and frightened. When his Christian and nationalist beliefs are exposed to the yellow light of the interrogation cell, he is inclined to abuse, or bluster. All of a sudden, he feels himself to be very small beer.

The rules for the victim are not easy to follow, and require great committment to the worth of his cause. The greater the committment, the easier the resistance.

Behaviour of the victim

1. He must never be provoked.
2. He must not match rudeness with rudeness.

3. He must never try to score a point.
4. He must never be witty, superior or intellectual.
5. He must never be deflected by fury, despair or the surge of sudden hope than an occasional question might arouse.

The victim of Establishment violence has the right to silence. It is his best defence. He must:

1. Match dullness with dullness, routine with routine.
2. Deep down, he must cherish faith, Christian and in the destiny of his revolution and his people.
3. He must have a savage contempt of the English system and all its Welsh lackeys.

The value of the ideology when the chips are down
Welsh patriots can only hope to come out of this experience strengthened provided they know exactly what they *do* believe. This is the value of ideology, but the ideology of the revolution must be underpinned by the morality of Christian faith. Otherwise, the victim will break.

Substitute belief systems: the soft option
The clever manipulation of belief systems closely resembling Welsh nationalism (which, nevertheless manage to preserve the hold of the English state over Wales) is the core of the interrogation procedure. This is of such importance to the understanding of the clash of political ideas in Wales that it is the subject of an essay on its own account (see *Liberalism*).

L and

I hold and maintain that the entire soil of a country belongs of right to the entire people of that country, and is the rightful property, not of any one class, but to the nation at large, in full effective possession, to let to whom they will on whatever tenures they will; one condition, however, being unavoidable and essential . . . full, true and undivided allegiance to the nation, and the laws of the nation whose land he holds.

Fintan Lalor, Irish patriot and philosopher

It is indeed difficult for those Englishmen who have destroyed their own country as a place fit to raise a healthy family to understand what the land of Wales means to us. For them, land is an object of profit. It exists to be exploited. All else is sentiment. The Englishman believes that provided he makes enough money by mining his own environment, it is always possible to buy his way into somebody else's. Not only is it possible, *it is his right*. This attitude has powerfully fuelled Welsh nationalism. Love of the land of Wales is an unchanging part of the Welsh character. It is significant that the language is far richer in vocabulary describing landscape than English. Poetry shows that the Welshman was articulate about his country, "gwlad", long before Tennyson and the Romantics made landscape poetry a feature of English literature. It is not surprising that the Englishman cannot really understand the bond between land and people which gives almost a mystical quality to Welsh nationalism. It is a dimension of the conscience quite beyond him. For him, land is to be possessed. For the Welshman, land is something to be celebrated. Can the Englishman guess that his insensitivity is stirring deep passions in Wales? The last to admit this would be the estate agents, the lawyers, the "developers", but for every farm, every cottage, every tract of moorland that is alienated, be sure that more than one Welshman grinds his teeth in anger. The English are sowing the wind, but they do not care. "Economic forces" render the Welsh powerless. Let them wring their hands in frustration! The vast eternal plan, the "market", will one day make of the Welsh an historical curiosity. In the meantime, at every sale, the Welsh Tory lawyer rubs his hands with glee over his fat fee and the thought that he has driven one more nail into that loathsome idea —the Welsh homeland.

No doubt the violence of the reaction of common people will one day come as a genuine surprise to this breed of men. They will protest, in innocence, that "Wales has fallen into the hands of extremists" who wish to abolish "freedom" and "free enterprise". (Funny, isn't it, how freedom comes to be equated with mindless exploitation?) "Their schemes are sinister, and should be stopped. Solid, responsible men should put a spoke in their wheel!"

While Welsh nationalism is surprisingly liberal in every other direction, on this one issue, we have to ask, is there room for compromise? It is nonsense to believe that we can push through a rapid reconstruction of this country without the repossession of the homeland, but in the last analysis, economics have got nothing to do with it. It is a matter of love, hate and fear, and these unruly passions will surely guide our actions where economics would not. The land of Wales and the seas around it are the absolute possession of this people. They are the support of the born and the unborn. They are *inalienable*. Can we afford to compromise in this matter?

Let nationalists resolve to *nationalise* all the lands and seas in and around Wales, but having done so, let us ask a number of questions concerning the use of the lands of this people. Once repossessed, how are the interests of both the land and the community best served?

1. Is the concept of freehold likely to be in the interest of a community benefit society? Under modern planning conditions, has not freehold become, in effect, a conditional lease?

2. If the Republic were to be the only true freeholder, is it any harm to the community that the ordinary householder continues to use his property and to dispose of it as he sees fit? Does this hold true for the farmer or the industrialist?

3. Can it be lawful for any Welsh citizen to own land in this community? Others may lease it under stringent conditions, but can they ever own it?

4. How much land must be devoted to crop, pasture, forestation and water catchment by the year 2000 to
   (a) support a population of 3 million to be self-sufficient in grain, cattle, sheep, dairy produce and root vegetables?
   (b) conduct an export trade in meat, forest products and water? At what level should these exports be?

5. With rising foodstuff prices to be anticipated in the Age of Scarcity, would it be profitable to bring marginal land into cultivation? What effect would this have on the character of the Welsh countryside?

6. What measures need to be taken now to bring current agric-ultural land into top condition, in anticipation of the demands to be made upon it during the Age of Scarcity? How long would it take? Do we know where neglected tracts of land are, and the reason for their degeneration? What form of registrat-ion and grading do we have?

7. If these measures were to include:
   * deep ploughing
   * drainage
   * re-seeding
   * re-planting of hedges, windbreaks and wild life refuges
   * provision of organic fertiliser
should these measures (which benefit the whole community) be expected to be financed by private farmers? Could they, in fact, do so? Can the community continue to regard agriculture and the condition of the soil as nothing to do with them?

8. As much of the work associated with rehabilitating land, hedges and ditches is, in fact, labour-intensive, where is that labour to come from? Is it proposed that this be supplied at normal agricultural wage rates? Or is it proposed to use

conscript labour to enrich the capital of Welsh soil?

9. Does the community have the food storage facilities to store extra produce during glut conditions and release it during conditions of shortage, so stabilising prices of acquisition and disposal? Who is going to pay for these storage facilities? Where are they to be situated and how are they to be serviced?

10. What requirements does an agricultural plan put upon a transport plan? To what extent is agricultural traffic capable of concentration? Where are the points of concentration?

11. If the price of oil-based artificial fertiliser of natural phosphates is likely to rise steadily over the next twenty-five years, what plans do we have for the creation of urban composting plants? How would these facilities fit in with existing sewerage and garbage disposal patterns? Do we have anything approaching a national *integrated* waste disposal plan?

12. Since the economic viability of these plants turns upon an efficient compost bulk delivery network, do we have the facilities for frequent fast bulk delivery? Do we have the facilities for bulk handling, intermediate storage, and on-farm delivery? If methane gas is created during composting, what facilities would be required to feed it into a national gas grid?

13. Can these facilities be provided by private enterprise?

14. If the community has at its disposal more land than it requires for its support, what is the best way to dispose of the surplus? If uneconomic farms have to be abandoned, is this any great loss? How shall the land be kept in condition for re-use, if necessary?

15. What is the best way for the community to exploit its agricultural land, by:
    * individual farms
    * partnerships
    * planned area farming
    * joint ventures with urban entrepreneurs
    * community owned farms
Should these holdings be freehold or conditional upon standards of husbandry specified by the community?

16. What is our requirement for land needed to re-house the population of the decaying areas of industrial Wales? Given the average age and standard of dwellings in certain areas, when will this land be needed? Is there a case for the planned abandonment of certain settlements in Wales?

17. How much land will be required to offer decent housing to *all* young people upon marriage, over the next 25 years? Should new settlement be permitted in the coastal conurbations? Should it be directed along the North-South railway?

18. Is it proposed to go on using virgin land on the "blaenau", or to rehabilitate land at the valley bottoms? Who wants to live on the "blaenau" anyway? Should council estates created on the mountain tops be demolished? What does it cost in human as well as material effort to live on the hilltops?

19. Who is going to pay for the rehabilitation of bottom land? Can we expect private enterprise to do so?

20. Can rehabilitation schemes be undertaken by:
    * private enterprise under subsidy.
    * local councils.
    * at Republic level, by a Welsh Land Authority?

21. How much of the cost of demolition, rehabilitation and the provision of new services is accounted for by labour charges? To what extent can use of conscript labour reduce these charges?

22. What land should be specifically set aside for the recreation of the urban population? What are the lines of access? How much access can the flora and fauna afford?

23. Do we need to specify wild-life areas and wild-life trails forbidden to people? To what extent is it desirable to plant wild-life colonies within agricultural areas? Should the rush for agricultural production be at the expense of wild-life? To what extent is the character of land and people dependent on maintaining a "wild Wales"?

24. What are the new national lines of North-South communication going to do to land values alongside them? What would the construction of an electric railway between

Cardiff and Brecon on the main North-South line do to property values in Brecon?

25. Should these gains be communalised to prevent inflation in land values? In the long run, who will gain by unfettered operation of the free market in the disposal of lands rehabilitated at community expense or whose value has been enhanced by infrastructure investment?

26. Should developers be relied upon to determine the concentration of settlement in new and rehabilitated land areas? What is the connection between "development" and language use?

27. Should developers be responsible for determination of plot size and scale services, and methods of heating and insulation, or should the community purchase and prepare the site with all services, and then release plots to the developers?

28. Should estate agents, builders, contractors, architects, the executives of development companies, lawyers or others in their pay, be eligible to sit on public bodies where land use and planing permissions are decided upon? To what extent has local government become the preserve of these interests? Where are the maximum opportunities for corruption in local government?

29. How should the community regulate the supply of land coming on to the market? How should the supply of land be linked to the supply of development funds and building materials in order to keep building costs stable? How do we prevent "over-heating" of the construction industry?

30. Should responsibility for community heating systems be vested in private entrepreneurs (a) by default (b) by design?

31. Is the community well served by continued use of traditional building materials? Would not cast lightweight concrete roofs covered with aluminium or plastic be better insulators? Since we have an abundance of fly ash and excellent aggregate in Wales, why should we import timber?

32. How does the community influence Building Societies to accept new materials, methods of construction and layouts in new work? Is it true that the Building Societies are the

principal influence in eliminating adventurous designs and perpetuating mediocrity?

33. Can foreign credit institutions be permitted to hold the deeds to Welsh land as collateral for loans?

34. How do we phase out foreign land holding in Wales:
  * by outright nationalisation with/without compensation?
  * if "with compensation", what form does this take, and when is it payable?
  * by conversion of foreign-owned freeholds to leaseholds which are transferable or fall to the Welsh state upon the death of the leaseholder?
  * by forced sale to Welsh citizens? Who fixes the price?

35. How does the community finance the possession of foreign holdings? What instruments of credit do we need? How freely may they be traded and discounted? What should be their term? Should the proceeds be freely convertible?

36. If the community is to be well-served by planned use of land during a period of revolutionary economic and social change, is the system of freeholds really viable outside the sphere of private housing?

37. If it is envisaged that most agricultural and industrial activity is based upon leasehold from the state, should not the conditions of the lease be linked specifically to use and re-habilitation after use? Should not the community demand that the exploiter of the land resource should put up a bond as a guarantee of rehabilitation to standards laid down by the community? How many industrial sites do we know in Wales where the exploiter has arranged a convenient bankruptcy after he has wrung the last penny of profit out of the land, but before he has rehabilitated the site?

38. What is the role of the solicitor in conveyancing of land under a community benefit régime of land use? Surely, this question goes to the core of all matters associated with land use, since the vested interest of the lawyers runs to some £280 millions per year for England and Wales? (separate figures for Wales are unobtainable).

39. As a computerised community land register is absolutely

indispensable to any planned use of land, and as that register would take several years to load, are the best interests of the community served by eliminating the private solicitor from conveyancing? Is it not in everybody's best interest to establish a new *modus vivendi* in a community benefit state?

40. Is it really true that the vested interests of solicitors, estate agents, developers and contractors are diametrically opposed to those of the community? In a community benefit Republic, would they not operate within a different framework, but operate nonetheless? What would the planned economic rehabilitation of Wales do to their incomes? Would they decrease?

41. Since, in this line of questioning, we have established connections, implicit or explicit, between land use and the use of the Welsh language (by determination of areas of settlement), food, prices, wild-life and recreational use of our land mass, is it not becoming clear that nationalisation of the land (in the Welsh, not the English, sense of that word) is the acid test whether any political party wishes to set up a middle class state dominated by vested interests, or a true community benefit state? If this is true, why has Plaid Cymru been silent on this matter for 50 years?

42. If the "culturalists" in the national movement have as deep an attatchment to the Welsh language as they claim, can they support *laissez-faire* attitudes towards citizenship and land use? Is it possible to permit unrestricted settlement in the language heart land, the *Bro Gymraeg*?

43. Is it permissible to support big unit agriculture when small farm land so often has been the bastion of the language? Should not agricultural policy support co-operative farms (in our Welsh tradition —not the Russian misuse of that idea)?

44. If foreign firms are induced to settle in the *Bro Gymraeg*, what undertakings must they observe as regards the use of the Welsh language in return for their licence to exploit the factors of production in that place?

45. Is it not true to say that Plaid Cymru has failed to bring together national independence, public ownership of natural

resources and cultural pluralism within one revolutionary goal? Is it at all conceivable that Plaid Cymru can become a credible vehicle for change in Welsh society until it links together all these elements within a consistent revolutionary ideology?

46. It there any room for culturalism without revolution, in the land question as in all others? Is not culturalism without revolution a betrayal —treason to the Welsh people— and the certain invitation to foreigners to possess this land *in aeterna aeternatis*?

It has been said that the dissolution of the monasteries in 1536-7, with the subsequent release of large tracts of land for intensive capitalist exploitation was the signal for the birth of monopoly capitalism in these islands.

If this is true, is it not also true that the nationalisation and communalisation of land must usher in a new era in the attitude of the community to land ownership and use? Can this come too soon in the Age of Scarcity? Let us ask once again, is the land of Wales a matter for exploitation or celebration?

L iberalism

(AND SOCIAL DEMOCRACY)

Liberalism proclaims its creed to be "Christian, moderate and conditional". Although political liberalism would appear to be a spent force in Wales, the newly-formed Social Democratic Party seems bent upon inheriting much of the political philosophy of the old Liberal Party. Disillusion with the English English two-party system will force many to consider it seriously, wishing to break the two-party stalemate which has made any substantial movement in English political life over the last 30 years impossible.

Even if nationalists believe that the revival in interest in a third force within the political system of the English state is no more than a fashionable interlude punctuating a period of dec- - line before the inevitable crisis of the unitary state, it is useful to prepare an analysis of the Liberal-Social Democratic line, so that we understand the role it must play in that crisis. This is the point of the examination.

The attitude of Liberals to Wales happens to be contained in a carefully written pamphlet dated 1977, author Rupert Cavendish, *—Differences and similarities between radical Liberalism and Plaid Cymru*, published by North West Community Newspapers Ltd., Manchester, 25p. This is a useful text for the Welsh nationalist cadre, because it provides a good example of first level and subliminal propaganda.

Let us examine Cavendish's arguments:

The Republic versus culturalism
1. Radical Liberalism and nationalism went hand in hand in Wales in the last century. Cymru Fydd was its political express-

ion. It interpreted its nationalist mission in terms of native Welsh culture and linguistic tradition. It became the vehicle for Home Rule, and became so closely associated with Welsh non-conformity, on account of the Church Tithe and Dis-establishment issues, that every chapel became a Liberal Party Committee Room and every Sunday School a recruiting meeting.

Cymru Fydd collapsed in ignominy in 1891 precisely on the Home Rule issue, between those who believed that Welsh culture could only be safeguarded by separation and those who did not. Lloyd George, with an eye to his career, was in favour of the English connection. Plaid Cymru was born as a belated response 35 years later, out of the conviction that Liberalism could never deliver the goods. It could not protect Welsh interests without a Welsh state:

> Culture without self-government is like a spirit without a body, a bodiless spirit, it cannot take part and express itself in the world of living men.

It is precisely upon this matter of the Republic that liberals of all shades of opinion part company with Plaid Cymru.

2. Community politics

Cavendish makes a case for the similarity of outlook of national-ism and radical Liberalism. He claims that "community politics" is not about the redress of grievances, but about the "return of power".

> Power may be said to reside with the people, but in practice, a few have monopolised that power, and denied individuals the chance to work out their own salvation.

3. Confraternalism versus federalism

In an ill-starred pamphlet in 1960, at the summit of his intellectual dictatorship of Plaid Cymru, Gwynfor Evans wrote in *Self-Government for Wales and a Common Market for the Nations of Britain*, "a common market should exist between a self-governing Wales and England. That is how Plaid Cymru (sic) envisages the future economic relationship between the two countries. Self-government need not, and should not, disturb the economic union which exists today."

Cavendish believes that, "if a confraternal system were established, the possibility of deadlock among politicians from 4 different states producing economic stagnation is greater than in a federal system with a clearly defined constitution."

The Liberal Handbook, *Pathways to Power*, is quoted:

> Our ultimate aim is a democratic federal Europe, with . . . representation in the community institutions for nations like Scotland and Wales, and the regions of England.

4. Industrial democracy

Plaid Cymru's spokesman, Emrys Roberts, is quoted as follows:

(a) Small businesses to remain the property of their owners with effective worker representation on a management board.
(b) Enterprises of over 100 should be owned by their work-people who would elect their own management. Investors should be paid interest upon funds in accordance with a national scale of risk. Public representatives might be called upon to sit on their boards.
(c) Vital industries should be nationalised, and made accountable to their employees, who should be the largest single group on the Boards of Management, together with Senators and the Chairman. Management should be decentralised to local boards with local government participation.
(d) The Senate should control the return of capital to owners of expropriated assets.

After acknowledgement of the difficulty of spelling out the Radical Liberal view, (noting that both the Plaid and the Radical Liberals are "left of the Labour Party") Cavendish puts forward the Liberal position:

(e) While workers should become shareholders, and worker committees should elect directors, workers themselves should decide whether they should set up co-operatives:

> It would be wrong to give this power away. The people themselves must take it.

(f) Workers should share profits and the increase in the value of assets.
(g) The shares of outsiders should be replaced with bonds of equivalent value.

Cavendish points out that the Plaid policy is "less voluntary in character" than that adopted by radical liberalism.

5. The power of myth and rationality

In many respects this is the most important part of the
pamphlet for reasons that we shall later examine. Let us note
the flow of the argument. It begins with a statement by the
Liberal Director of Policy Promotion, Gordon Lishman.

> The basic differences are represented by the tension between rational-
> ity and myth: the tension between individual power on the one hand
> and collective, or national, power on the other; the extent to which
> Radical Liberalism is a broadranging alternative, covering the whole of
> society, rather than relating problems to one basic cause.

and proceeds with an "example of the romanticism of Plaid
Cymru" by quoting a distinguished activist, Mr Raymond
Williams, concerning Welsh private conversation which is

> often an unmitigated flow, to prevent other things being said. And
> what those other things are we hear more often among ourselves; an
> extraordinary sadness, which is indeed not surprising, and, at the edges,
> lately, an impacable bitterness, even a soured cynicism, which can jerk
> into life —(this is what makes it hard to bear)— as a fantastic comic
> edge, or a wild self-depreciation, as a form of pride —a wall of words,
> anyway— so that we do not have to look steadily and soberly at all that
> has happened to us.

Cavendish states that many leading Plaid figures "reject reason-
ing and logic as inadequate in understanding Welsh issues." This
important section of the Liberal argument ends in the
peroration:

> If nationalism succeeds, it will have been by an appeal to all the selfish
> instincts which people have . . . Economic separatism is a negation of
> Christian concern.

Plaid Cymru and Radical Liberals have "similar attitudes" in
respect of:

    anti-militarism
    internationalism
    decentralism
    redistribution of wealth
    community-based society

To Plaid Cymru, the nation gives the individual an identity. To
the Radical Liberal, emphasis upon the nation . . . is a tendency
associated with centralism and anti-community forces, and

172

therefore "suspect".

Analysis of Liberal propaganda themes
The Cavendish pamphlet is such a good example of English
Establishment propaganda that it is a required reading text for
Welsh nationalist cadres. In it, we will see examples of every
trick in the book.

1. Target population of Liberal propaganda
Let us first examine the type of words and the slant of the
appeal of this propaganda, and those at whom it is aimed. Much
Establishment propaganda is aimed at the self-justifying
individuals who are intellectually too lazy to do much digging
into history. It is designed to be full of ".'comfortable words",
vaguely progressive, definitely "against", while taking good care
to be moderate, rational and in accordance with non-violent
Christian values. In fact, it is designed for that great number
who prefer the line of least resistance in political activity. Let
us look at the words applied to Welsh patriotism on pages 12/13
of the pamphlet: "sentimentality", "reject reason", "romantic,
instinctive, mythical approach", "a type of nationalism . . .
impossible to reconcile with Christianity", "not concerned with
. . . individual Welshmen", "appeal to selfish instincts", "selfish
philosophy, policy and appeal", "economic separatism a
negation of Christian concern", "selfish as regards water".

These are carefully chosen *triggers* to be placed in the mind
of waverers.

2. The truth behind the words
Liberalism, for all its own fine words, carries along the unthinking, or rather those who are too cowardly to think through
to the unpleasant and unwanted conclusion, to the very point at
which, when in power, English liberals have the opportunity to
act in government. That is its purpose. Once in power, there is
first hesitation, the "an appeal for moderation", and finally
abject betrayal.

The opportunity presented by Cymru Fydd
Lloyd George took much of Wales along with him until Cymru
Fydd was deliberately destroyed in 1891, when it threatened to
give rise to a significantly powerful Home Rule agitation on the
scale of the Irish within the English colony that, in its coalfields,

created the energy base of English economic and military power. (Remember it was to be a full 20 years before Winston Churchill converted ships of the English navy from coal to oil fuelling). Viewed in terms of power politics, it was already clear in the 1890s that a conflict between the English and German Empires was becoming more than a possibility.

The coming war between the powers might result in the liberation of Ireland, but with Cymru Fydd destroyed, and Welsh nationalism in a state of disarray (from which it was not to recover for 40 years), it was certain that the Welsh coal and manpower basis of English prosperity could not be threatened. The liberals cleverly disguised the true stakes in the abortive 1891 meeting at Cardiff, which should have given birth to a fully-fledged Home Rule movement. The vehicle of Lloyd George's triumph was "culturalism". Welsh culture could be maintained without independence. In practice, Liberal care for "Welsh culture" resulted in the Welsh dead of the Great War, the coal strikes of 1926 and the Welsh emigration during the slump of the 1930s.

The Sankey Commission

The second example of Liberal betrayal took place during the Lloyd George Coalition government of 1918-1922. In 1919, the Miners' Union put in a wage claim and the demand that the mines (under government control during the war) should be nationalised. Lloyd George, realising that it was either forward to a new era, or back to private ownership, bought time with the famous Sankey Commission. To the surprise of everyone, in 1919, Mr Justice Sankey recommended for nationalisation. An electric current of expectation ran through the Welsh coal-fields, particularly since the first interim report was also in favour of an increase in wages, and a reduction of hours. It took Lloyd George three months to decide which side his bread was buttered. Then he announced that his government rejected nationalisation.

It is difficult to imagine the consternation and anti-climax in Wales. The community felt itself deceived. Disillusion destroyed Liberal power in Wales.

In retrospect, the Welsh had no-one to blame but themselves.

Since 1891, they had believed what they wanted to hear. They did not want to look back over the bodies of the Welsh dead of the 1914-1918 war, to that fateful first betrayal. But Liberal propaganda did work, and worked very effectively. The mines remained in private hands. Monopoly capital was safe for another generation. Liberal propaganda had functioned as a delayer. The "people" had been confused just long enough to enable the forces of capital to be re-grouped.

Looked at in the light of history, how ought we to view the present rise in the level of Liberal/Social Democratic propaganda in Wales?

3. The rôle of Liberalism under monopoly capital

In the light of history, we are now in a position to determine the role of Liberalism, and its political successor Social Democracy, under monopoly capital in the coming struggle for power attendant upon the decline of the English state. It will be financed by capital to confuse and delay. Cavendish's critique of Plaid policy on industrial democracy shows exactly how this is to be done.

Liberalism condems Plaid's attitude on:
* the obligatory nature of the take-over of worker power: workers should "decide for themselves". This means that there should be a debate for just long enough to allow "moderate" and "rational" men to call out the forces of "law and order".

The thing that really frightens Capital is a sudden, complete and irreversible nature of the takeover by workers. Liberalism's function is to delay and confuse, and eventually de-fuse, that fateful takeover at all costs. 3 months will be long enough to rally the forces of counter-revolution.
* the provision about compensation by the Senate: no doubt lest the Senate prepare any compensation procedure on the basis of real rather than inflated values, and in some cases pay none at all.

4. The core of the Liberal intention: To destroy self-confidence in the revolutionary movement, and hence frustrate the separation of the Republic from the English state

The English state is well aware that, by the close of this century, the final conflict will embrace not a political conflict between traditional mass political parties, but a revolutionary conflict between cadre parties: Whitehall against the nationalist parties in the Celtic lands, and the Communist and National Front in England. They would prefer to follow the Americans into a third world war rather than face this conflict at home, but if there has to be conflict, then the psychological weapons at their disposal must be in good order.

The English are now past masters at the science of repression. They have a long history of "containment" of nation liberation —in India, Malaya, Cyprus, Aden, East Africa and Ireland. They know that nations are not liberated by the masses, but by an élite force of patriots and freedom fighters. ("Terrorists" in English terms.) The masses can be manipulated. It is not so easy to destory a cadre. They have a conviction, often based on several generations of conflict within a core of patriotic families in the colonial society; they are organised and have the embryo of a counter-espionage system. The way in which their threat is neutralised is:

1. Use of local intelligence services to pinpoint "subversive" family and community groups.
2. On some pretext, arrest and pull in members of these groups for interrogation. The object is to break down the patriot, and so frighten him that he is rendered inoperative in the struggle, and/or to force him to implicate others, unknown to the intelligence forces.

In a manner of speaking, the psychological preparation of the target society is conditioned by the vital 96 hours immediately after a patriot is picked up. The forces of containment know that they have a limited time in which to work. Shifts of interrogators, lack of food, sleep and lavatory facilities, are part of the operation to break down the powers of resistance. They must therefore use ideas *already implanted in his mind by mass propaganda.*

The role of "liberal" propaganda is to instil doubt and uncertainty:

* nationalism is an aberration, a form of romanticism, it is so "unreasonable".
* nationalism is so "intolerant".

* a substitute politics already exists which is almost the same.

The interrogation methods of the English are not usually brutal. (They are too clever.) They begin with kindly, avuncular approaches. "Come on now, young lady, you've got it all wrong, we rather like you, we consider it the sort of company you keep!"

The kindly gentlemen then launch into the unreasonableness of it all. At the end, the poor girl must be left with the feeling that far from doing her harm, she has been rather helped by these people. They are careful, however, to secure a promise to keep them informed upon "the company she keeps."

Viewed in the light of the terrible 96 hours such a young person spends in the cells, liberal propaganda has important functions:

1. To run on so close a parallel to that of the revolutionary party that it will set up real struggles of conscience during the process of interrogation, and give the intelligence officers their first handle upon which to build their case.

2. It must destroy confidence in the rightness and moral value of the Welsh cause. We are taught in church that there can be no compromise between right and wrong. Upon the basis of our Christian tradition, we demand the liberty of our Republic. This belief has to be severely shaken by the accusation of "intolerance". To hold an opinion on political order (which, when merged with religious conviction, constitutes an irreconcilable force) is subversive to the English state. It must be shown to be "intolerant". The word must be used as a trigger to show the patriot that he/she is genuinely in error.

3. It must, finally, convince the young person, frightened, very much alone, hungry and in distress, that it is really "selfish" to want the prosperity of one's own community. Under normal circumstances, the idea that it is selfish for ordinary Welshmen to want their rundown villages to be as prosperous as those in Surrey or Buckinghamshire would raise a laugh. But for the frightened young person in the interrogation cell, circumstances are definitely *not* normal.

It is only when viewed in the light of the stress situation created by the struggle for the mind of the young that the full significance of so-called "liberalism" becomes clear. It is no accident, indeed, that the quotation appearing on the cover of Cavendish's pamphlet is that sentence of William Morris' which is invariably used to convince potential revolutionary cadres that they are misdirecting their allegiance. It is designed to implant defeatism, so that we know that whoever uses it is probably doing so for a purpose, and that purpose is not helpful to Welsh liberty.

> Only slowly did I learn how men fight and lose the battle, and the thing that they fought for comes about in spite of their defeat, and when it comes, turns out not to be what they meant, and other men have to fight for what they meant under another name.

Young patriots are to be pre-conditioned to a failure finally engineered in the interrogation room. The Welsh Republic will be won by *winning* battles, not by losing them. It will be won by a revolutionary élite with unshakeable faith and dogged determination.

True rôle of Liberalism

Liberalism, then, is the power of the Establishment in disguise. Behind that power stands monopoly capital. God help us if we forget that for a minute! Cavendish was certainly correct on one point: we *are* intolerant. In a life-and-death struggle for our land, our people and our values, young people of Wales, can you afford to be tolerant? Do you choose to live or to die? If you choose to live, then you have no option but to come with us!

Low Intensity Operations

This is the term originally used to describe new techniques to neutralize, contain and eradicate freedom movements in colonial territories. The old "patrol" techniques of conventional warfare were not effective against guerilla bands.

LIO is based upon a small low profile military presence. It adopts guerilla-type tacticts itself. The force is well trained, maintains good radio communication with base, lives "undercover" off the countryside, and needs few supplies. The key to the LIO concept is an extremely well-developed system of local informers together with minute record-keeping upon the personality and habits of suspected adversaries. Whereas the old patrol would operate on a "hit or miss" basis, LIO troops would probe, confirm, isolate, attack, upon the basis of local intelligence sources. Consequently the technique depends upon close liason with local police and the civil authority. Intelligence is the "Queen of the Sciences", and the LIO is totally dependent upon it.

Its chief theoretical proponent (and an accomplished practitioner) is Brigadier General Frank Kitson, whose books *Low Intensity Operations* and *Bunch of Five* provide useful accounts of the technique. Brigadier Kitson is a good writer, but a better editor. What is *omitted* from his books is what is significant.

Nationalist interest in LIO

The techniques of LIO are of interest to the nationalist in as much as they open a window upon current military thinking and mark another step in the transformation of the old liberal mass democratic capitalist state into the neo-fascist corporate state. We are concerned not only with what LIO is, but what it can become. In western democracies the Army used to occupy a useful and honourable role as an instrument prepared to combat external aggression.

The development of LIO marks a step away from that conception. The Army has now become an instrument for *internal* surveillance and subversion. These techniques need only minimal adaption to be potentially very dangerous.

It is a truism of history that disintegrating empires eventually import the apparatus and attitudes of colonial supression back into the home land. Thus the full horrors of the SS were hidden from the German population until military defeat brought the apparatus of terror back within the contracting frontiers of the Reich.

The Algerian War eventually brought back colonial methods to metropolitan France. These methods include:

* the systematic use of espionage against "suspects" in the metropolitan population. The Intelligence forces were a law unto themselves. Even politicians were unaware of their activities.
* the use of torture in interrogating "suspects". (OAS or other).
* the amalgamation of the Army, the local civil authorities and the media of propaganda into a new establishment (which was difficult, at times, to distinguish from that of the former Vichy régime —indeed many of the personalities were the same).

The perfection of the theoretical doctrines of LIO, the opportunity for their use and verification in Northern Ireland, and the appointment of emergency services officers in local authorities, are all developments which deserve the careful attention of nationalists.

The Age of Scarcity will create tensions in all societies. The intensification of the nationalist struggle in Wales and Scotland will offer irresistable temptations to a sagging Westminster régime to use the "latest methods" to contain and neutralize. We can expect further developments in the techniques of LIO to make them more applicable to local circumstance and conditions.

Military
Mentality

During wars and in their immediate aftermath there is much discussion of this phenomenon. A spate of books was published in the '50s upon the mentality of the German General Staff. After the Algerian War, many books were published by the French Left on its evils. After Vietnam, another torrent of books was published in America, expressing concern over the power of the military in the economic and political life of that country. How many books have been published about the mentality of the English Officer Caste?

Young nationalists are not equipped to appreciate the military mentality. They are content to detest it. Perhaps this attitude may prove deficient in the next twenty years. There is a need in the Age of Scarcity to have an appreciation of the military mentality, to understand it, to master it and to use it in the service of the community benefit state. We will explore this need later in this essay. For the moment, let us examine the phenomenon.

One has to go far back into history —to the period of the great migrations and the first use of the horse in warfare, to understand the development of the mentality of a military caste.

The speed, the power and the terror of the first disciplined cavalry bands spread as much confusion in the minds of their adversaries as the lightning advances of the Panzers had upon the French "poulu" in 1940. Cavalry was the decisive factor in warfare until Welsh archers at Agincourt proved that it was not invincible. The Age of the Missile had arrived.

Yet, in the years of its ascendancy, and for many centuries afterwards, the use of the horse in warfare bred an attitude of mind which we would today recognise as the military mentality. When a group of men are armed with primitive weapons, they are no more than marauding bands. Give these same men what they regard to be the ultimate weapon, and let them use that weapon in a disciplined and experienced manner, and you have gone far to create in the minds of their leaders an attitude of superiority bred of their supposed invincibility. This is the basis of the military mentality. We have come to one key factor, then, in describing the mind of the military caste. It is an organisation for domination where mental factors as well as the physical means are of importance. The military believes itself to be superior, and others accept this opinion at its face value because the military possess the ultimate authority —the power of life or death.

There are economic implications. Every military caste must have the resource to arm itself and the leisure to practice its arts. Originally, it needed large tracts of rolling grassland to graze its horses. Therefore, it must possess. It must force others to provide for its subsistence. Hence, the military mentality has economic and social implications of political consequence. The pattern of history is remarkably constant, though both technology and society has changed:

CONQUER by means of its military might.
SETTLE in order to provide the means of maintaining that superiority.
EXPLOIT the labour of the defeated in order to do so.
DOMINATE the defeated by breaking their will, by a show of material and intellectual superiority. By making them feel inferior, they become, in fact, inferior.

This pattern reasserts itself time and time again: the Norman subjection of the Saxons; the English subjection of the Welsh; the subjection of the Slavs by the Landsknecht; the Junkers' subjection of the Poles; the Palhavari's subjection of the Persians; the subordination of American society to the manipulation of the industrio-economic complex. At first glance, this last example seems incongruous. Yet is it not true that the military subversion of American society beginning in the war has now reached the proportions of near-domination? The military provide the flywheel to the American economy.

"Yes," the nationalist will comment, "this is why we detest the military mentality. We will have none of it!" In this sentiment, we would have the support of the Welsh population. The "folk attitude" to anything military is one of deep suspicion. This is, perhaps, a result of the deep social cleavage between the personnel and attitudes of the English officer class and ordinary people. Wales is still a conquered nation, and in the last analysis, nothing will eradicate a fact of history, ancient though it be. This goes a long way to explaining the attitude of the English officer class to Welshmen —they are not to be trusted. It is possible, perhaps, to advance to the rank of major, but not beyond, save at the price of repudiating the Welsh heritage.

Such, then, are the circumstances which determine Welsh attitudes to all things military. Military means degradation —of us by them. We trot out religious and philosophical arguments in order to give substance to this detestation, but one must ask whether the circumstances of history gave rise to the attitudes, or the attitudes provoked the circumstances. Which is the more true? Let us recall that before 1282, the Welsh were demonstrably among the most formidable soldiers in Europe, and we have the evidence of Welsh poetry that the need to defend one's liberty was taken for granted by the most carefree of Welshmen —the wandering bards. It was never in question.

Of what significance is this to the modern nationalist? Today, the very mention of the military mentality is enough to make the hair bristle. One does not willingly court unpopularity to raise the topic. Yet, it is a topic which must be raised. The Age of Scarcity forces Welsh nationalism to come to terms with the need for an army, and therefore it must come to terms with the military mentality. Even if it does not like it, it must do so in order to control it.

Let us simplify the rationale behind this need in a number of equations, thus:

| Welsh nationalism | = the distribution of power to the people in both its economic and its political aspects. This is to be a de-centralised power. |
| Decentralised power | = a great variety of weak institutions in which resides "the sovereignty of the people". |

also:
Decentralised economic power, shared by working people themselves = the alarm and envy of organised monopoly capital-ism, struggling to consolidate its power over the mind as well as the body of man.
This alarm grows *pari passu* with the success of the nationalist in distributing that power, and the development of the community benefit economy.

but
a great variety of weak institutions in a neutral and pacifist community = a standing temptation for the wild men of monopoly capital-ism in the home of monopoly capitalism. "The Welsh free-dom is weak, divided and vulnerable. Let us nip it in the bud!"

hence
a standing temptation = the threat of interference in the creation of the community benefit state, by sinister forces in English society.

185

fascist interference	= the re-imposition of the régime of monopoly capital by violent means. The English government has never flinched from using force (or the threat of force) against unruly Welshmen.
the threat of force	= the need to protect the achievements of Welsh working-class democracy step by step with its creation. The greater the success, the greater the threat.

Before any hasten to observe that such things cannot happen in "liberal" Britain, let them ask why it is that whenever "disorder" threatened the established English order, troops have been sent into Wales. If "it cannot happen here", why is it that machine-guns were placed at Welsh pit-heads in 1926? Let us recall that the "wild men" equipped an expedition and sent it to Suez a full decade after Atlee's government came to power. Welsh nationalism is about to set up a community benefit society which will stink in the nostrils of the English establishment. Nationalism is not engaged in the organisation of a strike, but in the creation of a community benefit society. It will do so in an atmosphere of tension to be anticipated in the Age of Scarcity.

Whether we like it or not, then, it would appear that we have to come to terms with the military mentality —that of our own soldiers, who exist to defend the achievements of their own people. How does the nationalist control that mentality?

* By intense ideological training. Let every cadet know exactly what it is he is defending:
    * liberty of the land and its immunity from aggression.
    * liberty of the people and their freedom from the social degradation and economic exploitation of a conquered people.
    * the neutrality of the Welsh state and people.
    * the community benefit society in all its manifestations.

It is expedient that the army be entrusted with the responsibility for the training of young people in healthy civic attitudes. The army should become the ideological powerhouse of the people. Hence, a Military Academy is required not solely on account of the technical specialisation of military training, but on account of its duties to the Welsh people in respect of consolidating wholesome beliefs which the education system has sought to instil. Conscription becomes the last and most vital link in the chain of public education, where attitudes are crystallised during adolescence.

* By the restraint of the workers' militia.

It will be very difficult for the military to get out of hand in a vigorous society where the working people are armed. Welsh nationalism will give ordinary people self-confidence. They will feel what they never expected to feel in their lifetime —the exhilaration of actually building a new community with their own hands. These men are unlikely to be disposed to touching their forelock as a mark of respect to a superior breed of men.

A military caste must exist in the midst of a serf population. There will be no serfs in the Welsh Republic.

Welsh nationalism is afraid of the military. Fear is the basis of distrust. We cannot continue in this way. The people must master the military and use it for its own ends. Without the army, Welsh freedom is an illusion. We are free but for a season.

Monetarism

The Depression of the '30s produced Keynes and his theories of employment generation by fiscal policy, by widespread government spending, tax cuts and subsidies to depressed trade sectors. It became fashionable to create growth by deficit financing (i.e., running into debt in order to create employment).

The Depression of the '70s has created a new fashion in public finance; the manipulation of fiscal policy. The apostle of monetarism is Prof. Milton Friedmann of the University of Chicago, and its leading practitioner was (until replaced), Mr Arthur Burns, Head of the FRB (the Federal Reserve Board —the "Central Bank" of the USA). Monetarism is the new buzz word.

This school of economists aim at creating economic stability and avoiding inflation. They believe that the targets for the growth of money in circulation should be no greater than the growth in the GDP (Gross Domestic Product —i.e., the product of goods and services generated within a state). If monetary targets are too high, they argue, they exceed GDP. Inflation will result since too much money will be chasing too few goods. If money is too tight, the economy will deflate.

This apparently simple theory is fraught with many complications. If an economy is slack, any monetary target will probably be somewhat inaccurate since it would have been drawn up about a year in advance. The difference between the money in circulation and the low demand for goods will leave headroom for inflation. If, however, output is rising, there is a danger that fresh demand will trigger off inflation, hence the money supply should be carefully regulated by tightening credit *before* demand takes off. The net result of monetarism, as a philosophy of control over an economy, is the maxim "If in doubt, don't".

This is about as useful as the doctrine of orthodox financing in the '30s, when there was a passion for balancing budgets and cutting government expenditure at any cost to employment. Finance ministries throughout Europe superimposed budget cuts upon deflating economies. In the '70s the monetarists who have completely, it seems, won the ear of the finance ministers, hold the bogeyman of inflation up as an incentive to dampen down demand even in an unemployment economy.

The whole system of monetarism is in any case dependent upon forecasts of demand. Economists in the English treasury have a worse record at forecasting than their colleagues in the Meterological Office. They are not alone in the capitalist world. Without effective economic planning, demand forecasts must be unreliable.

Indeed, the new fashion for monetarism in this slump is a reflection of the fashion for Keynsian fiscal multiplier policies in the last. They are both a substitute for a planned economy.

"Enlightened" economists are now of the opinion that:

AN EFFECTIVE
MONETARY POLICY + FISCAL POLICY = SUBSTITUTE FOR
ECONOMIC PLANNING

Capitalist economists will twist and wriggle, and adopt any expedient, providing they can avoid the planned economy. High capitalism is hostile to planning in public finance. Planning implies an economy where community benefit establishes the priorities of investment. The capitalist would prefer to set his own priorities. In the community benefit economy, all the leading target economic indicators are set many years in advance, and deviations result in corrective action to bring budget and actual into line. This implies community control over decision-making in investment, market size and market share, certainly in the macro-economy, and for the nationalised (and worker share participation industries) also in the micro-economy. This is anathema to monopoly capital, which would prefer to act in collusion with civil servants in the Central Banks and Ministries of Finance, in order to perpetuate their own power over decision-making.

Here we come to another little-noticed aspect of monetarism. Both monetary and fiscal measures originate in the Ministry of Finance or in the Central Bank. They do not originate in a planning authority. Indeed, in states where monopoly capital is strongest, there is no plan and budget organisation at all —e.g., in Britain and the United States. The British Treasury is the inveterate enemy of any planning ministry, however innocuous. One recalls George Brown's ill-starred planning department in the early '60s, when the Treasury used every trick in the book in order to kill it off as quickly as possible.

Nationalist attitude to monetarism

Monetarism in an economy such as that of the United Kingdom is absurd. Any policy which lays waste the barren fields upon which this community ekes out a precarious existence, even in good years, is intolerable. It has two major flaws.

Rate of re-investment more important than inflation

* The determinant for an effective economic unit is a combination of assets, a contented workforce and management working to a purpose, clearly understood within and without the enterprise. Creation of fresh assets from restraint in consuming wages and share-cropping is the key to future wealth. The pace of re-investment is more important than the pace of inflation. Indeed, the higher the rate of re-investment in the creation of more efficient means of production, the more likely an enterprise will be in mastering inflation, because it will make more efficient use of resources whose cost has inflated.

Inflation, then, is inevitable in the Age of Scarcity. It is built into the capitalist system. The way to beat it is to invest, not deflate. The very act of investing withdraws capital from non-productive investment (so-called "financial" investment in High Street "money shops" of one sort or another, and real estate).

* Monetarism is a class solution, whereby working people pay with their living standards for the capitalist mis-management of the economy. The beneficiaries of monetarism are the largest accumulators of capital. Wages are forced down, and inventory finance costs are cut back. The rate of return on investment increases as a consequence, and on account of the high interest rate on spare cash put out to market. In the meantime, the Public Sector Borrowing rate actually increases due to the compound effect of high interest rates to service existing debts. Monetarism produces a vicious circle of dear money, closures, losses in infrastructure industries, leading to heavier borrowing and higher rates of interest in consequence

No substitute for planning

The Age of Scarcity will increase the need for regulation of the economy. Welsh conditions will make this need acute. Nationalists will inherit the problems created by a decaying capitalist economy, and superimpose upon them those associated with the massive investment required to create the infrastructure for a community benefit society. Control over investment and control over the market are crucial to an effective planned economy.

Control over investment means a substantial measure of control over all significant investment and over the sources of funds —banks, insurance and pension funds. Control over the market implies manipulation of fiscal and monetary measures, as well as market sharing and the physical control over imports. In fact, then, a Welsh community benefit state will be the complete antithesis to the British welfare state. The English Labour party, in theory committed to socialism (the key to which is economic planning) has in fact created a welfare capitalist state. The Welsh community state, while not in theory socialist, in practice must create a planned economy in order to survive in the Age of Scarcity.

To the nationalist, then, Milton Friedmann's practical monetarism and Lord Keynes' fiscal policies are only tools in the service of a planned economy. They are not substitutes for it.

Monopoly Capitalism

In the strictest sense, this used to mean the creation of a monopoly in the part of a market, so that the monopoly could charge as much as the market could bear for the product, irrespective of production costs.

While it may still mean this, it has now come to mean very much more. Monopoly capital has come to be associated with the multi-national firm. Not only does this organisation corner a piece of the market for a particular product or a group of products on the national scale, but it is increasingly able to do so on a world scale.

These concerns have long ago passed the point of interest in profits. Their control of the market, and investment in capital-intensive plant, assure that profits will be made as a matter of course. The crude measure of profit for accounting or taxation purposes is no guide to their power. It is possible, by means of manipulating depreciation charges and, even more, transfer prices, for raw or semi-finished products between one plant and one country to another to obscure the profit figures. Therefore, such organisations can manipulate markets and products to pay less taxation than a truly national enterprise. To an extent, large enterprises must transform themselves into multinationals in order to survive.

This is the key to their philosophy. The inbuilt management caucus is responsible to no-one; banker, shareholder or government. The sole criterion for decision-making is the survival of the power of the group, therefore, the prestige of those who manipulate it. It is not so much an immoral as an amoral entity.

Products, processes and markets are switched around without the least hesitation in accordance with computer optimisation exercises, which are themselves part of the corporate five-year plan. These plans are on the whole created, projected and executed with a degree of efficiency which no government, communist or capitalist, can match. These organisations are monolithic, single-minded, secretive and completely impervious to public opinion. Governments may chase their coat-tails: they cannot catch them. They cannot rule them, apart from completely nationalising them. War means nothing, even if two halves of an organisation happen to be on different sides. Multi-nationals are by their nature uncontrollable.

Without any doubt, then, these organisations make many of the real economic decisions of the non-communist world. Ordinary people are well aware of the existence, and vaguely aware of the power of such organisations as the "seven sisters" of the oil trade, ITT, IBM. What they are not aware of is the power of many lesser-known organisations, particularly those which control the matters closer to their well-being, the food trade. For example, it is not generally known that 7 companies control the grain trade of the world.

The significance of these organisations is not their economic power. It is their political power, rarely openly revealed, but always a force with which to reckon. There are good grounds for stating that the governments of the US and the UK effectively abdicated control of foreign policy in the oil-producing regions to the oil companies. It was considered that what was good for the oil companies was good for Britain. This view was rarely challenged. It was a great pity that it was not. A more even apportionment of oil revenues twenty years ago might have deflected the wrath of the oil states.

Yet, this is a matter of detail. It is not the crucial question. Monopoly capitalism will automatically collide with political reaction. If the survival of the organisation is at stake, only those régimes which interfere *least* will secure the very effective direct and indirect assistance that these enterprises can give. Monopoly capital only asks for one thing —complete control of the market. Change is anathema. It will share a bed with any organisation that will prevent change. It is thus a powerful generator of attitudes. These attitudes have an unmistakeable imprint upon the minds and actions of senior civil servants. This is their greatest power. For the aspirations of Welsh nationalism, it is lethal.

The key concept in Welsh nationalism is worker participation in industry. Whatever the share that worker involvement is likely to take in Wales (and this matter has not been settled even in terms of a party programme), the very fact that nationalists propose to share control of large enterprises with their workers, who might (or might not), be in 100% sympathy with the ambitions of the enterprise, will be enough to damn Welsh nationalism.

It is of no use to question whether the power of any enterprise might not, in fact, be strengthened in the Welsh community by a measure of worker participation. The very fact that there is to be an effective worker shareholding will provoke the unrelenting opposition of monopoly capital. No doubt the savagery of this opposition will come as something of a shock to many nationalists, who, if they have given much thought to the matter at all, are not, *a priori*, implacably hostile to any organisation in Wales provided it offers reasonably secure employment prospects. Generally speaking, nationalists are anxious to pursue a "live and let live" policy with any organis-ation that is prepared to subscribe to a code of good conduct. Large scale nationalisation or sequestration of foreign enterprises is not popular in nationalist circles, since while such enterprises would be left without markets and finance, they would require management skills which are certain to be in short supply. There are too many state enterprises which would require this resource in a free Wales.

Indeed, a purely empirical evaluation of the situation would suggest that nationalism would only expropriate foreign enterprises in a number of circumstances:

No. 1   They were unwilling to turn over at least a ⅓ share-holding in their Welsh operations to a workers' share-holding authority.

No. 2   If that enterprise was to operate in a trade sector where the Republic demanded a monopoly itself in order to secure its own survival. A Welsh state would probably require a monopoly (or a near-monopoly) in the energy market. Control of the retail outlets (not necessarily the producer) must be vested in the state. A small state must have absolute control of its own energy and transport markets.

No. 3 If the enterprise had too large a share of the Welsh market, for example, in the purveyance of retail finance and insurance, an area completely controlled by English institutions. The monopoly of the English banks must be broken by Welsh retail and wholesale institutions.

No. 4 No foreign enterprise may own or farm Welsh land. This is an exclusive privilege of Welsh citizenship.

No. 5 If any enterprise, for example, producing refined oil or petro-chemicals, were to have part of its activities in the market-place curtailed or eliminated, there is still no reason why the products of the enterprise cannot be exported without hindrance from Wales, or indeed purchased by a Welsh state monopoly, at the prevailing price in the international market.

No. 6 Where an enterprise threatens closure of a plant which gave livelihood to a whole community by shift of a production operation elsewhere.

No. 7 Where manipulation of reserves or transfer prices was to the detriment of the state treasury. Any foreign enterprise in Wales must be prepared for very careful scrutiny of transfer prices.

No. 8 Where a foreign enterprise threatened to de-stabilise the market for labour or competed with state sector industries.

Welsh nationalism would appear to be best served by a flexible policy towards large foreign enterprises, rather than by pursuit of doctrinaire policies of socialisation or nationalisation. Providing certain social benefit criteria can be observed, nationalism has no wish to make a rod for its own back.

Monopoly capitalism, then, will forever be regarded with

deep suspicion in a Welsh Republic, but nationalists are above all realists, conscious of the limited power wielded by a state on behalf of a population of under 3 million souls. No doubt, in the days of our early weakness, Welsh politicians would be very careful to disinfect any contracts with these foreign bodies, and keep a close watch for signs of cancerous growth. Providing it adapts to our society, and keeps well clear of politics, no doubt co-existence is possible, unless and until any organisation "touches the sceptre". Any activity in contradiction to the community benefit would surely result in precipitate sequestration.

We may finally ask ourselves the question, "Is capitalism, that is monopoly capitalism, about to collapse?" Marxists confidently predict that progressive concentration of capitalism must inevitably result in severe dislocation of "the system", which is itself a prelude to collapse.

There is no sign whatsoever of this collapse. Capitalism may or may not be working well, but its power over human beings has increased, is increasing and will surely be consolidated with governments in a neo-fascist community. While we cannot in Wales alter the international order, we can opt out of it. This is what Welsh nationalism is all about.

Nationalis-
ation

When the state gets hold of the people's wealth and the people become proleterianised, you find wealth and power concentrated in the hands of an irresponsible organization, the anonymous collective. Wealth controlled by the Anonymous Collective is sure to be wasted, for everybody's business is nobody's business.

The Welfare State, **D J Davies**

Broadly speaking there are two methods of gaining a measure of control over an economy. These are sometimes used separately, sometimes together.

* nationalisation
* control of investment

In general terms the Labour Party favours nationalisation, and Plaid Cymru control of investment through planning. This is a difference of long standing, certainly since Saunders Lewis put out his pamphlet on a National Planning Council for Wales in 1933.

If the Labour Party, in 1945, had been a genuine socialist party in the continental sense, rather than an English reformist party, prepared to maintain a welfare capitalist state, it would have opted for both. It chose nationalisation as a substitute for radical reconstruction of the economy. It was a fatal error of strategy.

It is fair to say that after 1945 the Welsh working class pinned its faith to nationalisation as the means of creating a community benefit society. It was deceived, economically and politically. Its deception was an accurate measure of its political immaturity in the 40s.

Economically, because the Labour Party chose to nationalise infrastructure industries and services, many of which had to be rationalised and had been badly (and sometimes deliberately) run down before nationalisation. Despite that importance, they were unlikely to be profitable. The lucrative end of the market was the consumer area. This is where private capitalism was permitted to retain control over the market and make large profits. Since control of market decisions remained in private hands, no government could really control the economy.

The state infrastructure provided subsidised goods and services to the private manufacturer. Investment decisions were thus, effectively, outside the control of a so-called socialist government in the really vital export and fund-generating industries. This is the key to the economic failure of English socialism. In fact, this policy cannot really be called "socialism" at all. It was a conventional measure of infrastructure re-organization in the interests of the experience was by no means confined to the UK. France, like the UK, has a formidable public sector, whose effectivness is small in actual direction of the economy. Sweden, on the other hand, has a very small public sector, but nevertheless, through other means, has been able to exert a considerable measure of control over the economy. This paradox has not gone unnoticed by Welsh nationalists.

Politically, nationalisation was, in fact, a disaster for the working class. It put control of the bureaucracy of the nationalised industries into the hands of a breed of man who was the sworn enemy of the working class movement. It was not entirely an accident that Establishment control of the nationalised industries resulted in massive run-downs in Wales, Scotland and Tyneside. These happened to be the citadels of radical socialism. Funds were certainly available, even in nationalised industries such as coal for massive re-investment. For example, the Investment Manager of the NCB Pension Board, responsible by 1978 for £1½ billion (more than the total gross assets of the NCB itself) could certainly have invested in South Wales in the 1960s to offset the effect of mine closures.

Despite their depressed area status we find investment concentrated in politically "safe" regions. Nationalisation, incidentally, made it easier to disperse a national bourgeoisie from the Celtic lands, (where they might be harmful) to innocuous postings in the South-East. We should not under-estimate the effect this had upon the development of Celtic nationalism.

These sins of commission were coupled with sins of omission. The Labour Party repeatedly failed to nationalise institutions which could have controlled investment —the banks, insurance companies and building societies. Massive amounts of capital available for internal productive investment were channelled into external and unproductive investment. Those of the pension funds and insurance companies alone amounted to £50 billion per year in 1978 and the *Economist* anticipated that these would grow to £70 billion by 1985. (*Economist* 4th Nov. 1978). Property was favoured by trustees in preference to productive investment. Speculation, merger and foreign investment were the "go-go" areas of the economy, not jobs sustaining manufacturing. Of the £4½ billion controlled by trust funds today £1½ billion is invested abroad. These were hardly the policies of a "socialist" government.

The other serious omission was the failure to erect an effective planning machine and give it enough power and prestige to counteract the influence of the Whitehall Treasury. In every state there is a constant tug of war between the plann-ers and the auditors, between the Central Planning Organisation and the Ministry of Finance. It is strange that while Labour politicians must certainly have been aware of this, in the 30s and the 40s, they never instituted a plan and budget organisation that did materialize in the 60s, under George Brown, was ineffective from the start and soon eliminated by Treasury intrigue. Aneurin Bevan was quick to point out that the English Treasury was the bastion of political and economic conservatism, but the English Labour Party was in no mood to listen. The English Labour Party has always held Welsh radical-ism in deep suspicion.

Nationalist attitudes to nationalisation

It is in the context of recent history that we must examine our own attitudes to this matter. Clearly, the Welsh need and Welsh attitude are going to be very different from those of the English state. The key concept of the community benefit republic is the establishment of national and social priorities. This principle enables nationalists to view nationalisation in a very different manner to reformist socialists in a "British" context:

* We seek to institute a community benefit economy by means of planning and control rather than through blanket measures of nationalisation. This policy is now 45 years old and there is no reason to change it.

* Where control demands nationalisation, we will certainly not be averse to it, but it is not a substitute for effective control over a monopoly industry created for social or revenue generation purposes. However, it is much more likely to be only that degree of nationalisation necessary for the community to secure and maintain a controlling posture over the Welsh economy. We can envisage a situation where branch lines of a national railway system are licensed for private exploitation, or joint enterprises are attractive in the steel industry.

* Society will be able to use much more subtle measures of control other than nationalisation, whose potential has been scarcely scratched under English socialist rule. These would include extensive disclosure of product, intra-company transfer prices, market share investment and depreciation information. These disclosures coupled with a much more flexible and imaginative corporate taxation policy can achieve effective control of the market, while avoiding the hassle of direct management responsibility. In this sense, disclosure through a more elaborate corporate tax declaration form for selected enterprises is a substitute for nationalisation (when –and only when– it is coupled with strategic community investment, as we shall see below).

* Armed with this information, the community is able to make direct investments in manufacture, wholesale and retail sectors, sometimes on its own, sometimes in joint venture. Generally one would expect these investments to cluster around the consumption end rather than the producer end, because this is where both the profit and the action are likely to be. To borrow Marxist terminology, control over the means of

distribution is likely to be more significant to the nationalist than control over the means of production. In this respect we are in direct contradiction to English Socialism.

* In any event, when there is a straight choice between measures of outright nationalisation and the introduction of direct worker participation, we would prefer the latter, provided there is no danger to the community's overall control of the market.

This preference for worker ownership accords with nationalist ideas about fostering individual worker responsibility within an enterprise, (which, of course, is directly linked to the profit he is likely to derive from it) and the control over the private sector that the Republic may obtain in the early days of operation of the worker share participation scheme.

It will be recalled that until dividends pay for the worker's shares, the republic stands as trustee for the loans it has issued to him to enable him to make the purchase. In this way the community has an interest in every large enterprise in Wales. This is preferable to outright nationalisation. Nationalists seek to rule, rather than to manage.

Nationalist thinking is generally more preoccupied with the ends of community benefit, rather than doctrinaire attitudes about the means of securing them. Fortunately we are not committed to free enterprise or socialist policies as such, and this offers management flexibility as well as political advantage.

In general terms apart from re-possessing our land mass and certain areas of monopoly activity, the nationalist sees nationalisation as a sledge-hammer used to crack a nut. By itself, it cannot create the community benefit state.

Non-Alignment

Wales has exhibited a disturbing inclination to pacifism, which is one reason why Whitehall has found the idea of self-government dangerous. Even during the Imperialist wars of the last century, there was an undercurrent of sentiment against involvement. The most frequent grounds for objection were moral. The Welsh conscience was shocked by the idea of war, and disturbed that it should be an instrument for subjecting tribes, however primitive they were described to be, to imperial rule.

The experience of the two world wars has offered no reason to ignore this sentiment. Neutralism is practical politics. It has manifestly been expedient and profitable to be neutral. It worked for Ireland, Sweden, Portugal and Spain during the last war. Swiss neutrality was respected even in the most un-promising circumstances. The harbours of Wales are a temptation to any belligerent. The Soviet-American war, should it materialize, will involve extensive submarine warfare. In 1939 the Nazis had 14 U-Boats commissioned and at sea in the North Atlantic. It is alleged that the Soviet navy numbered some 300 attack U-Boats. This is not a reassuring prospect for Wales, should we be tied to a NATO power. If there was any hint of the Welsh ports being used by either belligerent, we would be subject to nuclear attack.

There are penalties to be paid for non-alignment, but upon close examination, they are more apparent than real.

* intense opposition to Welsh home rule by the Whitehall

Defence Establishment, but they will oppose it anyway. They don't like giving any of their marbles away.

* American hostility to the idea of the foundation of a Welsh state. It is unlikely that the economic and social implications of Welsh nationalism would appeal to those who direct US foreign policy, in any case.

* maintenance of a defence force and basic armament industry convincing enough to deter potential aggressors in the event of a violation of neutrality.

Here, the shoe begins to pinch. Armies are not popular in Wales, and we are, as a rule, only too glad to express neutralist sentiments providing it does not cost us anything. We are all very quiet, though, about a defence budget. Investments in an arms industry are not entirely dead money. The Swedes and the Swiss, in particular, have developed a formidable defence posture by concentrating research and development upon a small number of excellent weapons.

This policy has paid commercial dividends, as well as equipping a conscript army with which potential aggressors appear unwilling to tangle.

Oath of Allegiance

1. This is the mechanism which legitimises a power establishment, the giving and receiving of an oath of allegiance or fealty. Great care is exercised to see that any wielding the smallest modicum of authority on behalf of the English state swears allegiance to the person of the English sovereign. Any contradictions of that oath constitutes an act of treason, which is ultimately a matter of the hanging of the offender by his neck until he is dead.

2. Since the English crown obtained its authority over Welsh lands and people by conquest, and not by consent, then it is clearly an act of treason to the Welsh people and nation to swear fealty to the English monarch. It is therefore illegitimate for a Welshman to do so.

3. The swearing of an oath is not a little thing. A man takes his whole self and puts his life and whole faculty at the disposal of the English state with his promise. To require this of a Welshman is, by definition, an act of deliberate degradation. It forces a man to commit treason and deceit upon his own people, his own community, its values and well-being, in order to become the pensioner of the English monarch, and progress in the service of that monarch. Whatever else the swearing of an oath may be (or may be dressed up to be), it is certainly not a mere formality.

4. Is this practical in an age when unemployment forces men to join the English armed forces in order to keep body and soul together, and in order for young people to equip themselves

with a trade? Must we brand men of this sort in the same category as the notorious traitors to their people who parade their shameful allegiance to the English crown? How does a Welsh nationalist MP preserve his moral integrity? This is an old predicament, and one to which a ready solution presents itself.

5. Let every Welsh patriot who is forced to take an oath to the English monarch make, beforehand, an oath of allegiance to his own Republic, notarised before two witnesses, in a public place:

> I swear by Almighty God, that I give my total loyalty to the Welsh Republic, that is the community of hope, experience and value of the born, and the yet to be born. I declare in front of these witnesses here assembled that any promise extracted of me to serve another is due to force of conquest and abhorrent to me, as God know my mind and inner thoughts. So help me God to keep faith with my own people. AMEN

Parliament

In a famous quip, Aneurin Bevan once complained that "he had
pursued power through the local council to the county council
and finally to Parliament, but he always found its coat tails
disappearing around the corner." Bevan was not interested in
power for its own sake; he was certainly not an ambitious man,
determined to make his mark by using working-class issues to
advance his own career. He was a genuine reformer. He wanted
to hold the levers of power in order to put the main line of
government at the disposal of the people. He wanted to create
a genuine people's state. He failed completely and ignominiously. He failed because he worked within an English, not a Welsh,
context, and because he fervently believed that the English
parliament was the cockpit of the struggle. He was wrong on
both counts.

Looking back over 25 years, his trust in the English
Parliament is child-like. He shared this with the overwhelming
majority of Welsh Labour politicians of his generation. They
were men of integrity, who worked in faith and trust with the
Whitehall régime. These men were not scoundrels and they
were sadly mistaken. They believed profoundly that the
people's state could be won by parliamentary struggle. They
were scrupulous observers of the rules. They lived by them,
and they did not stop to question whether they were being
used or not. *Chwarae teg* was their downfall.

However, unlike his Welsh colleagues, Aneurin Bevan did have
the perception to enable him to gauge the size of the stake. He
knew that if the people could not win their struggle against

reaction in the parliamentary arena, "parliamentary institutions would themselves be engulfed".

The English Parliament today is an institution in the last stages of decay. It is in decay because it is so obviously a "stunt". It is superfluous, and recognised as such. Reaction was always able to circumvent Parliament when it came to the fundamentals of the power struggle. In Bevan's day it was possible, at great effort, to put through reformist legislation, but it was, and still is, impossible to change that system for a genuinely democratic system.

Without exaggeration, it is possible to say that the English government system today resembles that of France under Louis XV. It is a system generally recognised as in need of reform, but a system where vested interest and old ideas are so entrenched and stalemated that reform from within is impossible. The English state has come to resemble *l'ancien régime*. The Establishment believe themselves to be impregnable. The powers of the English state are considerable and expanding. Government, or rather "administration", as it has come to be, is carried out with every sign of assurance and even arrogance. The conditioning apparatus manipulating public opinion and the safety-net of the welfare state are powerful tools for keeping ordinary people in a state of bewildered, but harmless, dissatisfaction. "The People" are largely inarticulate, and a good deal of effort is expended to ensure that they shall remain so. In the meantime, Parliament is part of the deception. Mock battles are periodically staged, battles which are inconsequential and where the real issues of government are rarely raised, and promptly stifled.

On Guy Fawkes' Day 1977, the London *Economist* printed a leading article upon the condition of Parliament, under the title "Blowing up a Tyranny". It was a surprising article, not in what it said, (as this has been said before and often) but in the urgency in which it was said.

It showed more clearly than any publication to date that some sections of the English Establishment see the storm clouds piling up in the distant sky, and are frightened at what they forsee. Their cry is now one of parliamentary reform. Before we examine the nationalist attitude to this matter, it is useful to summarise the *Economist's* argument, which, although familiar, was cogent and powerful.

The main theme is the absolute power of the executive over parliament, exercised by the party whips over individual members, regardless of conscience or issue. The English House of Commons is today largely a powerless body, in effect a public relations device, to give the appearance of legitimacy to decisions made by the inner party caucus. It has:

* no control over the timetable of legislation which is decided by the executive.

* no control over disclosures of information —the executive acts in secrecy and Question Time is inadequate because:

    there is no ability to force an investigation through a select committee of MP's, hence no real power of interrogating the executive;

    there is no power to examine civil servants, who have effectively acquired the authority once wielded by the House;

    no detailed supervision of legislation, and certainly none over financial policies;

    there is no means of unravelling the process by which decisions are taken.

The *Economist* goes on to point out that there is no prospect of reform from within, because:

* the English parties are so firmly in the saddle that each believes that the next government may be under its own control, and neither party is going to give away a part of its absolute power.

* this is particularly so as either party can form a government upon the basis of $\frac{2}{5}$ of the total votes cast in a general election.

* hence neither party wants to change the electoral system.

* each party will use its own period of office to push through its own brand of minority legislation, devised by its own back-woodsmen and hangers-on.

* there is no longer any "House of Commons feeling" as a vested interest opposed to that of government.

* the legitimacy of the House of Lords is so tenuous as to make that august body an unlikely focus of opposition.

* the parties are so locked in the pursuit of their own interest that national or even community interest have little chance of success.

* the quality of individual members of parliament is a direct result of the long hours and wretched pay, so that by gradual degree, showmanship and TV is more significant than character or principle on the floor of the House.

* preferment of any MP to the charmed circle of the 85 or so members who are part of the executive has come to depend largely upon ability to keep one's mouth shut, in case any constructive statement should rock the boat.

* the supreme position of leadership is consequently open only to those politicians who have succeeded in offending the oligarchy least.

These are strong words indeed coming from the London *Economist*. The Welsh nationalist is apt to take a long, cool look at lamentations coming from such a source. A clue to the alarm behind this manifesto is to be found in the following sentence:

> Already there has been a huge growth of corporate power in Britain — trade unions, central and local government bureaucracies, lawmaking tax collectors —of a kind that can and will flourish only because members of parliament a) do not accurately and fairly represent popular votes, b) act as lobby fodder for rival partisan manifestos, not as Burkeian inquisitors of government and all other centres of power. If this decay in fair democracy continues, because both major British parties find it inconvenient to stop it, it will not be easy in 20 years' time to argue its merits against even a Pole, a Russian or a Chinese.

Was this a Freudian slip? We may safely assume that the growth in corporate power which so alarmed the editor of the *Economist* was not only that of the trade unions and others. It was, perhaps, the power of international monopoly capital, which has become so obvious that it threatens the whole capitalist system. This talk of parliamentary reform is merely a device to throw sand in the eyes —to strengthen the illusion that ordinary people can fundamentally improve their condition through parliamentary action. "People's rule" through genuine local and industrial democracy would be incompatible with the rule of monopoly capital. Yet this is exactly the Welsh nationalist's definition of democracy. It has little to do with Parliament. That these opinions voiced by the *Economist* are true is beyond question, but that is not —for us— the point.

In Wales, we have passed the point of no return. This may not yet be apparent from the voting returns, but these will follow the logic of our situation. For us, there can be no looking back, no poignant wishes to tinker with or reform the machinery of English government. If ever in doubt on this matter, the aspirations, career and failure of Aneurin Bevan are evidence as to what can be expected in that quarter. People's rule has not, cannot, and never will be established in Westminster, but it can be established in Wales, and we are determined to do it.

Indeed, as for the possibility of reform, the more likely probability is that the powers of the English executive (of either party, it really doesn't matter which) are more likely to integrate more firmly with monopoly capital in the creation of the neo-fascist state, a régime nominally democratic but actually ruled by the interests.

From this probability we seek now to cut ourselves free. Nothing but evil can result from any further relationship between Welsh society and the English state. That state and that society are in decomposition and beyond redemption. Their problems and their crises are too persistent, and are a reflection of a social malaise and a régime which are past hope. Nationalists, then, are not to be taken in with the cause of English parliamentary reform.

Nor are we to be fobbed off with a local charade of devolved community interest. We required People's Rule, and we have proof positive that this is not to be won in the English parliamen parliament, or conceded by it. It is a régime that we shall make for ourselves.

This does not mean that elections to that assembly are of no interest. They are of consequence, because whatever its imperfections, for the time being, Westminster, not Cardiff, will be the seat of the Welsh national struggle, and it must necessarily remain so until the Welsh people at last toll their own liberty bell.

When the Welsh are once again a free people, the form and style of the English parliament will be of no relevance as a pattern of our own development. Our own circumstances are so different, and the times and conditions under which people's rule will operate in Wales are so novel and fraught with danger that the manner of the English parliament is of no more consequence than that of the *Estates-General* of France. Effective people's rule is dependent upon local democracy, civic and industrial, and in these matters, Wales will have to set her own precedents. It is on these concerns that nationalists should now be focusing their attention. Parliament is part of a dying order.

Profit Motive

The ideological position of Plaid Cymru was never in doubt upon this matter for the first twenty years of the life of the party. Listen to D J Davies on this matter in his Essay *I Believe*:

> Personal property is important as a basis, not of political and social power, but of human dignity and independence, as giving each person the maximum responsibility and thus cultivating in turn courage, self reliance and the other qualities which are essential to a fully developed personality ... When people have personal property and are organized among themselves they can make the state their servant instead of their overlord. Here again I would stress the point that control must be brought down effectively to the individual worker and local group, instead of being merely nominal, as it so often is today, even in so-called democratic organisations.

The situation is not now so clear. To help determine practical nationalist attitudes on this matter we might ask seven questions.

1. What is the difference between small scale and monopoly capital? Where is the dividing line?

2. Can the Community Benefit State do without the profit-motive?

3. If not, what place does it have in the Community Benefit State?

4. What are the anticipated circumstances of the Welsh Community Benefit State, in which the whole question must be discussed?

5. If the profit motive is encouraged, will this not lead to the

rapid growth of an entrepreneurial class whose vested interest may not coincide with that of the Community Benefit Society?

6. Can we tolerate community services run on the profit motive?

7. Are we asking, and answering, these questions from a Marxist or a nationalist point-of-view?

1. The difference between monopoly and small scale capital is the power it confers upon its possessor. In the case of a monopoly employer or supplier to a community, that power is, in fact, greater than that enjoyed by the local or the state government over a particular area. The powers wielded over the mining valleys from Dyffryn Chambers or from Hobart House today exceed, in fact, the power of the Westminster Parliament. The powers wielded by the small scale capitalist (except where he controls land) are limited. Even if his activities are disliked, his size contains him. To obliterate small scale capital requires extraordinary coercive measures which alter the condition of liberty of a whole people. This coercion can only be maintained by brute force.

2. In any case, the Welsh Community Benefit State cannot do without small scale capitalism. It is part of its title deeds to make every working man a part owner of the enterprise in which he spends his working life. Hence the Community Benefit State immediately turns the workman into a small scale capitalist. In a word, this is what we are in business to achieve.

3. Quite apart from the ideological committment of nationalism we have the question of economic expediency.

The charade of mass democracy has obliterated the working man as a human being. He is either a commodity or a political nuisance to be manipulated in order not to resist decisions made in his name. No wonder he has not the emotional incentive to work!

Welsh Nationalism has enormous works of reconstruction to do. We are investing ownership of the means of production in the people, because we must offer ordinary people the re-assurance that they do matter in the Welsh Community Benefit State. No motive is as strong as individual gain, to reinforce this reality. We need to get a supreme effort from our working population. Hence we must make it worth while to do so. A fair share of the rewards go to the work people and government taxation of workers' profits will be low enough to make the gain worth while. This is the place that the profit motive enjoys in the Welsh Community Benefit Society.

4. In fact, the anticipated circumstances in which we shall find ourselves are not propitious. The Age of Scarcity is no longer something seen from afar. The room for manoeuvre is decreasing, as the "scorched earth" policy of successive English administrations destroys more and more of the industrial base of the Welsh economy. The problems of the Republic will be immediate and enormous. It will have neither the funds, the manpower or the administrative capability to reconstruct the economy without "the light cavalry" of private enterprise.

5. In the first decade in the life of the Republic, it is certain that private enterprise will prospect in certain sections of the economy neglected by the Republic, or where the state has tried and failed. In these areas, will not the state become vulnerable? Certainly, but there are two expedients which can prevent the development of monopoly capital.
   * Enforced worker share participation.
   * Strict internal control over the market and barriers to external participation in Welsh companies.

6. It is not only tolerable, it may be unavoidable, that some community services are run by private enterprise, and with the assistance of conscript labour and state grants or remissions of taxation.

7. The degree of satisfaction with which these questions are answered will depend upon the assumptions of the reader. Are the conditions to be approached from a Marxist or a nationalist point of view?

If Marxist, then, clearly the answers are intolerable, until we remember that even in Russia the destruction of war, revolution and civil war induced Lenin to institute the NEP (New Economic Policy) after 1924.

If Nationalism, then clearly we are more concerned with the end product for the community. Means are of less consequence than the answer to the question "Does it work?".

Nationalists bring their own particular safeguards in the form of Worker Participation, which the Marxist could not concede.

Propaganda

With this enormous power to manipulate the public and the equally gigantic power conferred by control over information through computers and data banks, the oligarchy that controls the mass media and the election information systems can set up a network of information and manipulation capable of keeping the individual citizen under tighter control and more thoroughly subjugated than Stalin and Hitler were ever able to accomplish.

The Alternative Future. **Roger Garaudy**

Since the adoption of universal suffrage, it has been predictable that the masses must be manipulated. Since 1917 the Western democracies which, until then, had never concerned themselves with ideology, found the need to make counter-propaganda against communism. During the decade of the '30s, this need was powerfully reinforced by the incentive of 70 million unemployed. A world war was on the horizon, and a third of the workforce had to be convinced that, even though they were in extreme poverty, yet "our side" was worth fighting for. These circumstances gave a powerful stimulus to the development of propaganda. From an activity conducted by a group of amateurs, it became a polished tool of government. The Americans established an early lead, and an Institute of Propaganda Analysis was already at work in New York by the late '30s.

The Cold War provided a further impetus. Communist propaganda is based upon a strong ideological appeal. To many Europeans, surveying their wrecked economy after the war, it had more relevance than the free enterprise economy of

America. After one war, there was an understandable reluctance to fight another to ensure that General Motors could add a 15 per cent interim dividend to their distribution. European democracies were vulnerable. They had no ideological basis. They could certainly proclaim their freedom, but this would be incompatible with the open supression of "subversive" communist propaganda. Yet to many in government at that time, it appeared that communism would erode democracy from within. The governments of the West were singularly ill-prepared to meet this threat. Propaganda certainly constituted a form of aggression, but this type of aggression could not be taken to the Security Council. So the threat of attack from within encouraged a change in the style of government. It became more secretive. Pressures for "civil service rule" were strengthened. Counter-propaganda was stepped up. Media manipulation was perfected, based upon the earlier theoretical works of the Americans. "Dirty tricks" departments sprang up, whose existence and methods would never have been tolerated twenty years earlier. Unnoticed by the public, the savagery of the propaganda war forced the western democracies to change their style of government from within.

In the event, these governments need not have bothered. The crude excesses of communism in establishing the Soviet Empire, and the cynical repression of the East Berlin, Polish, Hungarian and Czech revolts undid the work of communist propaganda more effectively than all media manipulation and all the dirty tricks departments put together. However, what had been done was not undone. Despite the post-war boom, there were increasing signs of the alienation of the working class. The propaganda threat to the *status quo* now came from within. This alienation was particularly marked in the English state, and was a subject of frequent comment by foreigners. Celtic nationalism was a by-product of this alienation.

Nationalism, the search for a human identity, is now combined with fear, the fear of being without a job and without self-respect. Academic economists had long forseen that the post-war boom must peter out. There were several factors which made it unlikely that it could continue:

* saturation of the markets of the industrialised countries.
* the rising share of economic surplus demanded by workers internationally.
* competition for resources by the arms race.
* inflation produced by the arms race and aggravated by the Vietnam war, and exported to Europe.
* the growing poverty of the third world; it could no longer afford to import western goods owing to deteriorating terms of trade.
* rapid exhaustion of the raw material base and hence the rise in raw material costs to industry.
* the onset of the Age of Scarcity.
* finally, the energy crisis, whereby the cheap energy upon which the industrial world had come to rely disappeared overnight.

These factors were certainly anticipated by Western governments, long before their importance was appreciated by the general public. Throughout the '60s, there was a vast increase in internal conditioning, particularly within the USA. The economic crisis at the close of the century would, it was feared, lead to a political crisis. This would lead to further Communist encroachment. This could be contained by two measures:

* extensive welfare schemes to be operated, whatever their short-term economic effect upon orthodox government finance.
* massive conditioning by propaganda.

Propaganda is now almost an exact science, a science in which the Americans have an enviable lead. Of the 114 textbooks on a typical reading-list (published in Jaques Ellul —*Propaganda — The Formation of Men's Attitudes*, Random House, NY), 64 are American, 34 French, 9 German, the English and Italians have 3 each, and the Chinese and Russians 1 each. The Americans, in particular, have come to anticipate the problems of the Age of Scarcity, and to practice techniques of manipulation of the public to a degree unmatched elsewhere.

This is the background to the fierce propaganda war in which Welsh nationalists now find themselves, a war whose seriousness, savagery and complexity they are still slow to appreciate, and whose opening battles they have so ignominiously lost.

The true nature of the mass man

Nationalists are concerned to apply the science of propaganda in two areas:

* to govern their own propaganda activity.
* to subject the conditioning apparatus of their enemies to close study, and to nullify it wherever possible.

In other words, we find ourselves in a state of cold war, a war in which winner takes all. The enemies of Welsh nationalism are well practised in their understanding and application of mass conditioning techniques. Their target is the ordinary Welshman. We shall not understand the success of assimilationist propaganda unless we understand the true nature of the ordinary man.

Whereas nationalist propaganda is directed at an imaginary figure, the "gwerin Welshman", the *Western Mail* directs its propaganda against the Welshman as he really is. This goes far to account for the failure of the one and the success of the other.

The working man is governed by the pace of the line. He works in a noisy environment. He lives in crowded homes. He often keeps the hours of a mole. He is conscious of being part of a mass, of his unimportance. He is exposed to a continual bombardment of news, a bewildering and frightening assortment of events with no particular pattern. His native organic society has been destroyed. He cannot fall back on it. There is no real working class society. There is only working class distraction, the club, the TV and the car. The man is rootless. He has no Christian faith. He can detect no plan and no purpose. Yet it is implied that he *ought* to have an opinion on current affairs. He is embarrassed. He cannot really say that he has no interest and no understanding. He prefers to leave politics to others. Yet he must have an opinion to save his face. He does not want facts: they get in his way: he wants value judgements. (Plaid only gives him facts: it is assumed he can draw the correct conclusions). He wants to feel that he is on the right side. Above all, he is lonely. This loneliness is well understood by propaganda experts. It is the key to opinion manipulation. This is the ultimate psychological reality that makes the working man vulnerable. In Wales, this loneliness, this rootlessness, is combined with a strong impression of inferiority, deliberately cultivated on account of his Welsh origin. These feelings set up stresses, some of which are deliberately engineered, since *stress is an indispensable part of the conditioning process.*

Let us listen to Jaques Ellul, a leading authority upon the psychological effect of propaganda in his book *Propagandes* (Pan, 1962):

> That loneliness inside the crowd is perhaps the most terrible ordeal of modern man: that loneliness in which he can share nothing, talk to nobody, and expect nothing from anybody, leads to severe personal disturbances. For it, propaganda is . . . an incomparable remedy. It corresponds to his need to share, to lose oneself in a group, *to embrace a collective ideology, that will end loneliness.* Propaganda is the true remedy of loneliness. It also corresponds to deep needs (more developed today, perhaps, than ever before), the need to believe and obey, to create and hear fables, to communicate in the language of myths. It also responds to man's intellectual sloth and desire for security — intrinsic characteristics of the real man.

The deepest need of the ordinary Welshman is to be re-integrated into a real society. It is a need provoked by his instinct and his tradition. The satisfaction of this need is the key to unlock the combination of his mind.

This is precisely what nationalism offers through small unit government and worker participation. Yet we continually throw away our advantages in trivial "grumbling campaigns". It is easier to deplore problems than to advocate solutions. That takes guts.

Nationalist will never understand the true nature of the struggle in which they engage, unless they understand the psychological bases of their enemies' activities. These have been very carefully devised.

* The working class must be broken up. The individual must be made insecure. His organic community must be destroyed. Community is a threat to Whitehall government and monopoly capital. It must be obliterated.
* A relaxed, easy pace is subversive. Men must be kept on the move, in tension, with the "guts ache". It keeps them malleable. Shorter hours are dangerous. They give time for reflection.

* They must be persuaded to feel that this is the only way to live. Any attempt to alter this goes against "the march of progress". Individuals must be kept in a state of apathy. Apathy is the take-off point for reconditioning.

* Hence the basis for assimilationist English propaganda is that there is an inevitability about modern big-unit economic developments, the EEC, small pit and works closures, etc. These are part of the natural order of the universe. You cannot resist them.

* It is smart and modern to go with the tide. English class society is good, because it shows that a man is getting on in life as he moves up the class ladder. Welsh classlessness is bad because it shows affinity to crude living, speech and company.

* The object population is "cooked" when these sentiments are widespread. Reconditioning can now begin through the media.

Once these psychological bases for English policy are established, the logic of the deliberate destruction of valley communities and small scale farming in rural Wales becomes comprehensible. There are those who cannot bring themselves to believe in the cold-blooded destruction of communities and the cynical manipulation of the population. The evidence is before their eyes. *Si monumentum requiris, circumspice!*

It must be clearly understood that in the Age of Scarcity, mass democratic governments are forced to wage permanent psychological warfare on their own people in order to render them governable. Far from wishing to breed responsible citizens, government must be deliberately designed to produce apathy. This frees the hands of the interests to do things their own way, without the annoyance of debate and consent. This war is combined with infiltration of any organisation which can serve as a possible nucleus of radical change, in order that it may be disrupted or destroyed from within. Propaganda has now become a tool of statecraft. It has become the principal tool in the preservation of the *status quo*.

Characteristics of sound nationalist propaganda

Over 50 years, political nationalism has developed a workable organisation for dissemination of propaganda. It is the content that is deficient. This shows a limited appreciation of the

221

psychological ground,

* The propaganda of any cause which has the media deliberately closed to it is totally dependent upon a firm ideological base. Ideology is the cutting edge of revolution. Nationalists have been singularly neglectful in this matter.

* This base must link economic, social and religious as well as national content. Political nationalism of itself has no appeal. Culture, by itself, is a definite turn-off.

* Propaganda devised upon this basis orchestrates the power of the masses. It takes ideas and discontent that is vague, and crystallises it into clear unequivocal demands.

* It furnishes the masses with immediate tangible objectives.

* It reinforces existing prejudices. Where prejudice is *implicit*, propaganda makes it explicit. Propaganda deliberately provokes division and confrontation. Appeasement is *out*. Expediency is *out*.

* It aims to integrate the individual within the group and demands him to sink his personality aspirations and hopes into the group.

* It appeals to the sense of co-operation dormant in every Welshman.

* It organises response within a carefully prepared framework.

* It achieves this by the creation of stereotypes, ideas carefully built up and released through the use of trigger words or slogans.

* It induces successive moods of exaltation or depression.

* It emphasises the individual's contribution. It is all up to him.

* There is nothing spontaneous about any campaign. Milestone events are devised, and the situation response ghosted well in advance.

* Never allow reflection time between milestones. The opposition will force accounter-attack.

* Everything is deliberately programmed towards a predetermined result. Tensions are created which can only be

222

released by an unthinking reflex. The campaign is focused on that reflex.

* Release must be through sharp decompression which should show a noticeable physical relaxation in the object population. Lingering decompression can be fatal.

Advantages of nationalist propaganda

The opposition, Tory, Communist and Labour, has two propaganda themes which are skilfully exploited.

* "The future lies with the big battalions". The Communist version demands integration with the international working class struggle against any attempt at reform of capitalism.

* The Tory version demands integration with the EEC as the securest refuge for monopoly capital. Once national life is strangled by external regulation, the internal threat is much diminished. "Together we survive, individually we hang."

* The Labour oligarchy tries to take a leaf out of each version. Their own house is divided on both counts. This division should be persistently and cunningly exploited.

* The nationalists will create a Welsh-speaking "master race". The nation will become, in George Thomas' immortal words, "a fevered room closed to all fresh currents".

To nationalists, this is too ridiculous, but it is a charge to be treated with extreme caution. It should be disproved by example, not by argument. Nationalist propaganda has natural advantages:

* despite the rape of Wales, there is strong emotional attachment to the spirit of community and co-operation. Local democracy and worker participation are trump cards, emotionally and economically. How often are they used?

* Nationalism offers a complete and simple explanation of Wales' miserable history of exploitation —English rule. What's more, it is a fact that official statistics cannot disprove.

* Nationalism offers a complete emotional cure to the powerful feeling of alienation. Emotional appeal is more significant than rational explanation, so personal involvement in the new society is a factor to be stressed.

* Nationalism offers the obvious tool for recovery —a Welsh economic plan, administered through a Welsh Planning Authority. This tool must have teeth. This is the key to its propaganda advantage. The opposition cannot wind up this demand because they are incapable of giving Wales a planning authority with teeth without destroying their own power.

* Welsh nationalism is deeply intertwined with religious feeling. Many scoff at this, but in flat contradiction to other revolutionary movements, it is very difficult in nationalist thought to say where religion ends and politics begins. This is an unrivalled asset if handled sincerely and genuinely. It is a fact of Welsh psychology that the degenerate English opposition cannot even understand, still less emulate.

As the Age of Scarcity makes itself felt ever more keenly in English politics, it is inevitable that we shall see a sharp intensification of the nationalist struggle.

In this fight, every man's hand will be turned against us. Every dirty trick in the book will be used against us. Our opponents are fighting for their privileges and their jobs. Every door will be closed to Welsh nationalist propaganda. What there is must be much superior to that of the opposition —even to obtain a hearing.

Once again, we come to recognise a typical Welsh situation: in order to survive in a hostile environment, we have to take the tools and techniques of the Englishman, reject what is irrelevant, but make ourselves the undisputed masters of what is useful to us. We must then apply these techniques economically and imaginatively, but with the energy to match. They have a rich society to fall back on —personally and collectively. If we do not triumph, we go under. That is the size of the game. Propaganda is the key.

Psychological Warfare

This term was originally used in the First War to cover activities whose aim was to lower the morale of enemy populations, and to stimulate a demand for the end of the war. It was also used in a slightly different sense to detach the loyalty of enemy-occupied allied populations to encourage resistance which would, in turn, harass the enemy and force him to deploy badly needed troops for garrison duty. From the start, it was a mass manipulative technology.

This is not the sense in which it is used today. Psychological warfare today is a recognised technique used by governments against *their own populations*.

With the concentration of economic power in vast conglomerations, the unfettered pursuit of profit has a progressive and distortive effect upon human beings. The more monopoly capital forces people to adopt lifestyles to which the human animal is ill adapted, and from which he recoils in disgust, the greater the pressure to step up the conditioning process in order to foster attitudes of compliance with this unnatural state. The effort to conform to the capitalist-inspired behavioural norm —("the gay young handsome middle-class consumer; the progressive, obedient and diligent young executive, who will go far") on the one hand, and the intrinsic instinct of the human being, on the other, generates stress. *Stress is an essential component of exploitation.* Without it, people would begin to form attitudes of hostility to the existing social order. Stress preoccupies them. Hence stressful lives are deliberately engineered by management, (particularly those of the multinationals) forcing human beings into enduring hours and habits of work, emulation and competition within work, and discord within the office —"back-stabbing". The more threatened the management feel, the more evil the working environment. Human animals are not naturally adapted to being herded into vast sheds or open-plan offices. The human animal is relaxed working in a small group, at his own pace, according to a self-imposed discipline or that imposed subconsciously by his workmates. Above all, he must feel he is benefiting from the activity he performs. That benefit must be emotionally visible. Despite appearances to the contrary fostered by the media (to cover up the emotional bankruptcy of the capitalist order) this benefit is not primarily economic. It is the satisfaction of strong emotional needs within the workplace.

The bigger the gap between the natural condition of the human animal and the conditions forced upon him, the greater the degree of supressed discontent. Neither capitalism or communism can afford that discontent. Hence the need to maintain the established order by turning upon the subject population means of manipulation originally designed for waging war. Governments are afraid of their people. The deepening economic crisis of capitalism intensifies that fear, and encourages the government of a crisis-ridden country to press into service any and every method of pacification and containment. Moral scruple as to means has long since gone out of the window.

Does this mean, then, that there is a conscious conspiracy directed against this population? We have no means of telling. What we do observe, however, is that there is an *unconscious* agreement on attitudes to be engendered. That there is a conspiracy of attitudes is undeniable. Many different people in positions of power combine silently to do, or to withold from doing. This is an insidious form of totalitarianism. It is precisely this sort of conspiracy that sent six million Jews to their death.

Post-war Welsh society has become so familiar with these techniques of manipulated prejudice that it almost accepts them.

* routine use of manipulative techniques of propaganda in the media —slanting of news and attitudes *against* working people in conflict situations ("the power of the unions", etc.), *against* nationalists who are portrayed as "harmless cranks".

* use of television as a soporific —in order to isolate the individual human being, cut him off from society, and funnel all sorts of "safe" ideas into his mind. To make him feel powerless.

* encouraging fake conflict in mass sport activities and allocation of an inordinate amount of time to sports coverage.

* excessive prescription of sedatives by over-worked physicians —a practice officially deplored, but unofficially tolerated.

* loosening of censorship regulations in response to "enlightened" opinion in order to encourage subdued sexual hysteria as a substitute for other forms of emotional satisfaction. The permissive society is no accident. It reflects the political health of the community. Potentially dangerous libidinal energy is channelled to politically harmless sexual distraction.

* loosening of accepted standards of prohibition in regard to drug usage in order to legalise "low addiction" drugs —to offer any form of satisfaction of emotional needs provided it deflects social discontent.

In each of these cases, be it observed, a very good "democratic" case can be made out by the régime. It takes, or abstains from taking, certain measures "in response to public demand and current enlightened opinion".

This, then, is the depth to which mass democracy has sunk.

The one method, beloved of Marxist folklore, that is conspicuous by its absence from this list, is any official encouragement given to the traditional opium of the people —religion. In fact, this would be unwise, as religious opinion might be embarrassing. Too many thorny issues would be raised. Just how thorny some are may be gauged from the example of Bishop Hugh Montefiore when he assembled his independent commission on transport in 1970 and published a report, *Changing Directions*, in 1971 which challenged officially accepted attitudes on transport policy on every point of importance. The conspiracy of silence surrounding this affair is eloquent on its worth.

What is the attitude of nationalists to mass conditioning?
In the face of this massive manipulative process, nationalists
are forced to respond. This involves an inordinate amount of
hard work:-

* To familiarise himself with the theoretical background of
communications psychology.

* To keep himself abreast of the thinking of military intelligence organisations on this subject. They are invariably the
pacemakers. This used to be classified information, but some
men within these hierarchies are now turning away in revulsion
and several accounts have been published of conditioning, destabilisation and vilification campaigns. It is instructive to learn
of the careful planning and high quality staff work that goes
into these campaigns.

* To organise propaganda exposing the vested interest of the
régime and its local satraps. The initiative in this matter in
South Wales does not lie with the nationalists. It lies with the
publishers of the news-sheet, *Alarm* in Swansea. The organs of
political nationalism have been beaten to the draw by others.

* To organise a powerful counter-propaganda of destabilisation.
The excuse for not doing this is that nationalism has no access
to the media, therefore all efforts are doomed to fail. This is
nonsense. The media are already suspect. Nationalists can use
this distrust to handsome advantage.

* The "travelling circus" of the "national road show" is a
method of concentrating slim resources upon a highly
professional show, kitted out in motor-vans, featuring top
quality entertainment, with a peppering of short, effective
propaganda punches by star professional performers —*who
may not be the same as nationalist politicians.*

* Concentrating all propaganda upon emotional response rather
than rational argument. Reason bores the ordinary man. Plaid
propaganda is so rational, and its justice is so self-evident, that
it provokes yawns, not applause. The objective of national
propaganda in Wales is the creation of a mood of seething
national outrage. This is not achieved with sweet reasonable-

ness.

Finally, let us never underestimate the enemy. The English governing class are cruel, brutal and completely without scruple. With these people, one does not "play the game". The object of the exercise is *winning*. They are not immoral, they are amoral. Psychological warfare is the mental equivalent of the massed artillery barrage, before the troops go over the top.

Reaction

Until a mere twenty years ago, if a Welshman had been asked to list the forces of political reaction, he would have had a parrot answer: Finance capital, the bourgeoisie, the Establishment, the Army and the Church.

The response would have been immediate and unthinking. These would have been forces that stood in the path of further measures which would have transformed a capitalist society into something which he would have called a socialist society.

It is doubtful whether the answer would be so prompt or so confident today. Much has happened which he does not understand, but which he feels disturbing. The pattern of alliances has changed. He is no longer sure of where he (or in fact anyone else) stands. The nationalist is in no such doubt. Circumstances have made up his mind for him. He has come to realise his order of priorities.

* To obtain the social, economic and cultural order which his own people have wanted for 50 years, he must first of all obtain national freedom for Wales. The forces of reaction can load the dice against him in a United Kingdom.

* The key demand of the nationalist is worker control over the means of livelihood. The needs of man must not be manipulated by the English Establishment in such a way as to destroy his prosperity and thereby that of his country.

* This crucial demand now enables him to identify his enemies very clearly. For the nationalist, the forces of reaction are now easily defined.

The new reactionaries are:

* the English parties, because they stand to lose most by Welsh freedom. They lose their existence in the form which they now enjoy.

* the politicians of these parties, because it is doubtful whether welfare capitalists could stand the competition of genuine worker control.

* the trade unions, who are now purveyors of a factor of production at the highest sum market forces will permit. By acceptance of a market role they have in fact accepted welfare capitalism. They have become a reactionary bureaucracy, which would lose its *raison d'etre* with the advent of worker control. They would be superfluous, have their lukewarm enthusiasm for anything but charade worker participation which would enable them to strengthen their power base. The trade unions are now buttresses of political reaction, because their self-interest forces them to be.

* Finance Capital has not changed its position. It seeks to conserve today's gains irrespective of tomorrow. It cannot and will not see that genuine worker control is the last remaining chance for capital before the flood gates of communism open and sweep it away. Genuine worker control would allow finance capital a share in economic activity, not because of love of it, but in order to maintain a period of stability during the learning process. Finance capital believes that it can deflect and manipulate working class content. In any case, it believes it has a trump card up its sleeve. Rather than share its power with ordinary people, it will call in the Fascists. Encouraging noises will be made right up until the eleventh hour.

* The "liberals" will go along with this manoeuvre. They will use words —"compromise", "negotiation", "fair play to all parties", "enlightened opinion", "evolution". They all mean one thing. At the critical moment, they too will swing behind the forces of monopoly capital because they regard the idea of community control over economic life as preposterous. Anyway the "learned professionals", so they argue, had better side with the devil they know.

* The Communists watch these manoeuvres with the interest of a cobra in a rabbit-pen. This, they believe, is the ultimate justification of the truth of orthodox Marxist-Leninism. The new crisis of the west will bring first fascism to smash the existing machines, and finally pave the way for a communist take-over, when the "contradictions of capitalism" overtake the Corporate State. The rabbits, they believe, are there for the taking. It does not occur to these people that, given any measure of choice, ordinary people value their personal freedom. They will not trade it for a crude oriental despotism. Welsh nationalism offers our people that choice. It sees community economic power as an ultimate guarantee of a genuine freedom. To the Communist, then, Welsh nationalism is a deadly enemy. It offers the substance without the despotism. It is therefore in league with any other reactionary that is bent on eliminating Welsh nationalism.

The ideology of nationalism identifies the forces of reaction in our struggle. Woe betide the nationalist who is not nimble enough to see from what quarters the blows will rain down upon him!

Republic

The Republic is the focus of all our hopes, and the spur to our ambition. Whatever fact of nationalist philosophy is touched on, the ultimate satisfaction can only be through the Republic.

* The Republic is the highest aspiration of the Christian tradition in the Welsh context. God created nations and peoples, each to bring their own peculiar gifts and each to offer their own mirror to God's goodness. Our mirror to God's purpose for each individual in a free and creative society is the Republic. Christianity is by its very nature republican and self-governing.

* The Republic is the symbol of Welsh freedom. The English monarchy is a permanent reminder of conquest. The Principality is a deception: a synonym for a country without influence, without self-respect, without prosperity and with no future but that of a lackey.

* The Republic enshrines our vision of a community benefit state where the interest of all is subordinate to the needs of the born and unborn community. Only this state is satisfying enough to hold off the grim dictatorship of communism.

* The Republic is every man's guarantee of self-fulfilment, because it will be born to liberate us from subordination, reject-ion and the exploitation of English society. It will thrive because it gives the individual the chance to manage his own working life at a factory and at a state level, in determining the direction and pace of economic effort. It will satisfy because it

will accord with the emotional needs of every man to be part of something —a need which all the manipulation of capitalism cannot satisfy since he is only a part of a market or a wheel of production.

* The Republic is the first society not dedicated to the pursuit of power —over the markets of others, over the fates of others. We seek merely to satisfy our own needs. The Republic is not built on greed. Therefore, we look to this new order as the bringer of co-operation, not of competition. This is the old capitalist trick of setting every man against his neighbour, so that a few may benefit.

* The Republic is the régime of compassion for a people abused, exploited and shamelessly uprooted. The greatest badge of our shame is that many have come to believe that there can be no other order of society in Wales. While we may have compassion for those who have been so exhausted by struggle, we can never accept the Welsh condition. Nationalism holds in trust for our people an alternative. We will not compromise that trust for anything less than this Republic.

R|evolution

/REVOLUTIONARY MOVEMENT

At first sight, it would appear ridiculous to think of Welsh
nationalism as a truly revolutionary movement. It it had been
so, then certainly its official leaders have been at some pains
these 50 years past to hide the fact. Wales, it is said, is not a
land of heroes. It is antipathetic to change of any variety.
Violence is a notion the very mention of which can lose votes.
(We all think of votes in Plaid). We are for evolutionary change:
for a change in attitudes fostered by grass roots control over
local organs of government. There will be "change by stealth".

Whatever the virtues of this attitude, in practice it has been a
conspicuous failure —and a tree is known by its fruits. The
simple truth is otherwise. By the very nature of its birthright,
political nationalism in Wales is fundamentally a revolutionary
creed in the continental sense. It has to be.

* It stands for the liberation of England's oldest colony. It has
to reverse 700 years of assimilation. That will not be done without overturning the political order current in these islands.

* It stands for the economic emancipation of the Welsh population by the means of worker co-ownership in enterprises
employing any considerable number of workpeople. This
cannot be done within the framework of a régime which is the
historical birthplace of monopoly capitalism, where the power
of the institutions is currently greater than that of the elected
representatives of these islands, and by a substantial margin.

* It stands for all those concepts of a community benefit
society which cut across every substantial vested interest in this

land: property, builders, banks, lawyers, estate agents, unionists and party machines, building societies and insurance companies. The community benefit state would put very tight limits to the activities of these gentlemen, controlling their apparatus in areas where it is held that the living community has a prior interest. These vested interests are like ivy growing around a tree to the point of suffocating it, destroying the living host upon which it preys, and, like ivy, it can only be destroyed by cutting the single supporting stem at the base of the tree.

In fact, Plaid Cymru *must be* a revolutionary party, and Welsh nationalism a revolutionary movement in the classic tradition. Part of its lack of credibility is to be explained by the fact that it preaches changes which even the most insensitive know for certain cannot be brought about within the framework of the existing political machine. The ordinary man knows this by instinct, and yet nationalists for two generations have assured him that this is not so. Is it any wonder that nationalism has been thoroughly distrusted by everyone with whom it has come into contact?

Socialism

Socialism is a system of ideas based upon the propositions that:

1. All men are created equal.
2. Environment is more important than heredity in shaping men's development.
3. Inequalities of wealth are inherently bad, and wealth should be redistributed to iron out the most glaring differences.

These propositions have held unquestioning sway over Welsh political thinking for two generations. There is yet another, which was not gleaned from Robert Owen, Sorell, Blanqui or Marx, namely that change from one form of society to another must be evolutionary and painless. The idea that violence is the midwife of revolution has no following among Welsh socialists.

At this time, the world of the socialist in Wales is falling apart. All the gains that he believed he had made over 50 years are suddenly in jeopardy, and the foundation of this belief is seriously in question. What are these gains?

1. On the whole, these are primarily material. (The spiritual has been out of favour in Wales since the 1910 Revival). They concern welfare payments, a health service, and free education (now, alas, of doubtful quality).

2. They also concern the socialist "right ordering of society". Apart from nationalisation of the infrastructure, gains in this area are decidedly more ephemeral.

* There has never been a successful system of economic planning.
* The influence of monopoly capital over decision-making is as strong as ever.
* The bureaucracy is firmly in the hands of the old power establishment of Army, Foreign Office and aristocracy.
* Their own movement is split between those who want to go on and those who want to go back.

Last of all, and most humiliating, socialism has failed to prevent a recurrence of that unemployment, exploitation and indignity which gave such remarkable impetus to its birth and rise in the Welsh community.

Socialism, like the chapel, is a spent force in Wales. It is a dead religion, but it has not yet loosened its grasp. Wales still clings to its putrefying corpse, for the fear of the alternative — Welsh nationalism, because, outside nationalism, there is now no alternative. This fear is primarily the fear of revolution —the fear of that iron broom that will overturn the outsider, that will cleanse every nook and cranny of Welsh life, and the Welsh mind. There is now much of the inertia factor in the power of socialism in Wales. But let us delve further into the nature of the beast.

Socialism, as we have experienced it, is the classic example of a mass movement whose control has slipped into the hands of a few —the caucus of the English Labour Party. Power is central-ised in a caucus, not diffused in the local organs of party or government. This is an example of the way in which doctrine affects practice. Socialists believed in the power of the central-ised state to impose a new society. Aneurin Bevan claimed that the purpose of acquiring power was to give it away to its right-ful owners —the people. He spoke as a Welshman. The Labour Party was ruled by Englishmen.

Accordingly, the socialist state followed a consistent policy. It undertook the nationalisation of industries that commanded the economy one hundred years ago —and it permitted the English establishment to staff them and direct their policy. Its own policy of centralisation was used against it by its own enemies, in whose hands it concentrated more power than they could have dreamt of obtaining by themselves. That national-

238

isation in "Britain" failed, then, is a result that should have surprised no-one. Wales has suffered badly in respect of closure of mines, railways and steel plants, and will certainly continue to suffer further "run-downs".

Secondly, adherence to mass democracy led inevitably to the welfare state. This was a substitute for a community benefit state. It covered up the evil results of monopoly capitalism without destroying its ability to harm the community. The immediate impact of the welfare state upon Welsh life was very good, but the long-term implications of welfarism are less happy. It strikes at the heart of true social democracy because it erodes personal responsibility. The welfare state is undeniably an advance on what went before, but it pays scant attention to what is to come after. Welfarism without responsibility breeds a proletariat. It does not breed citizens. A proletariat is capable of manipulation. Socialism, while seeking to liberate the worker, has in fact chained him more efficiently to the capitalist system —because he has become a dependent personality. He is not an independent personality. It was, and still is, possible to operate welfare policies which abolish real need, but which nevertheless force the recipients to act responsibly, but it is unlikely that English socialism will implement them, for fear of the electoral consequences. Irresponsibility is aggravated by the egalitarian strain in "British" socialism. There has been a conscious desire to level everyone down. This is a policy dressed up as an equal-opportunity democracy. It has had unhappy results in two fields, education and taxation.

The Welsh grammar school may not have been a perfect institution. The education imparted was narrow and academic, but what it did, it did well. It provided a serviceable academic education to a generation of Welsh working class students. These schools "offended against the light". They were not egalitarian enough. The pursuit of doctrine has destroyed what was good without putting anything better in its place.

The destruction of the grammar school has backfired in two senses. It has not produced equality of opportunity, and has reinforced the class structure of "British" society. Boys from middle class homes who would previously have gone to grammar schools where they would have mixed with working class boys to become part of a classless society during their formative years have been put to public schools, often much to their parents' distress. Doctrinaire socialism, therefore, has been of direct benefit to the public schools, where the conditioning apparatus is hardly likely to produce a generation of leaders "in tune with the aspirations of the working class".

The costs of supporting decaying industries and pursuing doctrinaire reorganisations have been borne by high taxation. While this policy may have been pursued with glee a quarter of a century ago, it too has backfired. High taxation has re-inforced the socialist irresponsibility. It does not pay to work hard at a personal level, and at a company level it has been of benefit to the multi-national corporation. These companies can evade national taxation by juggling with depreciation, product lines and transfer prices between plants in different countries. The medium-scale national producer cannot do this, and is put under pressure. Paradoxically, therefore, socialist policies of heavy taxation have acted as a powerful catalyst in the further development of international monopoly capital.

Socialism as we have experienced it in Wales has led to an increase in the size and power of the bureaucracy, the least democratic instrument of government. The cost of this bureaucracy is the least of its evils. Its real significance is that it is a barrier to any sort of change. The financial habits of a bureaucracy are based upon last years' budget plus or minus. There is little opportunity for zero budgeting annually, where a whole organisation is called to rethink its objectives. These financial habits influence its thinking habits.

These are the results of 25 years of socialism as we have experienced it. In times of plenty, these results, although distressing, one can live with. We no longer live in times of plenty. Indeed, the Western world will *never* again live in times of plenty. The halcyon days are gone.

The Age of Scarcity magnifies the ill effects of English "socialism". Now let us examine what socialism has not achieved in Wales.

The English socialist state has not challenged the power of monopoly capitalism to distort society for its own gain. On the contrary, as we have seen, it has powerfully reinforced the power of monopoly capital in economic and social terms. It has preconditioned the working class to accept it. The drive for bigness was specifically encouraged by a socialist government a decade ago. This is a denial of a fundamental socialist concept —the power to direct investments must rest with the community, not in the hands of private capital. The institution one would expect a true socialist state to possess —a powerful central planning authority —is conspicuous by its absence. This goes back to matters of doctrine. Aneurin Bevan recognised that without this body, there would be no real transformation of "British" society. The English Treasury was an inveterate opponent, because it would have reduced its powers to those of auditor and accountant. Clement Attlee would have no part of it. It is difficult to imagine how any nation can survive the Age of Scarcity without community control over investment and priorities.

Thirty years after the first post-war Labour government, the factors of production, labour, land and money are still subject to the laws of the capitalist market, not to those of a community benefit economy. English socialism had the opportunity to change this and has failed to do so. It has intervened in the market for labour, land and money with prohibitions, but it has not taken effective measures to put the factors of production under community control. The only beneficiaries have been the bureaucrats, because prohibitions have to be policed.

The socialist state has done nothing to free the organs of communication from the control of the enemies of the working class movement. One of the needs of a community benefit society is to free the channels of communication, or else they will surely be used to condition the mind of the common man. The media are now immeasurably more powerful with the use of television.

In short, socialism in Wales has created the worst of all possible worlds. It has been doctrinaire and inflexible about matters upon which it could well have given ground, and accomodating where it should have held fast. Now it is being challenged by the forces of nationalism.

The Welsh nationalist attitude to English socialism

Despite the show made by the noisy lefts in the organs of Welsh nationalism, socialism has always, in the last analysis, been rejected as the guiding philosophy of our cause. The nationalist foresaw quite clearly what the likely effects of English socialism would be on Welsh society before its power was consolidated. Listen to D J Davies on this matter:

> So-called popular government today, instead of being a means towards individual self-government, has become a means whereby the individual escapes responsibility and decision, even in matters vital to him, shifting the burden on to someone "paid to do the job".
>
> 1945

> When the state gets hold of other people's wealth and the people become proletarianised, you find wealth and power concentrated in the hands of an irresponsible organisation . . . wealth controlled by the "anonymous collective" is sure to be wasted, for everybody's business is nobody's business."
>
> 1950

> Personal property is important as a basis of . . . human dignity and independence, and is giving each person the maximum responsibility, and thus cultivating in him courage, self-reliance and other qualities which are essential to the fully developed personality . . . When people have personal property and are organised among themselves they can make the state their servant instead of their overlord.

Nationalism rejects socialism on intellectual and pragmatic grounds. The nationalist bases his entire belief upon the responsibility of the individual within an organic society, that is, a nation which has a past, a present and a future. Responsibility is expressed through units of government of human size in civic government and the workplace. The one cannot be divided from the other. We believe in the direct participation of the citizen in government. Therefore, mass democracy is anathema to us. It is a contradiction: mass democracy must result in a dictatorship, but unlike that of an outright autocracy, it is more difficult to remove, because it gives the illusion of being democratic.

Consequently, in the nationalist community, power is diffused to its rightful owners —the people— from whom all legitimacy flows. The state is a leader, a planner, an arbiter, but it is not a tyrant. In consequence of this fundamental belief, nationalists must now be driven to consider precisely those points where English socialism has so conspicuously failed.

* Strategic investment should be carried out by a planning authority through the medium of a five-year plan, which has been *chosen* by the people as one of a number of alternative plans. The nation must control the choice of alternatives —not the bureaucracy— since it is the common people who will have to pay for them and live with the consequences of their choice. The plan is hence a legitimate instrument of government: *vox populi suprema lex est.*

In direct contradiction to the socialist, then, the nationalist is continually driven back to the individual, as he works through the inexorable logic of his beliefs. We must emphatically reject the idea that blind economic forces control human life. Accordingly, it becomes difficult to entertain support either for the absolutism of the capitalist market or the mass dictatorship of the proletariat.

Socialism in Wales has certainly humanised our lives, but this is a matter of degree. It has not changed the rules of the game. This is precisely what the nationalist is bent on doing. This is why he has to face the implacable opposition of both the social-ist establishment and monopoly capital, who, in defence of their vested interests, have joined together in an unholy alliance to defeat him. In many ways, Welsh nationalism will found a state more social than the socialists, and with perhaps more genuine enterprise than capitalism has been able to allow, but these will be the accidental results of creating a community benefit republic.

* The national plan must be accompanied by a popular participation in decision-making in the workplace as well as the unit of local government. The worker controls —effectively controls at that— a portion of the capital of all significant enterprises.

* As well as participation in decision-making, the citizen must participate in the direct execution of the plan, in his workplace and, when called upon, in civic labour brigades. (Universal conscription of young people is a natural extension of this principle). In a true social democracy, citizens are not able to

make decisions about the work of the nation and then walk away from their consequences.

Socialism, as it has been practised in Wales, is now clearly an obstacle to the establishment of that commonwealth. It has to go. We hold that no form of socialism can be of benefit to Welsh society unless it has been transformed and transfigured into our native form of socialism, cleansed in the furnace of the Welsh Revolution of all foreign impurities.

Taxation

High taxation is one of the pillars of the Keynesian neo-centralist state. It is necessary to finance government spending in order to maintain high expenses of government and growth, in order to maintain high employment. It has been enthusiastically embraced by reformist socialist parties in Europe, because it accorded very well with their own beliefs and with their emotional attachment to a "soak the rich" taxation policy. This emotional aspect should not be underestimated.

This type of policy has been employed consistently in Western Europe. It has had some surprising effects, some of which may not have been foreseen by its originators. High taxation has certainly had the desired effect on society. There are no longer the great discrepancies in Europe which are found in the new "run-away capitalist" economics of some Middle Eastern countries. But this has been achieved at a price.

Gradually, government has built up a great dis-incentive to effort, both personal and corporate. The responsibility of a man to look after his own has been blunted. Yet this is precisely one of the qualities required in a genuine democracy. High taxation has bred apathy —the feeling that whatever one does, the state will take away the gain. It is easier not to bother. This way of looking at life spills over into people's attitudes about the power of the state. It is subversive to a living democratic spirit. It also encourages citizens to be dishonest with the state, as the state is with them. It is a factor in the alienation of the people.

This malaise is largely responsible for the "British" work-shy reputation and is surely the most serious effect of Keynsian taxation policies, but it is powerfully reinforced by the encouragement they give to the inexorable accumulation of corporate power.

High taxation is of direct and immediate benefit to the large company, and in particular the multinational. It prevents smaller companies acquiring reserves, and puts them permanently in the pocket of the banks. This, in turn, puts the smaller company at the mercy of changing monetary policies which appear arbitrary, and for which it is very difficult indeed to make forward contingency plans. Hence, small business is discouraged by the fight against monopoly capital for markets on the one side, and by penal taxation on the other. The multinationals can switch product lines and markets at will. They can manipulate investment, depreciation charges and (in particular) transfer prices for components and semi-finished goods between plants in different countries, so that very little "book" profit is registered in high tax countries, where multinationals have corporate headquarters.

These practices are frozen into the economies of most European economies, and they are having a pernicious effect upon their populations, because they put them increasingly at the mercy of a few large conglomerates. Monopoly capital has now acquired such a grip over the economy that the politicians and bureaucrats, whatever their opinions, are forced to integrate with the corporations, or take the unacceptable political risk of high unemployment. High taxation, then, is a direct and material cause of the neo-fascist state.

What sort of taxation policy does Welsh society need?
We need a revolutionary change in tax policy both in its intention and its effects from that of the English socialist state. Welsh taxation policy must start from completely different hypotheses.

1. The primary aim of taxation is to assist in creating a climate where genuine social democracy, enterprise and worker-share participation can thrive. The benefit of working people owning half the capital of their enterprises must be clear and unequivocal.

2. Hence, while the Keynesian neo-capitalist state relied upon direct taxation to cover the costs of government and development projects, the community benefit state cannot and should not do so. That vast sums will be required to rehabilitate the Welsh economy cannot be in doubt, hence it is inevitable that the Welsh state must itself directly engage in commerce and industry. In particular, it must take the opportunity it possesses to fence off whole sections of the market to private capitalism, particularly in those areas where foreign monopolies have a stranglehold on the Welsh market. Some likely candidates readily come to mind: oil, pharmaceuticals, sugar, tea, contraceptives, steel building sections, clay bricks, grain, electrical cables, lamps and accessories, cosmetics. Upon further examination, it is clear that some of these commodities have, in any case, a major bearing upon a community benefit society, and are high upon the list of items requiring special attention for social reasons.

The Welsh government, then, is committed to earning its own growth capital; it is not committed to robbing others to obtain it.

3. Taxation in Wales should be used as a flexible instrument to channel investment into the right type of industry in the right place at the right time. Unemployment black-spots are an obvious immediate target for tax-free status. The whole Blaenau area could be made into a free port for selected industries in selected clusters of plants.

One does not envisage a single tax rate to be applied, as in the English socialist state, in blanket fashion. To all industries whatever their social merit, but a stepped rate from zero corporate taxation in free zone areas to high taxation in non-productive exploitation industries which repatriate profits.

One of the principal tasks of a stepped taxation system is to encourage infant plants on the strategic investment list. This list covers native Welsh enterprises engaged in setting up re-habilitation industries or new industries in certain government-defined areas of activity —particularly if these plants happen to be the mines, worker co-operatives or, as we have seen, workers' share participation industries.

In brief, Keynesian neo-capitalist taxation is negative in application and result, while nationalist taxation is positive in intention and execution. It must be clear that a taxation policy geared to the real needs of the Welsh community cannot be implemented by a colonial government. It would harm the metropolitan economy. Wales cannot have the type of taxation or customs policy it needs unless it has unfettered sovereignty. It must be outside both the English state and the EEC multi-national-manipulated super-state. Half-measures are doomed to failure.

Trade Unions

For 150 years these organisations have performed a useful role in the struggle to secure adequate wages for working class people. This role has changed, is changing, and will certainly have to change further, in the light of conditions anticipated in the old industrialised countries at the end of the century.

The traditional role has been that of bargainer between the helpless mass of the working population and the employers. It was primarily economic, concerned with wages and working conditions.

In communist countries this role has been transformed. Since power was held by the people, so the argument runs, "the people" cannot exploit "the people". The role of the union is to work within the planned economy, accepting that the wage for any grade of labour is centrally decided in view of the current priorities of the socialist state.

In these countries, therefore, the unions have shed their bargaining function. They have become advisers (and sometimes manipulators) of the workforce.

In the old industrialised countries of the West, on the other hand, unions have, in effect, become built-in to the system of monopoly capitalism. They control a commodity. Depending upon the degree of unionisation and the economic climate, they are just one more part of the capitalist apparatus: they have a commodity for sale at the highest rate.

Moreover, such is the lethargy of the worker, that all unions now tend to be staffed by officials and a bureaucracy with very sketchy claims to democratic election and decision-making.

Therefore union bosses tend to have much the same pre-occupation as their counterparts on the other side of the table — they are primarily interested in consolidating their power and prestige. As long as they are acting as "principals" in wage negotiations they have a function to perform. Their personal powers stem from the importance of this function.

For the established union bureaucrat, the shop steward is a dangerous rival. He represents the grass roots. The ordinary worker is as much alienated from the large nation-wide, industry-wide, unions as he is to the corporation. The shop steward is near, amenable, and definitely and visibly elected. No wonder the unions cannot surpress "unofficial strikes". From this point of view, the old South Wales Miners federation was a better union than the National Union of Mineworkers. It was more susceptible to local feeling.

To a degree, therefore, the modern trade union justifies the orthodox Marxist criticism —it is a vehicle for reformism. It is concerned with alleviating the lot of the working man within the system of monopoly capitalism. It has, to an extent, become "reactionary" in the classic sense of that word —a vested interest, concerned, together with other interests in maintaining a position of privilege.

By the end of this century, the dramatic changes in the economy due to the onset of the Age of Scarcity will have raised the cost of materials and capital. The progress of auto-mation and structural changes in industry will put severe pressure on the wages fund within the enterprise. Wages will tend to stagnate.

The unions will then have a choice: *either* they further consolidate their position within monopoly capitalism and settle for the best they can get from the monopolies, *or* they are forced by fierce pressures from below to adopt a more independent attitude.

Into this old conflict, we must now inject an exciting new dimension —workers' share participation.

Dr D J Davies wrote passionately about the belief of the early nationalists in genuine worker participation. During the 30s it became one of the pillars of nationalist orthodoxy. Un-fortunately some nationalists are now so attuned to "accomodation" that they would be glad to forget all about it.

Yet, as we shall see, it could become the key that finally unlocks the door to power.

Nationalism and the unions

For some years there has been a one-sided courtship between nationalists and the Welsh trade unions.

If this alliance materialized, nationalism would, overnight, find itself in a very powerful position. Several interested parties, therefore, are doing their utmost to ensure that the course of true love does not run smooth.

Let us first of all examine the situation from a theoretical point of view.

1. As long as the ageing bureaucrats in the unions adhere to the orthodox Marxist viewpoint that nationalism is a barrier to the emancipation of the working class there is little prospect of an alliance. Fortunately these doctrinaire opinions are held by an ageing minority who are fast approaching retirement age. There will soon be the possibility of an updated version of the doctrine of "socialism in one country". It will be a distinctly national version of socialism, but it will be by far the best version on offer.

2. The younger and more flexible unionists are slowly coming to appreciate the danger in which they stand. The growing concentration of decision-making in the hands of the large corporations (private and state owned) must now be giving cause for concern. The effective working alliance between monopoly capitalism, the government bureaucracy and the parties makes the transition to a neo-fascist corporate state probable by the close of the century. The complete inability of the Establishment to reform itself from within is also quite clear. Therefore the thoughtful trade unionist is forced to conclude that the only hope of genuine social democracy involves cutting the umbilical cord.

The Union has to go. Within a free Wales, social democracy can survive; within a United Kingdom trade unionists can only anticipate that they will be drawn tighter and tighter into the corporate state. The American trade unions have gone far down that road already. There are enormous pressures within the

English TUC bureaucracy propelling them along this road.

3. Worker Participation has been the principal pillar of Nationalist social policy since the 30s. Moreover the shortage of manpower in a free Wales forces *any* government to take heed of organised labour. The balance of power will be quite different to that in the Union. Therefore paper assurances about the survival of social democracy are backed by powerful expediency for any Welsh government.

So far we have been concerned with theoretical considerations. The hard facts of practical politics appear to spoil this rosy picture.

* If nationalism is concerned with a genuine emancipation of working people through worker share participation, there are very serious objections to placing that power in the hands of the unions. They have been horse traders for so long, that one must seriously question whether they could transform themselves overnight into shareholders' representatives. The union bureaucrat is primarily concerned with wringing the best available bargain out of "the management". What happens when the participators have a half share in management? Can the whole union movement lose its extractive mentality overnight? Can new wine be poured into old bottles?

* "Free Collective Bargaining" will be as dead as the dodo by the turn of the century. If nationalists come to power in Wales, there will be powerful incentives to kill it off. The half million workers in Wales will be too few for the tasks of reconstruction. There will be tremendous inflationary pressure on wages. Even after the conscription of young men and women into State Labour Service, the Republic will be forced to introduce wage restraint leading soon to a state wages scale. Otherwise economic catastrophe appears inevitable.

One is forced to ask how a union bureaucracy will regard this. Can unions voluntarily reduce their bargaining role to an hours and conditions role? Will they not thereby destroy their own power?

* It must be admitted that upon this interpretation of the future course of events, although nationalists are not Marxist,

our interpretation of the role of the unions and the central fixing of wage levels would appeal to have much more in common with Socialist Bloc practice than Western style "wheeling and dealing" unionism.

* This of course begs the questions which are central to the whole discussion,

No 1. Can Unions so change themselves as to become responsible advisors to worker participators? Can they exchange their bargaining role for a directors role?

No 2. Can nationalists bring themselves to trust the trade unions to permit them to do so? Do nationalists themselves want a genuine social democracy based upon genuine worker participation, or will they be content with a Welsh version of the English state structure?

The birth of the Welsh Republic may well turn upon answers to these questions.

Transport

Transport policy is the acid test of attitude of a government to the people it is alleged to serve. Transport is not a technical, nor an economic matter. It is a matter of political choice. This nationalist evaluation of transport policy starts from this assumption, noting:

1. No aspect of transport policy has ever been put to a vote, or any form of consultation in Wales. "Popular demand" for any service cannot be equated with what the public would want if they were free to choose the alternatives.

Community benefit can hardly be said to have been a consideration in Welsh transport policy which has never been opened for discussion by the English government. Wales has to take the transport allocated to it. At best, in the first years of this century, it was government regulation of services the transport industry found it profitable to provide. In its last years, the transport industry will provide those services determined by Whitehall to be in the interest of the English state, not the Welsh community.

2. Transport is indissolubly linked with energy policy. The Whitehall government has the same historic attitude to both in Wales. Destroy their domestic base utterly on "economic grounds". We have noted that in energy, Wales has a surplus of electrical energy and a deficit of transport and heating capacity in the economy *as it now exists*. We have also noted that for the reasons there mentioned, transport costs must increase substantially over the next 20 years, making it problematic

whether working people can continue indefinitely to use their motor cars freely.

3. The nationalist attitude is therefore one of vigorous intervention in the field of transport policy

* to make the best use of the resource we have —abundant electricity. (about 10,000 gigawatts in 1977).

* to provide a community-oriented service directly linked to Republican energy policy.

* to enable working class people to keep private cars for their pleasure and convenience.

* to regulate the use of the roads by freight vehicles much more closely and in any case to force the 20 million tonnes of long distance road traffic to external destinations on to the railways on piggy-back wagons, and to transfer the 34% of all lorry loads within Wales to rail (i.e., about 20 million tons) accounted for by crude numerals, the 12.4% of loads (about 7 million tons) accounted for by coal and coke (1977 figures Table 102 — *Welsh Economic Trends*, 1979).

4. Nationalism does not necessarily view this as opposing private enterprise ventures in road or rail, but it does mean that the Republic would loosen the stranglehold of traditional Welsh vested interest (public as well as private) in the movement of goods and people.

5. Intervention means the opposite under Welsh nationalism from the role of the Traffic Commissioners in the 1920s and '30s. The Road Traffic Act of 1930 fastened a rigid control over new entrants to the transport industry. The Traffic Commissioners (a classic quango) on the Tribunals set up as a result of this act listened attentively to the existing vested interests, the large operators and the municipal government Traffic Departments.

The nationalist view of a commission is of a man answerable to the Senate for his decisions, whose duty it is to implement positively the policy of the Republic within a given area.

6. These cardinal aims of a community benefit policy can be realised around several foundation enterprises which are

fundamental to the Republic to make it viable as a nation state:

* The creation of an electrified railway spine through the centre of Wales, built from its inception as a mover of the heaviest and most bulky lorry-loads in "piggy-back" on rail wagons.

* The creation of a fast interurban tramway system composed of internal light interurban vehicles for the whole of the northern and southern littorals. (210,000 manufacturing jobs are South-East of a line from Barry to Pontypŵl. Journeys to work alone account for many movements).

* The creation of urban goods transportment depots and delivery within city limits by overhead fed electric goods trolley vehicles.

* Rigorous licensing of all freight journeys of regular pattern by the Traffic Commission, and strictest enforcement of the "lorry off the road" policy.

* Invitation of private enterprise to contribute capital and management to these systems and to privately owned branch railways and post buses operating from the railway and other traffic arteries.

* A state owned on-line real time computer controlled network of terminals to record every regular freight movement by road, rail or ship, to provide data for tariff fixing and control over the transport economy. This system would be the biggest single asset of the Republican transport system, and all others depend for their efficient and profitable operation upon it.

7. Who are the enemies of a Republican community benefit transport policy?

* Welsh nationalism seeks to permit the use of a motor car by working people (if they wish to own one) at a time when it will become increasingly difficult to do so. This is not how it will be portrayed by the motor industry, the dealer network, the manufacturers and distributors of every piece of bolt-on junk dispensed by the industry which feeds off the popular idolatry of the twentieth century.

* The contracting industry which directly benefits from motor-

way maintainance contracts, whose maintainance costs will
increase by ⅓ when the axle load of motor lorries is increased
by an extra 0.826 tons over the existing 10 ton/axle load for
32 ton articulated vehicles and over 9 tons/axle for the rigid 30
ton motor lorry. Road construction costs will increase by 5%.
These are the figures which explain the furore over the EEC
higher axle loading controversy. Consider that UK roadway
maintainance costs in excess of £544 million per year in 1971.
This is the size of the vested interest.

* The old civil service establishment of the English state has
traditionally been anti-rail, because of the power of the oil
interest, the motor industry (accounting for £3.8 billions of
added value in 1980, and employing 769,000 workers) and the
dislike of the throttle hold of the rail unions might have on a
heavily trafficked rail system. The afterglow of these Whitehall
attitudes would be felt even in a Welsh free state.

Conclusion
The means to the solution of the Welsh transport problem lie
within the ability of the Welsh people to implement, if they
are minded to do so. The electricity, the coal, the steel and the
skill exist within Wales to build and operate a community transport system. What is lacking is the organisation, the
opportunity and the will to do so.

Figure 5

THE TRANSPORT OF GOODS BY ROAD TO AND FROM WALES BY ORIGIN AND DESTINATION OF GOODS: 1977[1]

thousand tonnes

	Origin of goods entering Wales	Destination of goods leaving Wales
North	417	428
Yorkshire and Humberside	793	879
East Midlands	1,021	802
East Anglia	430	463
G.L.C.	612	1,159
South East (excluding G.L.C.)	1,282	1,881
South West	3,808	2,907
West Midlands	5,263	5,139
North West	4,190	5,696
Scotland	109	365
Traffic within Wales	57,940	57,940
Total	75,865	77,659

Source: Department of Transport

(1)   1977 Continuing Survey for vehicles over 3½ tonnes gross weight.

In 1977 hauliers carried an estimated 78 million tonnes of goods from Wales. While 75 per cent of this was internal traffic, nearly 20 million tonnes left for other regions of Great Britain. The largest single recipient region was the North West of England, closely followed by the West Midlands, these two received nearly 11 million tonnes from Wales; the South East (including the G.L.C. area) and the South West between them received 6 million tonnes. While both the tonnage of traffic and the pattern of origin are broadly the same for goods transported into Wales, the West Midlands was the largest single supplier.

Figure 6

TRANSPORTATION OF GOODS BY ROAD INTO WALES BY ORIGIN OF GOODS: 1978

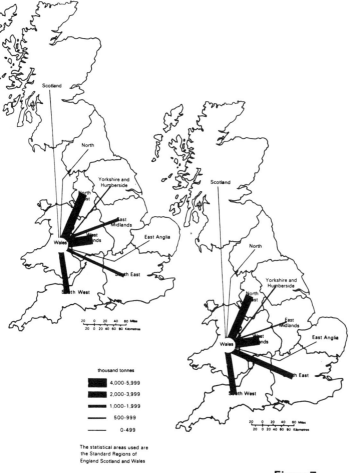

thousand tonnes

- 4,000-5,999
- 2,000-3,999
- 1,000-1,999
- 500-999
- 0-499

The statistical areas used are
the Standard Regions of
England Scotland and Wales

Figure 7

TRANSPORTATION OF GOODS BY ROAD OUT OF WALES BY DESTINATION OF GOODS: 1978

Figure 8

WELSH PROPORTION OF GOODS TRANSPORTED BY ROAD IN 1977 (for vehicles over 3½ g.v.w.) ANALYSED BY TYPE OF GOODS

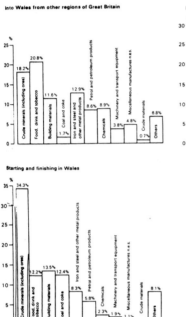

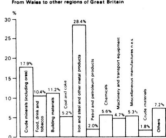

Treason

Nationalists have, for 50 years, been afraid to use this word. This is, perhaps a commentary upon their own uncertainties. It is like a garden hose, invertently turned on. They are afraid to pick it up unless they get a wetting. Yet the concept of our nationality, and of the community benefit state which must spring from nationalism cannot be taken seriously unless honourable and dishonourable attitudes to Welsh nationhood are defined. Welsh nationalism is a moral order. It is a matter of conscience. Welsh nationalism is *not* about a linguistic order. It is *not* about an economic order. It is *not* associated with a particular mode of government. It is *not* dependent upon a particular relationship between the governed and those who govern in their name. It is about a way of life. That way of life is primarily spiritual in that it is based upon a set of Christian values. It is about an order of priorities contingent upon them. Any action which offends those priorities or betrays them is defined as treason to the Welsh State and people. Far from this definition being a hindrance ("not wanting to offend") it is a powerful weapon in the armour of those who fight for the liberation of Wales. It is a weapon of conscience. Against that weapon, control of the media, armoured cars, mounted police and the tramp of marching battalions cannot prevail. In the end, the quiet voice of Christian conscience will overcome them all.

For the Christian, there are certain actions and attitudes which are unacceptable. In some cases treasonable behaviour is unconscious, and although none the less harmful in its effect, is excusable. It stems from wrong attitudes fostered in society by long acceptance, unchallenged. In some cases they are criminal because they set out, with deliberation, to destroy not merely the life of an individual, (which we call "murder",) but the life of a whole nation —born and unborn. A nation is the creation of God. Like the family and like life itself, it has sanctity. It is God's work. Definition of what is treasonable to this nation, by this token, conveys a definition of what is of greatest value to it. It is therefore not an academic point, but a practical consideration, to govern day to day affairs.

Let us see to what extent this may be clarified.

* It is an undeniable fact that in 1282 the English king Edward I, did wilfully and through the lust for power, conquer and subject the people of Wales to the power of the English crown. This was an immoral and criminal act. It is still to this day, accepted or unaccepted, a criminal act. The age of the crime does not legalize its results. Murder is murder whatever the time since its commission. It is treasonable, then, to admit the legitimacy of English control over Welsh affairs.

* To promote attitudes of mind, in our own people, or in others, which would condone this state of affairs is not permissible. It is treasonable since it gives aid and comfort to our enemies —those who seek to perpetuate this condition, from whatever motive.

* To accept commissions of government over the Welsh people by any in pretended authority over them is treasonable, because, through long custom, it appears to legitimize that rule in the mind of the simple.

* To earn one's living by devoting one's energies to the upkeep of the apparatus of an alien government is an act of treason.

* To accept favours, however deferred, in order to combat those who work for the freedom of the Welsh people is a gross act of treason. It does not constitute an action by default but premeditated treason with malice.

If these are to be the definitions of treasonable conduct, it will be said that none are without taint, and we must surely be mad because it would be next to impossible to maintain these attitudes in everyday life.

That is precisely the predicament of the Welshman —the intelligent and ambitious in particular. It is difficult for him to earn a living, a meagre one at that, unless he bows his head to accept a régime which embodies a standard of values totally at variance with his own. In other words he is forced to treason to eat. Moreover, he is actually required to swear his oath to up-hold this authority. No wonder that many Welshmen are schizophrenic! Treason to his own people engenders guilt, and guilt corrodes character. Without patriotism a Welshman is a poor thing indeed. It is the unwavering intention of English rule to destroy his integrity.

It is the duty of the nationalist (and a very painful one) to challenge this order. There can be no compromise between good and evil, between truth and lies, between loyalty and betrayal. Treason against our own community automatically means adherence to an order of society which supports monopoly capitalism. It is therefore nonsense to speak of a "socialist duty" to support the "international class struggle", in case of a working man, or to prefer a "wider circle of service", in the case of those who have the chance to do better for them-selves. If a man cannot be loyal to his own society, to his own home, however humble, what trust is to be placed in his claims to some splendid service beyond that home?

One of the difficulties associated with the concept of Christian duty towards Wales, and treason against it is the mis-use of the idea of "democratic choice". Those guilty men who are well aware of their betrayal refer to the sentiment of a people who have refused the idea even of a national assembly let alone that of Welsh Statehood.

A crime is still a crime whatever the sentiment of the on-looker. The fact that any majority do not at this point in time accept the duties of nationality is of no consequence. God's law is not a matter of majorities but of absolutes. The techniques of persuasion have not changed since the trial of Christ. The people of Jerusalem welcomed Jesus riding upon an ass in triumph into the holy city on Sunday, but they asked Pilate for Barabas in place of the King of the Jews on Friday. A few cheer-leaders placed strategically in a crowd by a skilful and determined enemy can always sway a mob. If a rabble can be swayed to send the Son of God to his death, how much simpler it is to play upon the fears of ordinary men to have them denounce their birthright.

The concept of Welsh patriotism and of treason are two sides of a clean mind. Nationalism is a movement concerned, above all, with attitudes. This is the most subtle, but also the most fundamental campaign of all. Good healthy Christian attitudes held in common by Welshmen are a deadly threat to the English state and to the capitalist order. Is it any wonder, then, that the most vicious campaign of all will be fought over this one word?

Welsh Language

It is through its society that a nation introduces its culture to man. This is why a close organic society is so important —indeed, is priceless . . . Safeguarding a nation, defending a nation, is to defend those living societies which are as yet undestroyed, those are the cup of our culture and the well of our civilisation. To keep them from destruction and to develop fully the inner possibilities, this is true nationalism.

Emyr Llewelyn, *Adfer Enaid y Cymro*,
Llanbedr, 1974

This essay seeks solely to define the ideological and political consequences contingent upon adopting a Welsh heartland policy, as outlined in Clive Betts' *Culture in Crisis* (Ffynnon Press, 1976). Those who want to have greater familiarity should consult chapter 15 and 16 of that book. In brief, Betts advocates the establishment of 3 zones within Wales, whose industrial, social and educational arrangements are designed to safeguard, stabilise and eventually to reverse the anglicisation of Welsh life, without any enforced cambricisation and the alienisation to the Republic which that would entail.

The Betts analysis

Zone A. 70%+ of Welsh speakers. Where the working language of government and industry would be Welsh, equipped with its heartland education authority, where all education, primary, secondary and tertiary would be in Welsh, and immigrant children would be assimilated by crash instruction (under 11) or bussed out to a Zone B school (over 11).

The industrial organisation to incule a heartland industrial development board with higher incentives to establish industry, and a supply of Welsh-speaking managers and supervisors, trained by the Board and made available to entrepreneurs. The connection being that Welsh can be maintained as the language of work only so long as management is Welsh-speaking.

All communication to and from central government would be Welsh only. Development would be refused in work or in housebuilding if it threatened the language.

Zone B. 50%-70% Welsh-speaking ability. **Transition Zones.** While English would be the accepted work language, colonisation by all-Welsh industrial units would be encouraged with the same financial incentives as provided by the heartland development board. Written material in government would be bilingual. Education would be primarily in English after primary education in Welsh, with Welsh secondary school options. Welsh instruction to equivalent of 'O' level standard would be compulsory in all schools.

Zone C. Anglicised areas. While Welsh would be the national language and all material displayed by the government would be bilingual, the language of the community would be English, with provision of optional Welsh primary and secondary education. Welsh instruction to 'O' level equivalent standard would be compulsory in all schools.

Palatine status for The Bro Gymraeg

Betts' proposals are practical, as anyone with working experience in multilingual countries would appreciate. (It is only here, in Wales, that the officially induced fears of discord cause any eyebrow to be raised at what is, in most multi-lingual communities, the norm of accepted government behaviour). It is not this aspect of these proposals which, with variations, plus or minus a point or two, are becoming accepted in Welsh and English-speaking Wales, that here concern us. It is their implications for government.

Nowhere does Betts suggest it, but the direct implication of his proposals is the creation of these palatinates, in the classic sense of that work, being a territorial unit of government enjoying prerogatives which elsewhere belong to the sovereignty of the Republic alone. This implication is of such crucial importance to the good order and government of the Republic that it must be weighed most carefully.

* The boundary of Zones A and B and the anglicised areas very nearly forms the route of the recommended North-South Union Railway, Welsh to the West and English to the East. It completely ignores the existing county structure, but curiously does follow the north-south "wealth line" that distinguishes poor West Wales from richer Eastern Wales.

* It raises in acute form the position of the hardy anti-Welsh communities along the English Marches —most unwilling subjects of the Republic.

* It introduces a third dimension to the work of the All-Wales Development Authority, local planning boards and extra-territorial presidencies in charge of transport, utilities and state arsenals.

Even-handed language polices relax tension

There are good reasons to start the political evaluation of the language question completely at the other end of the spectrum, in the English crescent stretching from Rhuddlan, Delyn, Alyn and Dee, Wrexham Maelor, part of Montgomery, Radnor, Breconshire and Gwent. Some of this area is Welsh by sentiment, some distinctly not. It is good government that wherever there is a distinct community, it is better to hive it off as a self-governing Palatinate where all the benefits of the Republic apply, but where powers of local decision-making are considerable. The English do not practice this form of administration in Wales. They try solution by "electoral geometry" (clever manoeuvres like the creation of South Glamorgan or the splitting of constituency boundaries so as to favour the Establishment loyal to the English Crown.) They appear to have forgotten the history of the Hapsburgs. Wherever one has to resort to boundary-rigging, it is clear that the impetus of the state ideal has died, and clever solutions may postpone, but can never ward off, the Revolution.

It would be wise that nationalists immediately concede County Palatine status to the Marcher counties, and seek to foster genuine local democracy. The Welsh state ideal is so strong that generosity is in order. Once the Marches realise that they are to be left in peace, and stand to benefit from the good housekeeping of the Republic, fair and evenhanded, tension will be released and many troubles averted. One may anticipate the enrolment of the sons of the Marcher landowners into the state service of the Republic. Their grandchildren will be Welsh-speaking, and as firm in their allegiance as any other.

The key to the Welsh heartland political problem lies, then, not in the Bro Gymraeg, but in the English Marches. We can now contemplate the full Palatinate Status for the Bro without misgiving. It is possible to defuse the time-bomb of the special status to be accorded to the Bro by offering exactly the same status to the Marches.

Linguistic quietism

The real danger to the Welsh language is hinted at in the close of the quotation which heads this essay. Mr Emyr Llewelyn, like others before him, might be persuaded that "true nationalism" is concerned solely with the Welsh language to the exclusion of all else, and constitutes some form of "linguistic quietism". This puts a rural self-sufficient existence in the Bro as more pure and worthy than the crude realities of the political infighting in the coarse and socialist working class areas of Wales. This idea is disloyal to the Republic. In the last analysis, without the Republic, there will be no language, and any who opt out of the struggle, whatever their degree of attachment to their culture, do disservice to their own cause, and to their whole nation.

Worker Participation

Functionless capitalism should be eliminated and the land, labour and capital should be in the same hands —in the hands of those that work. Without this, and the idealism which produces the best possible work (and thus ultimately benefits the community) will not be engendered, for a man will not put the whole of himself into his work unless he feels that he owns and controls the finished product.

I Believe. **D J Davies**

This is the new buzz word of the Western world. Its meaning can range from insipid chats with tame workers' representatives to total control of an enterprise by a co-operative of workpeople who *employ* the management.

It is the new bogey of monopoly capitalism, and a great deal of effort is being spent to dilute "wild ideas" and render them "manageable".

Yet it is an idea which even monopoly capitalists need to consider with sympathy. With each further step taken towards the establishment of a more perfect monopoly, one should ask, "Are my thousands of workpeople going to *enjoy* working here more or less?"

Logically, why should workpeople enjoy working for a corporate machine? The more impersonal the organisation, the more indifferent its workpeople, the more insensitive to relieve monotony with disruption. Although it is now but a shadowy possibility, let us ask the question seriously: *Are we prepared to fight the communists to enable my organisation to continue making profits?* Of course, by a sleight of hand, capitalism has come to be associated with freedom. This trick may have worked over the past 50 years, but the attitude of the young now makes the answer to this question seriously in doubt, because many no longer do feel that freedom and the capitalist system are the same thing.

Despite the intense hostility of the very few genuine capitalists, and the very few career managers, to worker participation, there are grounds for suggesting that sharing their power with their workpeople might be their best chance of survival. It might, incidentally, make their life a lot easier.

In Wales, the problem does not loom as large as it would in an advanced economy. Most large employers are state-owned, although the alienation of their workpeople is, if anything, more intense than in the private sector. There are far fewer organisations employing, let us say, over 100 employees than in the South-East.

Nonetheless, worker participation has been on the agenda of Welsh nationalism from its early days. Unfortunately, it has come to be regarded as a grey area where it is best to make no committment.

The pioneers of nationalism had no such restraint. They recognised that healthy working relationships were the key to a healthy society, politically, economically and in terms of human satisfaction. For them, the new Welsh society would be built primarily in the workplace. Therefore it was not a cosmetic exercise, a public relations gimmick, a further expedient to reconcile the individual to his place in a machine, an aid to higher productivity. The commitment of a man like D J Davies was not to an exercise in manipulation. Davies and his associates wanted to fit work to the man, not man to a slot in the system.

In other words, Davies wanted ordinary men to fulfil themselves through their work. For him, participation was genuine. He believed that this was not to revert to the rural workshop — he believed that a steelworks or a mine could and should be run co-operatively. He did not mean to abandon it but to humanise it by altering the basis for its organisation, and distributing its fruits.

For the first generation of nationalists, then, "participation" meant essentially control over the capital; if not complete control, then certainly a big enough stake to work their purpose.

It is upon this very point that nationalists now prevaricate. Nationalism is now so preoccupied with its image with the establishment that it is prepared to ditch an embarrassing old-time religion. Yet Davies spoke from the heart. His message made an appeal to the reality of the working class in Wales.

There would be no shuffling of feet, if nationalists concentrated their attention on the tasks ahead.

A free Wales is committed to an enormous task of industrial reconstruction. No way will this be possible without the enthusiasm as well as the genuine participation of the small working population of Wales. The working class hold the real key to power in Wales. Temporarily it may seem as if Westminster and the great interests hold power. This is an illusion. Smart "modern" nationalists may now scoff at Davies and other pioneers as naïve, but their accommodating attitudes sadly miss reality.

What are the *minimum* requirements of effective worker participation in Welsh industrial life?

1. A compulsory purchase of 49% of about 100 *selected* private and public sector enterprises, based upon flexible criteria: turn-over, profitability, importance to the economy or number of employees. The State Board of Trustees shall determine the worth of any enterprise and the price of any share. Small enter-prises are not generally significant, and are better managed privately.

2. The Welsh state will lend the workers the purchase price for a shareholding of about £1,000. The state will pay the donor enterprises with state-secured bonds at fixed interest rates maturing at five, ten and fifteen year terms. These bonds are negotiable within Wales, but not without. Under this arrange-ment no cash changes hands.

3. The state will hold the shares in trust for their owners until the accumulated dividends amortise the workers' debt.

4. Working people are encouraged to buy shares in their own enterprise, but also in any other on the donors' list. They have to have served for 3 years in that enterprise. Their shareholding follows them if they change jobs, but upon retirement, the

shares are re-purchased by the state in return for an annuity, and returned to the workers' fund for redistribution to the working population.

5. Any undistributed shares are available for purchase by members of the Welsh Republican Army, or new qualifying workpeople. Undistributed shares are held by the Board of Trustees.

6. The proxies are held by the State Board of Trustees until redemption, but the trustees may use their voting rights at general meetings of the enterprise only upon consultation with workers' representatives and the trade unions, and in agreement with them.

7. Trade unions are specifically excluded from managing or owning workers' shares.

These provisions would eventually circulate the capital of all significant Welsh enterprises within the working population. Yet, the scheme achieves much more than this limited objective.

* It puts tight control over the commanding heights of the private economy into the hands of the Board of Trustees during the crucial first decade of freedom. By channelling new issues, rights issues and share splits through the trustees, the state has acquired a substantial control over investment.

* It gives the working class a period of apprenticeship under stable conditions to enable them to exercise their new responsibility as shareholders. When their share purchase price is amortised, their decisions are their own.

* This ensures that control does not drift into the hands of an irresponsible minority, or into the hands of the trade unions. If the unions were invested with trustee obligations, this would finally cement them into the system of monopoly capitalism, rather than force them to pursue their role as watchdogs of the working class.

Under these conditions, the long process of genuine participation can begin. As Wilhelm Reich has pointed out in his *Mass Psychology of Fascism*, a working population, manipulated and exploited, will not immediately be capable of controlling its destiny. Under communism, all power is vested in the party as perpetual trustees. Under Welsh nationalist rule, we want to diffuse it gradually to the body of the people.

Working Class

Labour is a fundamental reality of human life, and ideally, it is the means
by which man humanises nature . . . labour is significant not only
economically, but as a means of human development: and if our life in
the universe has any purpose, that purpose must be for us to grow and
develop it as human personalities.

I Believe. **D J Davies**

We . . . believe that we can only get the workers to join together and move
towards a new and better society by giving them a living sense (not a mere
idea) of the unity and permanence of the historic Welsh nation.

Our Attitude. **D J Davies**

Everyone is a champion of the Welsh working class. Clearly, if
we are to believe the politicians, no section of the population is
more loved, honoured and appreciated for what they are, than
are the workers of this nation. Yet Welsh workers are among
the poorest paid, most insecure in their jobs, and have the least
beguiling prospects of any living in these islands. Why the
paradox? In great measure, this is due to the myth of the working class in Wales, a pernicious myth that every party carefully
maintains and to which each party in turn dutifully contributes.
The most assiduous myth-makers of all are the Welsh nationalists. The attitudes cultivated about "the workers", dependent
upon the occasion, and the degree of flattery which is
expedient at the moment, would include an amalgam of the
following:

* the workers are innocent, beguiled and put upon by capitalists, Whitehall and anyone else of an evil turn of mind.

* the workers are the true repository of ultimate political

truth and Welsh culture. Provided they can be liberated from outside interference, all will be well.

* They are stout fellows, who know which side their bread is buttered, and are not going to be taken in by any set of cranks.

* they are the direct descendants of times and men whose mood was one of savage militancy tempered with despair.

One has the uncomfortable feeling when any politician in Wales speaks of his own electorate that they are an imaginary people. Are these people not more remote than the Hottentots? Surely the majority of the working population in Wales is now almost completely deracinated, dependent, manipulated and not a little afraid. As for the genuine working class culture of a century ago; eisteddfodau, chapel, choir, trade union and lending library, it has almost completely vanished. Indeed, it would be difficult to speak of a Welsh working class "culture" of any sort, apart from the club, the pub and the game. Television has replaced culture. It is obsolete.

These are the people nationalism is trying to enlist and has tried to impress for 50 years past. One might as well bite upon a stone. There is nothing, not one spark, to be got out of them. Perhaps, in addition to idealising, stereotyping and exhorting, nationalism is a little afraid of the people. Who are the people? Do they really have to be placated and served up with the same sugary gruel year in, year out? What is the real hunger of this people? Are nationalists really afraid to hear what it is, lest it contradicts them? Dare we really set this people free?

Before we dare to answer these questions, let us ask what it is that Welsh freedom really has to offer the working people of Wales —particularly the young workers, who will have to live with nationalism and all its works for a very long time.

We have nothing to offer them except sacrifice, shortage, perhaps direction of labour, and certainly low wages for a full decade, before we can begin to put this country in some sort of order. We can offer the working class self-respect (and you can't eat that), a genuine workers' participation in industry (which will show little by way of extra spending money for money for many years to come), hope of a better future (Whitehall can cap that with another offer, the illusion of

massive oil revenues and "give-aways"), and a certain together-
ness, in facing the common burden of rebuilding our life
together.

But surely, this in itself is something quite new. It is
valuable. For the first time, politicians will be telling the
obvious truth, and we will be trusted, as no-one has been trusted for a very long time in Wales.

The single crumb of comfort that nationalists can draw from
50 years of campaigning is the knowledge —the invaluable
knowledge— that the working class knows that he has been
taken. At the ultimate moment of truth, when all the gewgaws
and the tinsel have been pushed aside, and the give-aways have
been discounted, the ordinary man knows full well that he is
manipulated, cheated and that a very low opinion is really set
upon him by those who hold the ultimate power in these
islands. They key to this situation is to use this knowledge, to
be very frank, and appeal to the sense of co-operation (never far
below the surface of this people) in heaving the working class up
by its bootstraps. Nationalism has been afraid of the truth. It
has sought to join the merry-go-round of flattery and deception,
when the tasks a free Wales would be called upon to face are so
manifestly more onerous than any soft option the English
parties choose to offer. It is no wonder that nationalism has
bitten on stone these fifty years past.

EPILOGUE

The prince who would wish to subdue this nation, and govern it peacefully, must use this method. He must be determined to apply a diligent and constant attention to this purpose for one year at least; for a people who, with a collective force, will not openly attack the enemy in the field, nor want to be besieged in castles, is not to be overcome at the first onset, but to be worn out by prudent delay and patience. Let him divide her strength, and by bribes and promises endeavour to stir up one against the other, knowing the spirit of hatred and envy which generally prevails among them.

Gerald the Welshman. *Description of Wales*

Gerald the Welshman wanted a job —a job within the gift of an English King. In the pursuit of this job he undertook several commissions for this king, and wrote a book —*The Description of Wales*, about his travels through Wales before the conquest.

After the passage quoted, he went on, in detail, to recommend starving the Welsh people out of their resistance and the planting of castles and strongpoints to enforce her submission. Three chapters are devoted to these topics. Essentially, with periodic updating as to circumstance, this book, and the principles ennunciated in it, have been applied in Wales (and subsequently in every English colony) ever since. Gerald's advice on suppressing guerilla warfare has been used unchanged in Malaya during our own time. It is recorded, incidentally, that Gerald never got his job. In 1186, he was passed over by Henry II in favour of another. It is said that Henry distrusted the Welshman.

In many ways, this ABC seeks to undo the work which this vain, gifted and treasonable Archdeacon of Brecon wrought against his people 700 years ago.

Gerald was the example of a man who would sacrifice his own people for career advancement, and then turn around and wonder why it was that his career had not, in fact, advanced.

We have explored in these pages many of the attitudes, strategems and tools of oppression which have, and still do, shackle the mind of this people, and it is our minds that we must first cleanse before we seek to rebuild our lives.

As this book goes to press, 700 years after the conquest of Wales by an English king, the people of Wales yet again find themselves starved out, with 15% recorded unemployment in many of our communities, and a much higher level, hidden, unrecorded. In the last analysis, the Welsh have no-one to blame but themselves. They reap as they have sown. Just as Gerald found out 700 years ago, and just as Sir Julian Hodge has found out only last year as he tried to gain full banking status for his bank, in the last analysis, any who seek to maintain themselves and their affairs in Wales, whatever their services to the English state, will in the last instance be distrusted because their persons and their work will raise institutions potentially dangerous to the English interest. The ordinary people have turned this way and that, keeping their heads down, and seeking only to survive in the homes, at whatever cost. They do not want to be involved in politics, still less a separation from England. They would swallow any humiliation, any privation and any cancer of decline, provided they would be left in peace to enjoy their own. Now their jobs have disappeared, and in the eerie stillness of silent workshops, they ask themselves "why?"

They are without respect and without support, driven hither and thither like cattle, because they have shown themselves weak and inconstant in the only thing that mattered: their determination to assert their own national interest to the extent of running the English out of their country and their lives, and doing for themselves what, in their simplicity, they had trusted to others to do for them.

Let them now throw off sloth and false friends together, and face up to their sorrows and their joys within the stout walls of their own Republic —a poor thing, perhaps, but their own. They can touch it, talk to it, and build it with their own hands.

278

If they did but know it, it has been in their own minds all along.

When first, in the book *The Rise of the Welsh Republic*, I set forth the condition and self-discipline required of this people, to heave themselves out of their shameful backwardness, a cry went up that the very evident effort to do so would be unacceptable to ordinary men and women. Look around you now, good people, and ask yourselves, "What, sincerely, is your prospect under the rule of the English? Is it really so much worse to set up shop for yourselves?"

Under the Republic, you will certainly sweat for every crumb that passes your lips, but you will work together, and in the joy of men who do for themselves, with no master. In the meantime, you will lift yourselves and your children out of the poverty and degradation of a society which must beg others to feed it. We will, in Wales, after great suffering, achieve on our own, and through the strength of our own right arm, what we have begged and grovelled before others to give us.

The attitudes set out in these pages will enable the young, in particular (who have no hope, except it be in a Welsh Republic) to bring our people to a right mind, in their view of their own lives, and of the condition in which they now find themselves. The first and most important battle is in the mind. Let us think as Welshmen, and as no other, of our own interest, and no other.

May God be with all our young people in their bitter distress, guide their thoughts and harden their resolve to throw off the English domination and, in the joy of freedom, establish together the Welsh Republic!

AMEN

BOOKS FOR
FURTHER STUDY

PARTY SOURCES
Principles of Nationalism Saunders Lewis. Reprinted by Plaid Cymru in 1975 from the original lecture of 1925.
Towards Welsh Freedom The collected works of Dr D J Davies. Gee and Son, Ltd., Denbigh, 1958.

These works cover the period of the late 1930s to 1951.

The Welsh Coal Industry D J Davies and H P Richard. Plaid Cymru, 1948.
A Trade Union Congress for Wales Ithel Davies. Written some time before 1945 —published by Plaid Cymru.
Wales against conscription jointly by Gwynfor Evans, Dr Tudur Jones, Emrys Roberts and Lynn Moseley. Undated, probably 1956. Published by Plaid Cymru.
Non-Violent Nationalism Gwynfor Evans. The Alex Wood Memorial Lecture. 1973.
The Lessons of Yugoslavia: Industrial Democracy for Wales Robin Oakey. ISBN 90-30-77-11-3.

These are a fair selection of seminal works which, I believe, have decisively shaped Plaid thinking. The young party worker cannot fail to observe the difference in the quality of Plaid literature after 1950.

GENERAL READING
Propaganda —the Formation of Men's Attitudes Jacques Ellul. Vintage Books, 1874. ISBN 0-394-71874-7. The best all-round analysis of the theory and practice of propaganda in the West.
The Alternative Future —a vision of Christian Marxism Roger Garaudy. Penguin Books, 1976. A brilliant intellectual analysis of present-day capitalism.
The Coloniser and the Colonised Albert Mernini. Souvenir Press ISBN 0 285 64771-7. 1974. Portrays the emotional consequences of colonialism.

Business Civilisation in Decline R Heilbronner. Penguin Books.
ISBN 0 14 02 2015-1. An excellent short survey of the crisis of capital.
Fascism —a reader's guide edited by Walter Laqueur. Penguin Books
ISBN 0 14 02 21190. Particularly the essay on ideology by Zeev Sternhell.
A good analysis of the development of fascist ideology.
To the Finland Station Edmund Wilson. Fontana Books. An old but
valuable survey of modern political theory.
Low Intensity Operations Frank Kitson. Faber and Faber.
ISBN 0 571 09801 0. Required reading in the mentality of the military
anti-nationalist authorities.

The concluding chapter of Michael Balfor's **Propaganda in War, 1939-1945**
contains an interesting insight into the general views of the English
government upon slanting news.

The first chapter of **The Double Cross System** by Sir John Masterman,
Sphere Books 1973, should give grounds for reflection for those concerned
with party security and counter-espionage matters.

Now you must read the full, gripping story of John Jenkins' bombing campaign, M.A.C. and the Free Wales Army as told in Roy Clews' bestselling book, published last year:

This is the controversial book that one MP took to the Director of Public Prosecutions; that the police confiscated from the printing works of the publishers; that kept its author in a police cell; and that the Welsh Books Council is STILL refusing to distribute.

WHILE STOCKS LAST (it has sold extremely well because of all this!) we are able to make a special offer for orders sent direct to the publishers:

        £2.50 per copy POST FREE

or   £4.80 for 2 copies POST FREE

or   £7.00 for 3 copies POST FREE.

Send your order now to:

       Y LOLFA, TALYBONT, CEREDIGION SY24 5HE.

Also by John Jenkins:

20x15" two-colour poster. Means in English: "Blessed are they who are persecuted for the sake of justice." **40p**

Four-colour Celtic Christmas card, with envelope. **10p**

Ar Ben Waun Tredegar
Dacw 'Nghariad i Lawr yn y Berllan
Cân y Bugail
Bugeilio'r Gwenith Gwyn
Fflat Huw Puw
Ar Lan y Môr
Ffarwel i Langyfelach Lon
Lisa Lân
Gwenno Penygelli
Mae Gen i Chwaer Mari
Llongau Caernarfon
Migildi Magildi
Harbwr Core
Marwnad yr Ehedydd
Moliannwn
Rownd yr Horn
Rwy'n Caru'r Ferch o Blwyf Penderyn
Titrwm Tatrwm
Tra Bo Dau
Trwy'r Drysni a'r Anialwch
Wrth Fynd efo Deio i Dywyn
Y Bardd a'r Gwew
Yr Eneth Gadd ei Gwrthod
Ym Mhontypridd mae 'Nghariad

24 o ganeuon gwerin gorau Cymru
24 best loved Welsh folk songs

MABSANT   £1.45

24 most popular Welsh folk songs, newly arranged for voice
and guitar, with explanatory notes in both languages.

WELSH PERSONAL NAMES
Heini Gruffudd   95p

Over 1,000 Welsh names for children, with meanings, historical
notes and pictures. The fullest list on the market.

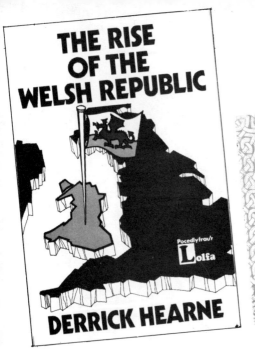
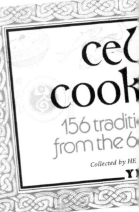

THE RISE OF THE WELSH REPUBLIC
Derrick Hearne   90p
A "model" of life in the first ten years of a sovereign Welsh
Republic established in the near future, in the Age of Scarcity.
A serious, ambitous work covering government, economics,
education and defence.

THE JOY OF FREEDOM
Derrick Hearne   £1.85
A collection of wide-ranging essays attempting to lay the basis
for an "Ideology of Welsh Liberation" strong enough to
challenge English imperialism and its manipulation of the
media.

PARLIAMENTARY ELECTIONS IN WALES 1900-75
Beti Jones   £2.85 (hardback)
The election results of this century in one volume, together
with a history of the franchise, potted biographies of MP's,
pictures, maps and an index to all candidates.

THE WELSH EXTREMIST
Ned Thomas   **£1.75**

Essays on Welsh literature, politics and society today. According to one reviewer, "probably the best and most important book on what is happening in Wales that has appeared in English." 4th reprint.

CELTIC COOKBOOK
Helen Smith-Twiddy   **85p**

A collection of 156 traditional recipes from the six Celtic nations, clearly and prettily presented. One of our bestsellers.

WELSH IS FUN
Heini Gruffudd & Elwyn Ioan   **85p**

The ideal introduction to spoken Welsh for adults; funny — 17 cartoon-lessons— but thorough, with exercises, grammar and a full vocabulary. Sold over 40,000 and now in new, completely revised, paperback format.

WELSH IS FUN—TASTIC
Heini Gruffudd & Elwyn Ioan   85p
The follow-up to *Welsh is Fun*, but funnier (or bluer?) still;
packed with cartoons, with a useful revision section. New
paperback format.

LOOK—UP THE WELSH!
Heini Gruffudd   45p
At last a really full, modern phrasebook for visitors to Wales,
fully illustrated with photographs.

CORNISH IS FUN
Richard Gendall & Tim Saunders   75p
A new, popular course in living Cornish, based on *Welsh is
Fun*.   (P.S. "Irish is Fun" also in the pipeline!)

*To order any of above, just send the money with 10% extra to
cover postage to us (address below). Our 32-page Catalogue
has a full list of all our publications and will be sent free, upon
request, by return of post.*

> Y LOLFA
> TALYBONT
> CEREDIGION   SY24 5HE